The Authors and the Publisher offer in good faith the information regarding the survival skills and techniques described in this book. They point out that some of these may be dangerous in certain circumstances. They therefore disclaim any liability for any injury which may result from employing these skills and techniques.
Readers should also note that these skills and techniques are intended for use in the context of emergency survival situations only. When practising any of these skills and techniques the relevant laws of the State, as well as all landowners' rights, must be strictly observed. The Authors and the Publisher are unable to accept any responsibility for proceedings or prosecutions instituted against any person or persons as a consequence of the use, correct or otherwise, of these skills and techniques.

All rights reserved.
Copyright (C) 1987 Barry Davies/Philip Beynon

This book is sold subject to the condition that it shall not, by way of trade or otherwise, be lent, re-sold, hired out or otherwise be copied in part or whole by any means without the publishers prior consent.

ISBN 0 9512298 0 X
SALES CODE 1014

First published in 1987 by
B.C.B. INTERNATIONAL LTD.,
Rhymney River Bridge Road,
Cardiff CF3 7AF. U.K.
First reprint 1989.

Printed in Great Britain by
FIVE ARTS (PRINTERS) LIMITED
Cardiff.

Typeset by
AFAL, CARDIFF.

The line drawings in this book
are by SURMA GRAPHICS

FOREWORD

Survival – by which we mean the ability to survive – is a dying art. Paradoxically, the very factors which assist our survival in normal circumstances are those which weaken our ability to cope with the abnormal, the unexpected. Too much easy living, too much urbanisation and too much television have taken away from many of us knowledge that was second nature to our forefathers. Their living was simple, difficult and rough – but they knew how to look after themselves and how to get a living from the land.

Of course, we have many advantages, but in attaining them we have created an artificial environment for many people. And if that artificial protection is stripped away – by accident, disaster or unforeseen emergency, then many people are virtually helpless.

But the last few years have seen the rapid growth of a new interest in the matter of survival. An uneasy feeling seems to be stirring that we are getting too far away from our roots in Nature. Many of us feel a need – perhaps unconsciously – to be near to the land again, if only temporarily. We want to be able to find or provide our own shelter and our own food. We want to create our own warmth. For some of us, life's present uncertainties awake a desire for the ability to be self-sufficient, so that possible emergencies can be faced with self-confidence. Another group treat survival as a kind of sport, while explorers, mountaineers, fell-walkers and sailors, along with campers, hikers and orienteerers, already know its value well. They appreciate the dangers which can all too quickly arise from foul weather, an injury, an accident or becoming lost.

But whatever their reasons for being interested – actively interested – in survival, they are on our wave-length. Survival has been one of the primary factors in our lives. We hope that this book will meet some of the needs of all of the people interested in survival. And since we believe that women are among the greatest of natural survivors, we ask them to read "she" for "he" whenever the latter is used! Then, perhaps, we can also hope that we shall meet all of the needs of some who are going to be survivors.

Should this be so, we shall have succeeded in our wish to demonstrate that Survival is the Art of Living.

CONTENTS

Introduction to Survival 1

Survival – The Basic Equipment 7

Survival Situation – Assessment and Planning 22

First Aid for Survival 29

Fire Lighting 55

Survival Shelter Construction 71

Types of Fire, Stoves and Cooking 90

Survival Navigation 108

Water Procurement 124

Location Signalling 145

Plants as Food 151

Animal Food: Hunting, Traps and Snares 187

Aquatic Food 205

Travelling for Survival 221

Index 233

CHAPTER ONE

INTRODUCTION TO SURVIVAL

In a survival situation your circumstances or environment will have been changed – usually unexpectedly – so that you are faced with danger. There will be threats to your survival. Some will come from the world around you. Others – at least as dangerous – will try to emerge from within yourself. They may be obvious. They may be insidious. If help and rescue is not immediately available, it is essential that you are able to recognise and deal with these threats if you are going to be a SURVIVOR.

You will find here a wealth of detailed information on practical survival equipment and techniques, with which you can succeed in most situations. In recent years, great advances have been achieved in the design and manufacture of clothing, equipment and supplies. Equivalent advances have taken place in the development of techniques for their use. But however good the equipment, however effective the techniques, your chances of surviving depend entirely on how well you can employ them.

It is a sad fact that man's psychological reactions to disaster or danger often render him unable to make the best use of his available resources. Your first step must therefore be to control and direct your own reactions to any survival situation.

Information in the field of survival psychology is far from complete, but there has been sufficient research and assessment to provide an understanding of some of the major factors involved, and of their effects on the survivor's mental attitudes. In our normal, familiar world, most of us are able to learn from past experience. We then use our knowledge to work towards successful adjustment to later changing circumstances.

Unexpected conditions of danger and stress, however, can inhibit this ability to learn and adjust. This can happen to an extent that has led to the deaths of many very able, apparently sensible people. Of prime importance among the psychological requirements for survival is the capacity to accept immediately the reality of any new emergency. Doing so allows you to retain the ability to choose the appropriate reaction. This capacity for acceptance is NOT a passive attitude. It is positive. It is rooted in self-confidence. It is true belief in the value of your own survival techniques.

Studies have demonstrated clearly that survival information contributes a great deal to the belief in one's own capacity to survive. This belief is all-important in dealing with fear and panic. Survival information will minimise fear and check possible panic.

****

What are the psychological factors confronting us in a survival emergency, which threaten self-confidence? We can identify them as the "Enemies of Survival." They include Pain, Fatigue, Boredom, Loneliness, and the effects of Cold, Thirst and Hunger. Either separately or in conjunction they work to induce fear.

Everyone has some experience of all of them, but only a very few people have known them to a degree which created actual doubt about the possibility of surviving. In a survival situation the feelings of cold, pain and the rest are basically no different from what we experience in more normal conditions. They vary only in their severity and danger.

The more you know about these feelings and their possible effects on you, the better will you be able to control them rather than have them dominate you. Later chapters will provide you with detailed practical steps you can take to tackle most of the problems they create. With this knowledge, and confidence in your own ability, you will be able to alleviate many of the difficulties. To protect self-confidence demands control over these enemies of survival, and over their deadly ally, fear.

The first step towards command of your survival situation is to recognise them and understand their effects – and you can begin that process now.

Pain

Pain is a natural occurence – a normal way of making you pay attention to something that is wrong with your body. But Nature also makes it possible to hold off pain – to diminish its effects – if you are so busy doing something important that you are unable to attend to the injury immediately. Pain may be made more bearable if you occupy your mind with plans and activities aimed at survival. If, on the other hand, you do not attempt to combat it, pain will weaken your drive to survive. Even if not serious or prolonged, it can get the better of you if you allow it. Pain demands a special effort of thought and will towards optimism and activity.

Cold

This is a much greater enemy of survival than it may at first appear.

The obvious threat from cold is the physical damage it can inflict. But it is far more insidious than that. It numbs the mind as well as the body. It enfeebles the will and reduces the ability to think clearly. It can do this in such gentle easy stages that a positive attitude to resist it and guard against it is essential before it takes effect.

Failure to recognise its threat can all too easily lead to a state of mind where sleep and the hope of warmth become all-consuming, devouring even your determination to be a survivor. The greatest of all its dangers is that cold can even remove fear. And paradoxically, this is perhaps the most dangerous effect of all.

Thirst

This is probably the best-known enemy of survival, especially in its extreme form. Well before this stage, however, thirst can begin to pre-occupy the mind. But like pain and cold, thirst can be kept in its proper place. Your will to survive must be strong enough and it must be backed by confidence. That confidence must rest on the certainty that, if water CAN be obtained, you have sufficient knowledge to set about getting it. Of great importance, too, is the rational use of any stock of water you may have. It must be used sparingly, but not so sparingly that you run the risk of significant dehydration. It is pointless, not to say harmful, to reduce your effectiveness in a survival situation while you still have resources at hand.

Hunger

The physical effects of hunger are fairly obvious, especially if prolonged. Its additional hazard lies in its adverse mental effects, one of which is to lessen the capacity for ordered thought. Both thirst and hunger lead to an increase in the survivor's susceptibility to the enervating results of cold, pain and fear.

Fatigue

Even a very moderate degree of fatigue has its particular method of debilitation. It achieves this by creating a careless attitude – in the sense that it becomes increasingly easy simply not to care what will, or will not, happen. Here is another of the great dangers to your survival – all the greater because it can arise from an unsuspected source.

Fatigue is generally thought to be directly related to the expenditure of energy. Certainly, there can be risks from over-exertion. But the belief that fatigue follows physical activity only is mistaken. It may well have been responsible for many deaths in many survival situations.

Fatigue can actually be due to lack of hope, or of any real goal. It can build up from frustration, dissatisfaction or boredom. It may be unconsciously used as an avenue of escape from a reality which seems too difficult to contemplate. But unknown reserves of strength can often be summoned, along with the will to go on – if the dangers and sources of fatigue are recognised and fought against.

Boredom and Isolation

These are another two tough enemies of survival. Their toughness is derived from their being, usually, unexpected. Waiting, with nothing happening, can play a very significant part in the matter of survival. There can be many hopes and expectations raised – only to be dashed to nothing. At night, for example, you may have to stay still, quiet and alone. This is the kind of moment when you become the target of boredom and loneliness – when they will attempt to sidle into your consciousness. You must defend yourself. Talk – to yourself if necessary – talk and make plans for the future. Talk about the future after your rescue, as well as the time until it happens. Devise problems to keep your mind exercised and occupied. Active, positive thinking leaves no room for boredom or loneliness.

Fear

Fear is an entirely normal – even necessary – emotion. It is the basis of instinctive reaction for anyone faced with an emergency creating a threat to life or limb. Behaviour and reaction are always influenced by fear, and, through them, so are the prospects for survival.

There is no advantage (indeed there may be an actual disadvantage) in attempting to avoid fear by denying the existence of danger. Acceptance of fear as a natural reaction to any threatening situation will produce two immediate and positive benefits.

> First: You will be able to dismiss the fear of being afraid, which is often a burden in itself. True courage may be found in people who freely admit to fear – and then go on to do their best in the circumstances they face.
>
> Second: You will find yourself more likely to be able to carry out considered rather than unco-ordinated actions. You will recognise that there is always something that can be done to improve the situation.

Both these benefits will greatly increase your prospects of surviving. How an individual reacts to fear depends more on the person concerned than the situation he faces. Perhaps surprisingly, it is not always the physically strong or devil-may-care people who cope with fear most effectively. The ones who are timid and anxious in normal circumstances may well respond more coolly and efficiently when under stress. Their chances of survival are very much increased. Fear must be recognised, lived with, and used to advantage if possible.

We have looked at most of the major factors which can generate fear. This is the moment for a summary of the mental preparation you can begin NOW. Take these steps, which will be valuable in decreasing and controlling fear.

1. Build confidence in yourself through knowledge of survival techniques and of your ability to make the best use of them.
2. Acquire confidence in your choice of survival equipment through familiarity of handling and regular checks on serviceability.
3. Develop acceptance of the absolute need to concentrate on the survival job to be done.

PERSONALITY REQUIREMENTS FOR SURVIVAL

Your survival may depend more upon personality or character – call it what you will – than upon any danger, any severity of weather or terrain, or any other aspect of the situation, even though they dictate the nature of your emergency. Will fear produce panic, or act as a spur to sharper thought and action? Will fatigue demoralise you – or be itself defeated by your ability to maintain necessary activity?

The answers to these and any similar questions are dependent more upon the person than the situation. Attributes important to survival are listed below. The more of these you have – or can aspire to – the greater your chance of success.

(a) **To be decisive** – after accepting the realities of your situation, assessing resources and considering alternatives of action.

(b) **To be able to improvise.**

(c) **To be ready to accept isolation if necessary.**

(d) **To be ready and able to adapt to your circumstances.**

(e) **To remain cool, calm and collected.**

(f) **To maintain hope for the best** – while making all possible preparations for the worst.

(g) **To have patience** – to be ready to wait for the moment holding the optimum chance of success.

(h) **To be able to take hardship up to your limit.** Few people know how much they can really take – but the limits can be extended by your recognition of, and preparation for, the worst that can happen.

(i) **To recognise your own special fears or worries.** Many personal fears have their roots in earlier life. They can be troublesome in dangerous survival conditions, but recognition limits their power to damage.

Every one of these attributes adds to the driving force which always lies behind all attempts at survival – **the will to live.** It is your overriding instinct. **Help it to help you.**

CHAPTER TWO

THE BASIC EQUIPMENT

You have considered some of the major threats to survival which can arise from within yourself. You have prepared – and must constantly renew – your mental defences against them. Now you must look at the survival situation from another angle. What positive, practical steps can you take at this time to be more able to combat the physical dangers which could emerge from the environments – possibly hostile – in which you may find yourself?

You can begin your practical preparations in two different areas.

The first is to acquire a sound understanding of basic survival skills – shelter construction, fire lighting, navigation, food and water procurement and so on. Each of these will be dealt with in succeeding chapters. The second involves the compilation of a personal survival kit together with consideration of the need to select and use clothing suitable for the activities in mind. These are the subject of this chapter.

The personal survival pack is of the utmost importance. It should be carried on your person at any time when the possibility of an emergency involvement exists. Your choice of its contents is crucial. That choice may vary according to the type of expedition or journey being planned.

You may well be forced to compromise in your choice – between what you may see as any possible need, and the limitation on what can be carried. Your decision on the items to be included in the survival kit can only be made after all items have been carefully considered. You must assess every item's usefulness, its adaptability and its weight or bulk. This assessment has to be made keeping in mind the strong possibility that the kit may be your only initial resource. You must select items on the criteria (i) that together they are small enough for you to carry at all relevant times and (ii), that each will increase your chances of surviving. Then they will be the catalysts to essential action. They will be the keys to open the store of natural resources – because they will be the tools with which your survival skills and techniques can be stimulated and utilised.

Listed below are a selection of possible components of a personal survival kit, together with notes on their uses. The items underlined are those which are strongly recommended for inclusion. Others may be useful in particular situations. In any event, the final selection will be influenced by your own individual skills and outlook.

In addition, it is worth thinking about "reserve" items. These can be kept at hand as possible substitute components. They would be used if the need arose to modify your kit before beginning a journey or expedition to any particular type of region. Different regions and climates will make different demands on your kit.

THE PERSONAL SURVIVAL KIT

Matches

A dozen or more kitchen matches, which have been completely immersed in melted candle wax will be both waterproof and wind-resistant. They should be carried in a waterproof container. They must be packed loosely, so that one can be withdrawn easily even if fingers are cold, wet or numb. A scrap of emery cloth will provide a dry striking surface, but it MUST be placed in the container so that it will NOT make contact with the match heads.

Matches are now commercially available which are either windproof or waterproof or both. These can be bought from most leading camping and outdoor pursuit shops. The better quality matches are packed in an air-tight container, each match being handmade and coated with protective varnish. These matches burn for about 12 seconds when lit. They will not go out even if completely immersed in water or exposed to the strongest winds.

Flint and Steel Firelighter

This is a rugged and dependable item of equipment, which will provide thousands of opportunities to light fires in all kinds of weather. It is best carried as part of a "fire set" which also incorporates other basic essentials for lighting fires in hostile conditions.

A good fire set will be equipped with a flint containing a percentage of magnesium, to produce large, intensely hot sparks. The striker will have hardened teeth to obtain effective performance when striking. It is a good idea if its leading edge is sharpened to provide a small sharp blade. This could be useful in many ways, but particularly in scraping tinder from clothing etc.

A small supply of cotton wool is also included. This is excellent tinder – and can be made even better if it is blackened, preferably with charcoal, before use. Another item in the set will be firemaking blocks. The blocks are a very good primary fuel. They burn slowly in block form but provide rapid ignition if crumbled.

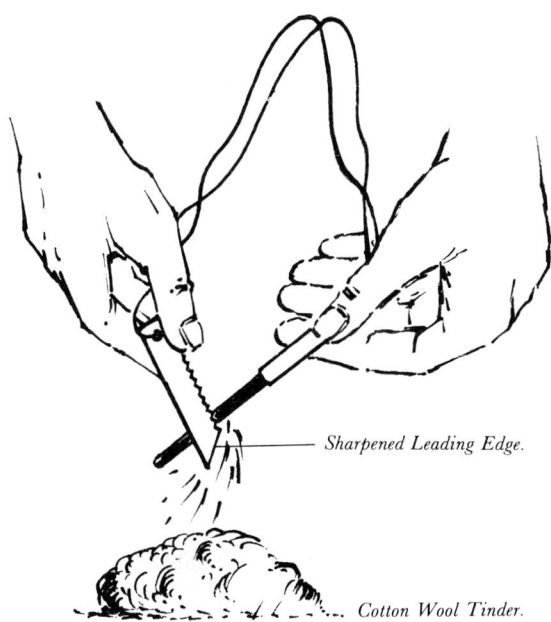

Sharpened Leading Edge.

Cotton Wool Tinder.

They should not give off poisonous fumes when burned and are therefore safer to use in any confined space.

The packing tin itself has various possible uses, including those of heliograph or animal-fat lamp holder.

Candle

A four inch candle weighs less than one ounce yet will burn for up to three hours if it is protected from the wind. The best choice is a candle made from 100% stearine (solidified edible animal fats). This will light in any temperatures, serve as emergency food – and lubricate items as diverse as a zipper and the hand-held socket of a bow-drill fire maker. It is practically indestructible, being immune to dropping or soaking in water. Besides providing light it will, if burning inside a tin, make a heater for a small, snug shelter, snow cave or igloo. When other fuel is not available, it may be used for cooking food or heating beverages. A candle will ignite tinder too damp to be lit by matches alone.

Blisters can be prevented if the candle is rubbed on the heels and toes of the socks should shoes begin to chafe. The melted grease will seal the seams of pre-heated leather boots. Finally, the candle, used with a tin can, makes a fairly good lantern which will operate in light wind and rain.

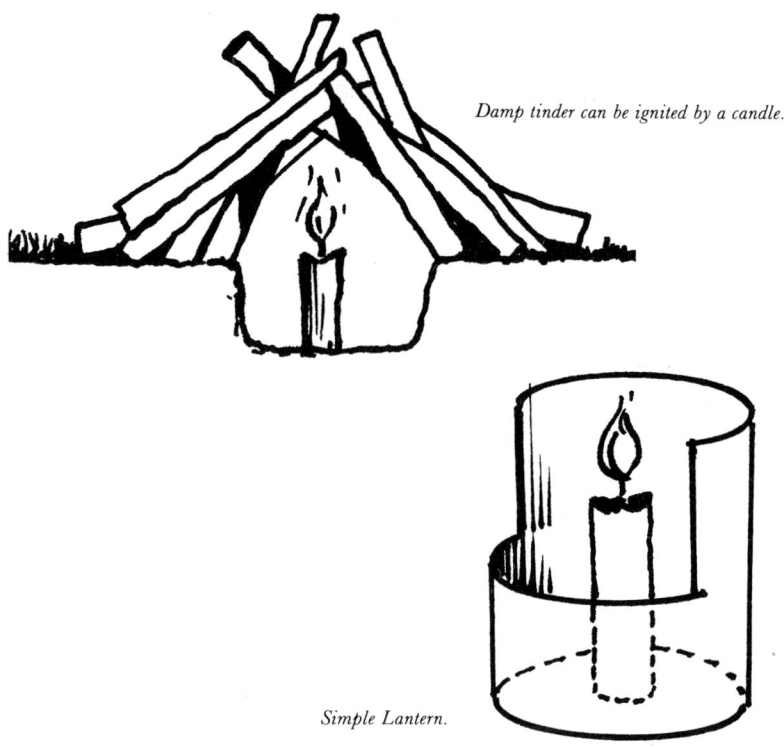

Damp tinder can be ignited by a candle.

Simple Lantern.

Contraceptives (CONDOMS)

The Condom is an item of survival equipment having one of the most comprehensive ranges of use. When held in a sock or shirt sleeve it becomes a water carrier. Note: it cannot be filled by simply dipping into a water supply. To use its storage capacity adequately, water must be poured in. If held as described above, it will contain approx. 1.5 litres when extended to a length of 30cms. It can be used as a waterproof container for small and medium sized items which need protection from damp, (e.g. dry fire tinder.) Two Condoms together can be used as a catapult. They may be inflated for use as emergency life-jackets, when, for instance, crossing a river of unknown depth. The Condoms chosen should be the inexpensive variety, non-lubricated and heavy duty. Your kit should include a minimum of three.

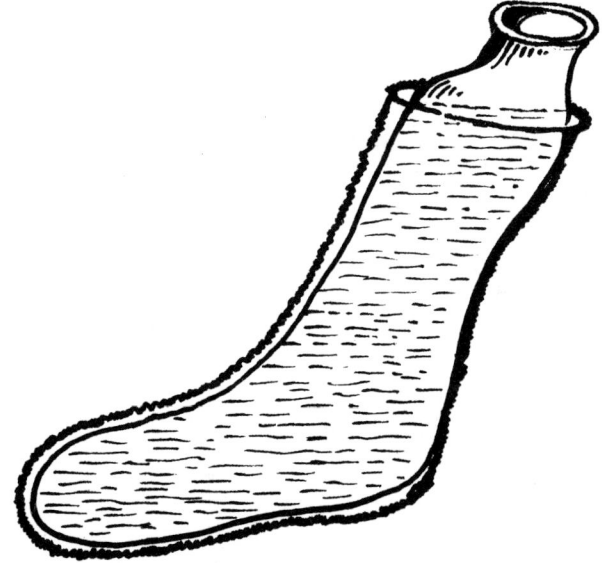

Using a condom as water carrier.

Needle

A needle with a large eye, about 2 inches long, (e.g. Chenille No. 16 or a sailmaker's needle) can be used for heavy-duty sewing of materials such as shoe leather, rawhide or heavy clothing. It will also be available to be magnetised for use as a pointer in an improvised compass. (See Survival Navigation.)

Compass

A compass is a priority item for your kit. A button compass is the ideal choice – easy to read but taking the minimum of space. The "Explorer" button compass is a good example, being liquid filled. A button compass should be fitted with some form of lanyard to guard against loss – a real possibility in view of their small size. There are several good alternative compasses available, even if most of them are considerably larger. It is all-important that a good quality instrument is selected.

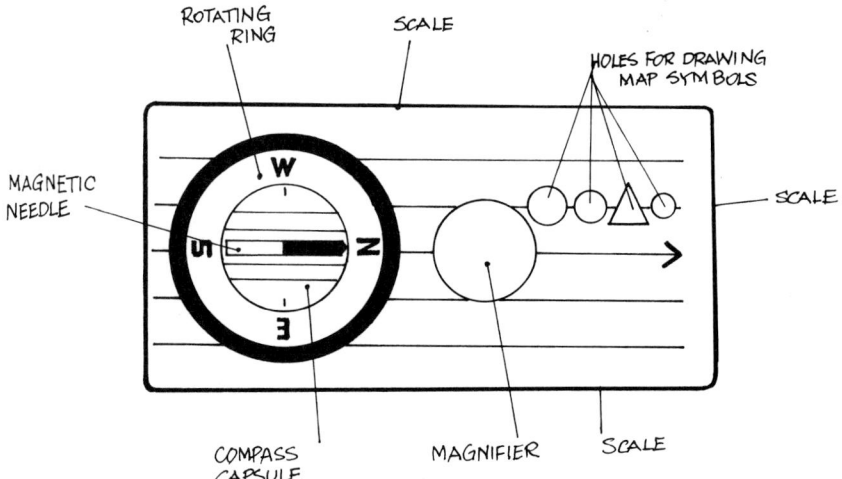

Survival Bag

One of the most frequent dangers to be faced in a survival situation is the involuntary loss of critical amounts of body-heat. This loss occurs through **convection, conduction** or **radiation.**

Convection involves the transport of heat by the movement of a heated substance. In the survival context, this means that the body warms the surrounding air (or water).

This then moves away, carrying the body-heat with it. It is replaced by cooler air or water and the process begins again. The repetition of this action produces the "chill factor" in cold, windy conditions. In most survival situations convection is the biggest single cause of body-heat loss. Convective loss of body-heat is greatly reduced if the layer of air next to the body can be trapped.

Conduction occurs when the body is in contact with any colder surface. Heat from the body will flow into and along the colder material through the areas of contact.

12

Radiation. The human body emits some heat in the form of low-frequency radiation. This is most effectively reduced by the use of an emergency blanket made of aluminised polythene sheet.

An orange polythene survival bag is the best choice for your personal survival kit. It deals most efficiently with heat-loss through convection. Once inside, the body is protected from wind and rain. Conductive heat loss can be minimised by placing the bag on insulating material (bracken, twigs, grass etc).

Heat-saving efficiency will be increased if you occasionally exhale into the bag, although the mouth and nose should not be covered. The neck of the bag can be drawn up under the chin for maximum protection. The orange colouring enables the bag to be

more easily seen by rescuers, giving it value as a signal marker. The bag can also play a role in obtaining water, (See Chapter "Water Procurement"), and possibly as part of shelter. (See Chapter "Survival Shelter Construction").

Wire Saw

The value of including a wire saw in your kit is obvious. A saw needs to be made from at least eight strands of wire if it is to have the strength it requires for lasting use. Keep this in mind when making your choice. Most of the better saws will cut wood, iron, bone and plastic. However, wire saws are relatively easily broken. Always saw slowly, not allowing the wire to overheat. When sawing is finished, the saw should be held straight and taut until it cools. For long term or one-handed use, make a bow-saw using a suitable green stick.

Used with rope or cord, the saw can cut overhead branches from ground level, so as to make a clearing in forested areas or bring down fruit-laden branches.

The smaller ring fitted at one end of the saw will pass through the larger ring at the other end, allowing the saw to become an efficient snare.

Water Purification Tablets

These provide a quick and convenient way of sterilising water. Each tablet will purify one litre of water in about ten minutes. The tablets will kill bacteria – but they do not remove any dirt present in the water. The treated water tastes of chlorine. Aim to carry about fifty tablets in your kit.

Knife

The most careful consideration should be given to your choice of knife, since it will be the main weapon in your arsenal during the fight for survival. The two basic types of knife to be considered are the pocket knife and the survival knife.

The pocket knife can be a simple single bladed pen-knife, but its blade should be strong and of the lock-back variety. At the other end of the scale is the Swiss Army type knife, which incorporates a wide variety of functions. It can include extra blades, scissors, can and bottle openers, screwdriver, and a saw among its many implements. It is strongly recommended that a small pocket knife should be carried as a matter of course whenever you travel into

the countryside away from habitation.

A survival knife is the alternative choice. During the last three years the growth of the survival knife industry has been little short of phenomenal, and almost every month sees the introduction of a new model. Most of these are of a sheath-knife pattern. Many have survival kits packed into a hollow handle or in a pouch on the sheath. The number and range of items included in the kit varies according to the model and its quality. The best survival knives range in price from £20 to £200. They offer truly remarkable assistance in any survival situation.

Unfortunately there has been a flood of cheap, poorly-made survival knives, mainly from the Far East. The greatest care has to be taken to avoid these when making your selection. They are likely to be of very little use at the very moment when they are most needed. The major criticism of such knives is the weakness of the joint between handle and blade, while the quality of the survival kit items included generally leaves much to be desired.

The ten items listed above will provide the basis of your personal survival kit, which may be built up with others from the following list of suggestions.

Fishing Tackle

A small fishing kit can be made up of about thirty metres of line, five hooks (size 14 or 16) and swivels, and ten weights (iron or brass). A brewer's cork can be used as a float. The cork, if charred, will provide face and hand camouflage – helpful if you are hunting. A plastic luminous lure is also useful.

Examples of snares.

Snares

It is possible to make four snares if you carry three metres of brass snare wire, but it is probably better to include ready made snares in addition to the wire. Ready made snares are cheap, and work more effectively. In either case, the snares should be rubbed with rabbit droppings before being set. They can also be used to catch water-fowl and fish.

The advantage of carrying spare brass wire is that it can be used for fishing traces, and for many tying purposes – in shelter building, fastening a blade to a stick, or for repairs of various kinds.

Many countries frown on the snaring of all forms of game.

Mention of snares is made here solely in the context of techniques for survival.

Other items which may qualify for inclusion in your kit may be found in the following list. All are of obvious use. The amount of space available will be the deciding factor for or against the inclusion of any particular item:—

Razor Blades	Scalpel Blade	Magnifying Glass
Energy Bars	Parachute Cord	Plastic Bags
Heliograph	Whistle	Safety Pins
Purse Net	Foil Container	Drinking Tube
	Thread	(Plastic, 20cm. x 3mm.)

You should also assemble a small personal medical/first aid kit. This should include the following items:—

Plasters	H-shaped Plasters	Suture Plasters
Burn Dressings	Large Wound Dressings	Aspirin
(Paraffin Gauze)	Mosquito Repellent	Cetrimide Cream
Antiseptic Wipes		(All Purpose Antiseptic)
Anti-diarrhoea tablets		

The recognition of the AIDS danger poses another problem. This is particularly relevant if the survivor is injured, and the emergency has occurred in a poor country, or one in which AIDS is widespread. The seriousness of any risk of becoming infected with the AIDS virus will depend on the factors making up your individual situation. The thoughtful survivor will certainly keep this threat in mind when planning travel in, through, or over, any country presenting a high risk of AIDS infection.

Assembling and Packing the Kit

The range of survival equipment is vast, with new items being added every year. You may well discover other items which would earn their places in your personal kit. When the final selection is made, there are two further steps to take before finally packing the kit.

The first is to prepare a list of all the chosen items. Now, study the list and again consider each item with care. Ask these questions about every one: Is it really necessary? Is its function duplicated by any other item? Remember always – the aim must be to keep your kit as small as possible.

This done, assemble all the pieces of equipment which have passed your tests. Make sure they are well packed and totally water-proof. The

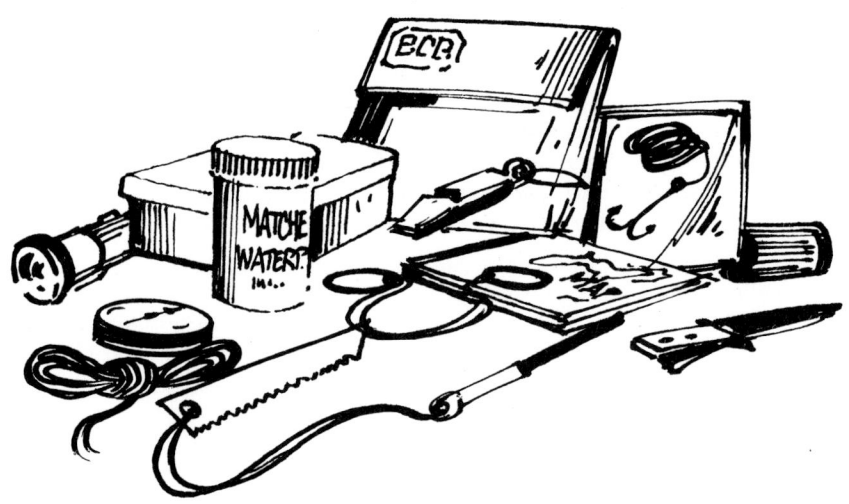

Typical Kit before packing.

simplest way of ensuring the latter is to seal the whole kit in an airtight container. A metal tobacco-type tin is ideal. Alternatives include, a waterproof plastic box, a re-sealable polythene bag inside a heavy-duty canvas pouch, a snap-seal plastic container (of the type used to pack tablets) or a screw-top metal cylindrical container. Once packed and closed, the container closure should be sealed with adhesive polythene tape.

It is important that the kit is not opened again until it is needed. The only exception to this rule would occur if you wished to modify the kit according to the type of expedition or journey which has been planned. For instance, if heading for an arid area, increase the items for water gathering and storage. A journey to a cold environment would call for items to provide warmth and the means to catch food. A jungle area would demand more, and probably stronger, tablets of different kinds.

Your final decision is simple, but of paramount importance. It is this. Whenever you are going to begin or even approach any activity or travel which may lead to a survival situation – take the kit with you and **KEEP IT ON YOUR PERSON.**

CLOTHING

So far we have dealt with the Personal Survival Kit, discussing in detail the need to assess each item with great care. Only after such careful consideration could one compile a Kit which could be expected to do its job properly. That job has two aspects. The first is to provide the survivor with the practical means to tackle the most pressing and threatening of his problems. The second, and by no means less important, is to give the survivor the confidence to enable him to meet those challenges effectively. This confidence is born of the knowledge that he is familiar with every item of his Kit, that each has been tried and tested, and that he has the technique and knowledge to make the best use of all.

Everyone involved in outdoor activities – at any level which takes him away from the well-trodden paths – should consider whether this general philosophy ought not to apply to ALL his equipment, clothing and supplies. Everyone who strolls, walks, hikes or marches away from the known, populous environment has to accept one fact. He is entering a situation where, for however brief a period, he has to rely on himself, what he is wearing and what he has with him. For as long as events follow their expected sequence this may be simple.

But the attraction of outdoor activity **is** that is it NOT controlled, NOT orderly, NOT organised. The inevitable conclusion from that

statement must be that, unless one wishes to be foolhardy, preparations must be made to deal with the unexpected. The unexpected might include serious deterioration of the weather, getting lost, suffering some kind of injury, or merely over-estimating your own capabilities so that a night outdoors is unavoidable, however unexpected or unwelcome it might be.

It is impossible to offer advice which meets individual needs, because individual activities and aspirations differ so widely. There are, however, general considerations which should be applied when planning outdoor activities. It cannot be stressed too strongly that a degree of planning (i.e. forethought) MUST precede every outdoor excursion, at whatever level. Death from exposure has claimed many who have not recognised this.

Extra spare clothing is essential if involved in an outdoor activity. This is particularly important in hilly areas. Worsening weather can be uncomfortable in any kind of country. If its effects are experienced on an exposed windy ridge, even a relatively warm wind produces a dangerous wind-chill factor. Extra clothing is important, too, for the times when rest stops are taken. The conditions may be comfortable while walking steadily, but once stopped, the body will cool rapidly.

A number of thin layers of clothing are more effective than a few thick garments. Light items are easier to fold and carry, and dry more readily if they do get wet. Thin cotton underclothes, covered with one or more layers of warm wear made from wool, fibre pile or fleece are ideal. The outer garment should be windproof, and preferably waterproof. It could be made from tightly woven cotton, polycotton, fibre-pile material or nylon. Nylon anoraks are inexpensive, light and easily packable. Their drawback is that they do not allow perspiration to escape. It therefore condenses inside the material. In very cold weather this could be dangerous, since the insulating properties of all other clothing being worn can be very much reduced if it is damp.

The better alternative for the outer garment is one which is made from a material which allows the water vapour from perspiration to escape. Some popular brand names of such materials include Gortex and Cyclone. Although expensive, they are highly recommended. For waterproof over-trousers, however, nylon should be adequate for most situations. When choosing them, make sure that they are wide in the leg, or are fitted with zip fasteners, so that they can be pulled on and off over the walking boots.

During outdoor activities the legs require adequate protection. Trousers made of substantial material are needed. Breeches are very suitable wear. These are made from corduroy and tweed – materials suitable for trousers, also. Denim jeans are definitely NOT recommended for walking outdoors.

Boots are the only footwear which can be recommended. A good quality pair of modern walking boots that are comfortable without being too heavy would be ideal. Climbing boots are not entirely suitable. They should be either water-proof in themselves, or capable of accepting a dressing which will make them so. The addition of water-proof nylon gaiters is also recommended.

All new footwear must be "broken in" by being worn for short periods at first. This allows the boot to adapt to your individual tread. Only when they have been broken in should you attempt any substantial walking. During use, they should be washed in clean water and allowed to dry well away from any direct or artificial heat source.

It is also necessary to carry at least two pairs of thick woollen socks or stockings. Add some sticking plaster for use if any blisters form. A spare pair of boot laces is imperative. Keeping your feet and boots in good condition is one of the basics of survival. Many people who were otherwise fit have died because of lack of foot care and protection.

These careful preparations, and the thought you have given to them, will bear fruit if and when any survival situation arises. You will be adequately protected. You will possess the resources to begin to make good use of your survival skills and techniques. You will not be frustrated by an inability to act. You will not be helpless. Most important of all, your survival kit will be the catalyst which stimulates thought and provides the will to start building your defences against the enemies of survival. **It will be, in fact, the means to help you to begin to help yourself.**

CHAPTER THREE

SURVIVAL

Situation Assessment and Planning

The first reaction to any dangerous emergency will almost certainly be instinctive – since self-preservation is the strongest drive we have. Danger – and the alarm and fear it engenders – makes the adrenalin flow, naturally stimulating and keying-up the body to an intensive effort if and when required. If you can accept fear as a natural, instinctive reaction, you have a greater chance of making good use of these bodily effects to extract yourself from the threatening situation. It is possible, for instance, to achieve a "personal best" performance if running from aircraft wreckage which is likely to explode.

However, instinctive actions have their limitations if the longer term is being considered. They only appear to be rational acts. They are, in fact, carried out without any conscious thought or intention.

The moment that the immediate personal danger has passed, observation and logic must take over. The overwhelming requirement in a survival situation brought about by any kind of emergency is to THINK. If you are to create the best chance of survival, you must make the very best use of every asset. The finest of these is – your brain. You must assess the situation and plan all activity so that it contributes to survival.

If you are not alone the first thing to do, of course, is to check carefully if anyone else needs help, giving first aid treatment as it may be required.

Having made sure that no-one is in immediate danger you should now act more deliberately. Establish and carry out a survival routine. This routine will be very valuable if you are alone, for it will provide a framework of purposeful action. If you have companions, it will help to minimise confusion. It will begin to bring about some semblance of order. Above all, it will offer an alternative to panic – a major enemy of survival – taking over.

If you are alone, carry out the steps of your survival routine in the order that best suits your circumstances. If you have companions, try to persuade them to join in. But however other members of the party may react – stick to the routine. Panic may well be infectious, but your cool,

Aircrash.

calm ordered attitude can be an effective antidote. Others will follow the right example when they see your lead.

1. Put on any appropriate clothing available. This will conserve body heat and/or body fluids, according to conditions. Never forget that protection from the cold is vital for survival. Layers of clothing which trap air will be warmer than one thick garment. Headgear is very important. Something like 30% of bodyheat loss can occur through an uncovered head. If you have no proper headgear – improvise something. Keep as dry as possible, since wet clothing can lose up to 90% of its insulating properties.

2. Collect and consolidate any survival equipment, food and water, together with any other useful items. Initially, interpret the phrase "useful items" as widely as possible. Even the most unlikely object may provide something which will become the key to unlock a particular problem. Adaptability is one of the names of the survival game. As an example, an electrical generator may not seem to be much of an aid in the provision of food – but it contains wire which will make workable snares and serve many other purposes.

3. Now look around and try to sort out your situation as it actually is. Forget any "if onlys", and maintain a strictly realistic approach. Take this opportunity to relax, and try to be more receptive to what you see, hear, smell and feel. Using the information gathered by the senses, begin to sort out priorities. Begin to put together the successive steps along your road to survival.

Among the first decisions you have to make is whether shelter is needed, against cold, wind, rain or snow. If the temperature is low, remember that the most dangerous threat will come from the cold, which can kill much more rapidly than lack of food or water. If you are in any doubt about needing weather protection, take the cautious option. Seek or construct shelter – even if it is to be only temporary. Find or make a shield against the wind to begin with – making full use of any natural features such as caves, the lee sides of rocks, trees, fallen logs, snow banks etc. Add cover from the wet as soon as possible. Do not waste time or energy building any sort of shelter if nature already provides it.

Making a fire may be another early need. The chapter on **Fire Lighting** will provide you with information about the various methods of achieving this. It is enough, at this stage, to point out that a fire has many values. It will be a signal of your location, a source of heat for all purposes, and, very importantly, a source of psychological reassurance and strength.

You will now have done everything possible about the immediately demanding requirements of your situation.

It is the moment to formulate your plan for future action based on the calculated priorities. This order of priorities will become clearer if you ask yourself – and others, if present – the questions below:—

Are you alone?

Are there any other survivors?

Are you, or is anyone else, injured?

If so, are the injured capable of moving or being moved?

What are the strengths and weaknesses of the party?

Has anyone any specialised skills or knowledge which can be of help in tackling any problems?

Are there any children or old people in the party?

What are the weather prospects?

Would it be possible to move through the surrounding terrain in safety?

Do you know your present position – or at least have some reasonable estimation of it?

Do you know in which direction the nearest help lies – and how far away it is?

What stocks of food or water do you have?

How long will they last?

What are the prospects of supplementing them from the country around you?

Is there more favourable terrain in sight, or within possible travelling distance?

What other essential equipment is available? (e.g. survival or first aid kits, tools etc.)

Have you any means of communicating with rescuers? (e.g. radio or distress beacon).

If you are in a group, discuss all these matters openly, excluding only any very young children as and when necessary.

Encourage everyone to give a point of view, so that the maximum range of information and opinion are available for consideration. Establish as many positive facts as possible. Use these facts – together with the best of the probabilities – to arrive at your decisions. If there is a group, try to arrive at joint decisions.

As a general rule, the aim should be to try to keep the party together, although there may well be pressing reasons for making a different choice. It may be that the best course is for some of the fittest and most experienced survivors to go for help if others are unable to travel.

Whether alone or with companions, it is essential to carry out this sort of examination of your situation. Once a decision is made, stick to it unless some major new circumstance arises which is sufficiently significant to warrant a change of plan.

Perhaps the earliest and most vital decision will be the choice between staying where you are and awaiting rescue, or attempting to make your way to safety. There is no single, simple answer. The circumstances of your survival situation will, to a greater or lesser extent, influence the choice you make.

You may, for example, become lost in the mountains and/or be threatened by the onset of foul weather. You may be a survivor of an aircraft, crashed or force-landed in a remote area. You may be the survivor of a shipwreck, cast either ashore or into a boat or dinghy. The variety of possible causes is endless, and the range of circumstances resulting is infinite.

The particular survival situation will dictate the nature of your response to each problem or challenge. You can make the most favourable selection from the options available **only** if you remain calm and bring a rational, informed approach to your problems. Some of the factors which will contribute to this early decision will be included in your responses to these further questions and accompanying observations.

(i) How long is it likely to be before you are missed, the alarm raised, and a search organised? What sort of difficulties might the rescuers encounter? How long will they take to find you and then reach your locality? To arrive at something like a realistic estimate, triple the total of these times. You must plan to survive for this length of time. You must do all you can to shorten it, by assisting your rescuers in various ways.

(ii) Have you left an accurate plan of your movements with a responsible person? If so, have you deviated from the plan to a degree which would increase the difficulty of your rescuers? Is it feasible to regain a position on your projected route?

(iii) If your emergency has arisen because of any sort of mishap to transport, it is a fact that searchers are more likely to spot wreckage –

of aircraft, ship or motor transport – than individuals. In addition, if you decide to stay and await rescue, you can do a number of things to make your location more visible. You will also be staying close to whatever resources are offered by the vehicle or its wreckage.

(iv) Even if no-one in the party is injured, any decision on attempting to walk out to safety must recognise that your pace will be that of the slowest and weakest in the group. Your calculations must include this, if it is a factor.

(v) Check the surrounding area, without wandering too far away, so that you are able to return without difficulty. You will probably be able to make a better assessment of the ease or difficulty of moving in the locality. You will also gain information regarding the availability of water, fuel and food.

Having taken time and trouble to collect the best information obtainable, be sure to make good use of it. Remember, always, that you are looking for the **safest** option – the choice that will give you the best chance of surviving. You must be realistic in assessing the situation. Generate and maintain optimism – but never minimise the difficulties. Accept them, and work positively to find the means to overcome them.

If your decision is to stay put and await rescue, your plans will be aimed at surviving until help arrives and doing all you can to shorten the time you have to wait. Help your rescuers in every possible way. Try to put yourself in their position.

Where will they come from? Where are they likely to start searching? How are they going to come? Using the knowledge you have gained about the area, try to anticipate what difficulties they may experience. What signs will they be looking for? How can you make those signs more obvious, more easily seen? You may not be able to go to meet them physically, but you can try to meet them mentally, which will help to choose the most effective methods of helping them to find you.

Positive activity in support of your own rescue will certainly help to keep apathy and apprehension at bay. What can be done is detailed in the Chapter on Location Signalling.

If you have decided to move, the information from the Chapter on Survival Navigation, will be needed.

Before you move, however, consider carefully what you can take with you. Your choice may have to be a compromise between what is available and how much can be conveniently carried. If you are in a group, make sure that all available protective clothing has been shared equally, and that everyone is as fully protected as possible.

Select what you are taking with great care. You will, of course, regard any survival supplies – first aid, food, water, survival kits, flares etc., as priority, adding to them anything which may be useful but is not bulky or weighty. Use the same criteria as you would for assembling your own Personal Survival Kit (see Chapter 2) – but with ingenuity and a wide eye for adaptability. You have to be able to survive while travelling. You have to be able to obtain/provide shelter, warmth, food and water, especially during overnight stops. Take the items which offer the best help in meeting these needs.

The decision to move might be with the intention of reaching safety and help without outside aid. On the other hand, your aim might be limited to achieving a most favourable position – such as a move from a cold, exposed highland area down into a sheltered valley. (Remembering, though, that the very lowest parts of a valley will themselves be the coldest). In this case, it is worth keeping in mind the feasibility of returning, later, if there are any useful items or supplies that you cannot move on your first trip.

Survival has as its parameters these essentials:—

First Aid – Protection – Water – Fire – Food – Location

You are able to assess your situation. You are able to place these essentials in correct priority by using your knowledge, skills, self-control and intelligence. Your will to survive is inbred. Foster this will with your Survival Techniques – and you will live.

CHAPTER FOUR

FIRST AID FOR SURVIVAL

The term, "First Aid", implies primary help and treatment given to a casualty until medical care or hospitalisation becomes available. The ability to produce first aid has enormous value in normal circumstances. This value is beyond measure in a survival situation, where there may be no prospect of skilled assistance, backed by proper resources, for an indefinite period.

Even though medical supplies may be inadequate or entirely absent, you may have to provide first aid for yourself or other survivors. Improvised equipment, used with even limited knowledge, can save lives. If it is backed by wider knowledge and practised skills, the same simple equipment can arrest deterioration of a casualty's condition, providing him with his chance of staying alive until rescued. It can even open the way to recovery.

As in every other aspect of a survival situation, the need for first aid has to be assessed, priorities established, and a planned course of action carried out. The situation itself will impose its own directions. There may be several casualties needing attention simultaneously. Familiarity with the treatment procedures detailed below will help sort out the order in which they should be treated. But whatever the circumstances, keep these general rules in mind:—

1. Keep calm. However serious an injury or dangerous a situation, panic will only impair the ability to think and so lower effectiveness. Time will be wasted – and time can mean life.

2. Avoid any unnecessary danger to yourself. This is not cowardice. You will be no help to anybody if you suffer needless injury. Any other injured survivor needs you to take care of yourself. So, stay fit to help him.

3. Think carefully, but as quickly as possible, before you act.

4. Do your best to reassure and comfort any casualty. Try to provide the sort of encouragement from which the will to live will grow.

5. Find out if there are any other uninjured or active survivors who can help to deal with the situation. In particular, look for any survivor with medical qualifications or better experience than your own. Even if

injured, this person could direct you so that your activities are more effective.

6. When assessing individual casualties, use your own senses to the full. ASK. LOOK. LISTEN. SMELL. Then THINK and ACT.

Ask the casualty to describe his symptoms and to tell you what he thinks happened and what he feels is wrong. If there are others present, check if anyone has anything relevant to add. You may be guided towards an injury by someone else's observation of what happened.

Look – Touch – Listen – Smell. These actions form the basis of your check on the casualty's condition – together with his description of symptoms. If he is unconscious, you will have to rely on what your senses tell you, assisted by anyone else's observations.

General advice for deciding the order of treatment, if there are several casualties, is given below. Any injured survivor should first be moved clear of further immediate danger. Those in positions of relative safety should be treated before being moved. You must assess the seriousness of individual injuries. You must assess how rapid a threat to life they are, and what help you can give. Bear in mind that the casualty making the most noise is not necessarily the most seriously injured. When assessing priorities keep in mind that the quickest killer is lack of air. Remember that air is obtained for the body by breathing through airways and then by the circulation of the blood. Serious bleeding is probably the second quickest killer, while shock can also be fatal if it is serious and untreated or aggravated.

Any survivor who is unconscious or appears to be choking should be given help as soon as possible. Check that each is breathing and has a detectable heartbeat or pulse. Absence of either or both of these vital functions means that the casualty requires **immediate** help on the lines given below. The urgency arises from the fact that the brain can begin to sustain damage after only three minutes without oxygen.

BREATHING

To determine if an unconscious casualty is breathing listen with your ear close to the nose and mouth. You should be able to hear and feel any breath. Watch out for chest and abdominal movement at the same time. If there is no sign of breathing, take immediate action to ensure that the air passages are clear.

(a) Supporting the neck with one hand, ease the head backwards with the other. Keeping the head back, lift the chin upwards.

This action will open the air passage and bring the tongue forward to prevent it from being an obstruction. Check quickly inside the mouth to find and remove any other cause of blockage e.g. dentures, vomit or other material. Once the air passage is open and clear, the casualty may begin breathing again. If this happens, and his heart is beating, put him into the coma (or recovery) position (Illustrated later in the chapter). If there is visible injury to the front or back of the head (which might indicate damage to the neck or spine), maintain the clear airway with the head back. Improvise some form of collar or head support to keep the head correctly positioned.

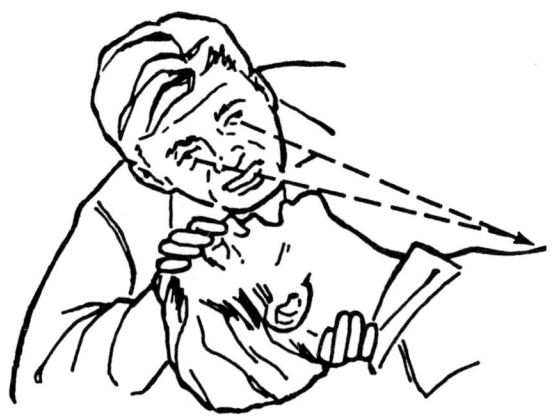

Assisted Breathing.

(b) If breathing does not re-commence the casualty must be given help with respiration. This can best be done on a mouth-to-mouth basis. Taking a deep breath, pinch the casualty's nose to prevent air loss, open your own mouth wide and seal your own lips around his open mouth. Blow into his lungs, watching for expansion of the chest. When the maximum expansion is reached, raise your head well clear and breathe out and in. Look now for chest contraction. When this has happened, repeat the procedure four times. It may be more convenient to use mouth-to-nose contact. In this case, the casualty's mouth must be kept shut to prevent the loss of air.

Following the fourth assisted breath, it is important to check that the casualty's heart is beating. The oxygen, having been taken up by the blood, must be delivered to the body's vital organs. Feel for the carotid pulse, in the neck.

If there is no heartbeat, chest compression must be carried out as in 2. below. **BE SURE** that there is **NO** heartbeat before beginning chest compression. Far more harm than good will be done if attempted chest compression interferes with an existing heartbeat, however weak.

If the heart is beating, continue giving assisted breaths at between 16 and 18 a minute. When the casualty begins breathing for himself, continue giving assistance at his natural rate until breathing is normal. Then place him in the coma (recovery) position.

CHEST COMPRESSION

Check that the casualty is lying on a firm surface. Kneeling alongside, locate the bottom of the breastbone. Measure the width of three fingers up and place the heel of one hand on the bone. Lay the other hand over the first. Keeping the elbows rigid, lean forward so that your arms are vertical and your weight bearing down on the casualty's chest. Depress the breastbone by between 4 and 5 cms. Lean back to release the pressure, so allowing the breastbone to return to its original position. Perform 15 compressions at the rate of about 80 per minute. (Count, one back two back three back and so on, leaning forward on each number.)

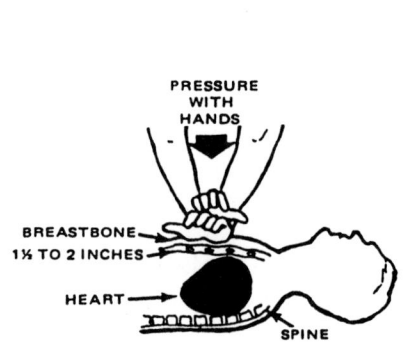

Chest Compression (Heart Massage).

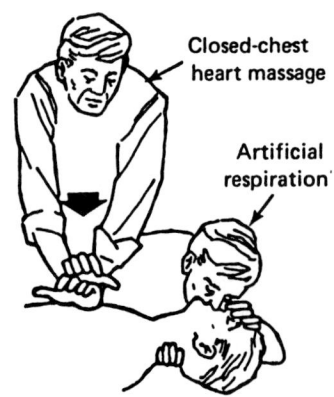

Alternating Chest Compression with Assisted Breathing.

In normal conditions, breathing and circulation take place at the same time. The casualty needs both, so assisted breathing and chest compression must be carried out together. If you are alone, the procedures have to be alternated. As soon as the first 15 compressions have been given, restore the open air-passage position of the head and provide two more assisted breaths. When this has been done, continue this cycle: 15 compressions and 2 assisted breaths for a full minute. Then check for any heartbeat. If none is present, continue the treatment, checking for heartbeat every three minutes.

If two active survivors are available they should each provide part of the treatment – one assisting breathing, the other providing the compressions. At the start, give 4 assisted breaths and follow these with 5 compressions. Then establish a pattern of 1 assisted breath followed by 5 compressions. Aim at a rate of one compression per second. Each assisted breath should follow the release of the fifth compression without pause. The check for heartbeat should be made after one minute and then after every succeeding three minutes. Discontinue compression when a pulse is felt. Continue with assisted breathing until the casualty breathes for himself. When breathing and heartbeat are both established, place him in the coma position after checking for other injuries.

If the casualty is a child, less pressure must be applied. Use the routine as above, but place only two fingers on the breastbone instead of the heel of the hand.

CHOKING

Any survivor showing serious signs of choking is in need of immediate assistance. These signs may include being unable to speak or breathe, the skin going pale or blue, the casualty grasping his throat. The condition is usually caused by something lodged in the windpipe which prevents free passage of air to the lungs.

Removal of the obstruction is an urgent requirement. A conscious survivor should be encouraged to cough it away. If this is ineffective, check inside the mouth to see if the blockage can be cleared by a finger.

If the choking continues, gravity and slapping should be tried to shake it free. Do this by helping the casualty to bend forward so that the head is below lung level. Now slap him sharply between the shoulder blades, using the heel of the hand. This may be repeated three more times if necessary. Check inside the mouth and remove the obstruction if it has been freed. If it has not, try to clear it using air pressure generated by abdominal thrusts.

If the casualty is conscious and upright, stand behind him and put your arms around his waist. Clench one fist and place it with thumb side against his abdomen. Make sure it is resting between his navel and the lower end of the breastbone. Place your other hand over the fist. Make a firm thrust upwards and into the abdomen. Do this up to four times if required. Pause after each thrust and be prepared to remove anything dislodged from the air passage.

Treatment of Choking (Adult).

Back Slapping following Abdominal Thrusts.

Should the choking still persist, repeat the four back slaps and the four abdominal thrusts alternately until the obstruction is cleared.

An unconscious casualty requiring the thrusts must be turned on his back. Kneeling astride him, place the heel of one hand between the navel and breastbone, and put the other hand on top. Deliver the four thrusts as above. If the obstruction persists, and the patient stops breathing, begin assisted breathing and chest compression as above.

If the sufferer is a child, employ the same procedures but with less force. The child may be placed face-down across your knees.

It is stressed that these techniques need skilled guidance and practice if they are to be employed effectively. As with most other survival techniques, the ability to use them quickly, accurately and with certainty is only acquired through practical experience. The St. John's Ambulance Association provides such instruction in most areas of the United Kingdom.

Make use of this facility – and you will be equipped to handle the

Treatment of Choking (Child).

difficulties of the sort of situation described above. Continued practice will make these procedures into disciplined drills – which could be drills by numbers. They need to be acquired so well that they can be carried out in the dark – or in any other difficult condition.

35

THE COMA POSITION

Generally, an unconscious survivor who is breathing and who has a reasonable heartbeat, and is without other injuries demanding immediate attention, should be put into the coma (or recovery) position. This position, illustrated below, is the safest because it minimises the risk of impeded breathing. The tilted-back head ensures open air-passages. The face-down attitude allows any vomit or other liquid obstruction to drain from the mouth.

The spread of the limbs will maintain the body in its position. If fractures or other injuries prevent suitable placing of the limbs, use rolled clothing or other padded objects to prop the survivor in this position.

BLEEDING

Bleeding should be stopped as soon as possible. There are three options available.

(a) DIRECT PRESSURE

Place a dressing over the wound and apply firm but gentle pressure with the hand. A sterile dressing is desirable. If one is not available any piece of clean cloth can be used. If no dressing is ready for immediate use, cover the wound with your hand. If necessary, hold the edges of the wound together with gentle pressure. Any dressings used should be large enough to overlap the wound and cover the surrounding area. If blood comes through the first dressing, apply a second over the first, and if required, a third over the second. Keep even pressure applied by trying on a firm bandage. Take great care that the bandage is not so tight that, like a tourniquet, it restricts the flow of blood.

If the wound is large and suitable dressings are to hand, bring the edges of the wound together and use the dressings to keep the wound closed. To arrest the flow of blood from a very large wound, make a pad of the dressing and press it in to the wound where the bleeding is heaviest.

The object of this treatment is to slow down or stop the loss of blood until the body's own defences come into play. These defences include: (i) the fact that blood will clot relatively quickly if the flow is slowed or stopped, and (ii) although a cleanly cut blood vessel may bleed profusely if left untreated, it will tend to shrink, close and retreat into its surrounding tissue. Sometimes these natural methods will succeed in arresting bleeding entirely unaided.

Reassurance and rest play their vital part in the treatment since they can lower the rate of heartbeat and so reduce the flow of blood around the body.

(b) **ELEVATION**

If there is no danger of any other injury being aggravated, an injured limb is best raised as high as is comfortable for the casualty. This reduces the blood-flow in the limb, helps the veins to drain the area and so assists in reducing the blood loss through the wound.

(c) **INDIRECT PRESSURE**

If a combination of these procedures does not succeed, the use of appropriate pressure points must be considered. It is necessary to recognise the type of external bleeding, because pressure points can only be used to control ARTERIAL bleeding. Arteries carry the blood outwards form the heart, in pulses of pressure. At this stage, the blood has been oxygenated and filtered of its impurities, therefore:—

      (a) Arterial bleeding is revealed when bright red blood spurts out in time with the heartbeat.

while (b) Blood from the veins flows out steadily, with less pressure, and is darker red.

A place where an artery runs across a bone near the surface of the skin constitutes a pressure point. There are four pressure points readily available to control heavy arterial bleeding – one in each limb. Those in the arms are on the brachial arteries. These run down the centre of the inner side of the upper arm.

Pressure points for the legs are on the femoral arteries, which run down the inside of the thigh. The pressure points can be found in the centre of the groin, and can be compressed against the pelvis. This is

PRESSURE POINTS

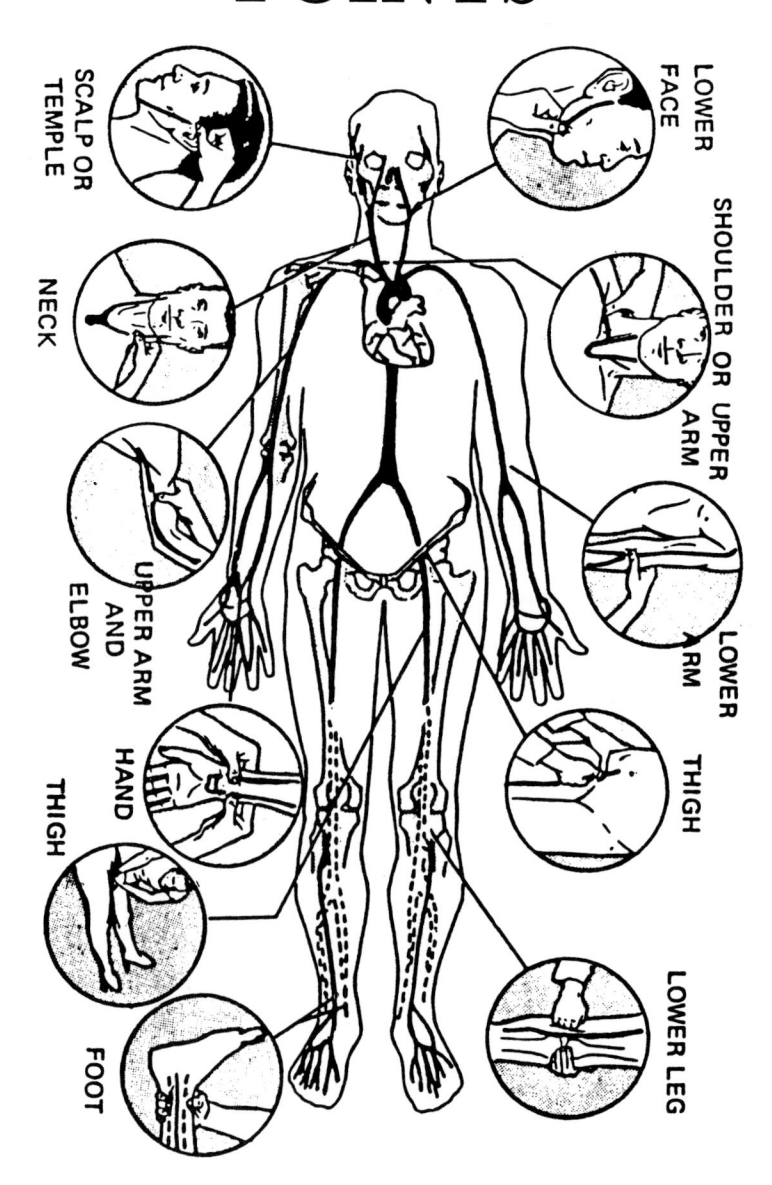

easier to do if the casualty's knee is bent. When using pressure points to control bleeding make full use of the opportunity to dress the wound more effectively.

PRESSURE APPLICATION

(i)   Locate the fingers or thumb over the pressure point and apply sufficient pressure to flatten the artery and arrest the flow of blood.

(ii) Redress the wound.

(iii) Maintain the pressure for at least ten minutes to allow time for blood-clotting to begin. **DO NOT EXCEED 15 MINUTES PRESSURE** or the tissues below the pressure point will begin to be damaged by the deprivation of arterial blood. It is essential to release the controlling pressure after **15 minutes.**

Try to prepare mentally for the unlikely – but possible – moment when you may yourself be injured, conscious and alone. Have ready a self-help routine:—

(i)   Lie down and rest – out of the wind if possible.

(ii) Apply direct pressure to your wound. Put a dressing, improvised or otherwise, on it.

(iii) Tie on a bandage tight enough to maintain firm pressure without restricting circulation.

(iv) Elevate the injury if possible. Keep as still as possible to relieve pain.

Your effective use of techniques to control bleeding will be infinitely improved if you have previously received skilled practical instruction. Serious bleeding, like breathing and circulation difficulties, can pose the most urgent of threats to life. Rapid and correct action to deal with them may be literally a matter of life or death. Attendance at practical courses like those offered by the St. John's Ambulance Association will equip you to provide just such action – the action to convert a casualty into a survivor. And remember, the casualty could be you . . .

INTERNAL BLEEDING

In the aftermath of an accident, there may be casualties suffering from internal bleeding. This will be revealed by the symptoms of blood, blood in the faeces or urine, or blood loss from the ears, nose, mouth or rectum. It can be as damaging as external bleeding, but there is little that can be offered by way of first aid. The only treatment is reassurance, protection from cold and lying down at rest. A drink of water is allowable if there is no abdominal injury. If the casualty loses consciousness, place him in the coma position.

SHOCK

Although the reasons for shock can be complex and varied, and it can be a serious – even fatal – condition, its recognition can be very simple. First aid treatment can be very effective. Its basic cause is the loss, or unavailability of, circulating body fluids. The fluid loss can be unrecoverable as in:

– loss of blood through external or internal bleeding.

– loss of plasma due to continuous "weeping" through surface capillaries damaged by burns.

– dehydration caused by recurrent vomiting or diarrhoea or shortage of drinking water.

In these cases the body withdraws fluid from the circulatory system to replace that which has been lost.

Unavailability of blood can also be due to "pooling" caused by an involuntary reaction of the nervous system to extreme pain, to fear, or to other emotional disturbances. Illness and severe injury can also produce this reaction which has the effect of lowering the blood pressure.

Whatever the cause of shock, the symptoms are always the same. The casualty will become increasingly pale, cold and clammy. He will feel restless. His face will assume a pinched, anxious appearance – eventually even ashen, with sunken eyes. His breathing will be rapid and shallow. He may be gasping for air in a vain attempt to make insufficient blood carry oxygen around the body. His thirst will increase and he will feel weak and giddy. These signs become more marked as the blood loss and the severity of shock increase. The pulse will become increasingly faster and detectably weaker.

Note, however, that if the pulse is SLOW and weak, then it is likely that the shock will be due to emotional disturbance rather than physical injury. If observed, this is a very significant symptom, for it demonstrates how great a part emotion can play in causing shock. It can be the only cause in some cases. The symptom also emphasises that shock should be treated with responses to both its emotional and physical causes.

EMOTIONAL TREATMENT

(i) Handle the casualty gently and carefully.

(ii) Provide immediate comfort and reassurance – and continue both throughout the treatment.

(iii) Rest the casualty in the quietest obtainable surroundings, moving him as little as possible.

(iv) If practicable, the casualty should lie on his back, head low and turned to one side, with legs raised unless injuries or breathing difficulties prevent this. In this position available blood will be supplied to the vital organs.

(v) Provide protection from the cold and wet. Loosen any tight clothing that might impede circulation or breathing. Do not provide any external heat (e.g. warm stones, hot water container) – they would divert blood to the skin, away from the heart, lungs and brain.

PHYSICAL TREATMENT

(a) Check for and identify any injuries. Arrest any bleeding as quickly as possible, using the methods described above. Immobilise any fracture discovered (see below). If pain-relieving tablets are available, consider their use.

(b) If the casualty is conscious and has no stomach injury, supply him with a warm drink.

(c) Should any breathing difficulty develop put him in the coma position, and watch carefully to see if there is any deterioration calling for assistance with breathing.

(d) A slow, bounding pulse could suggest head injury or some other interference with the functions of the brain (e.g. carbon monoxide poisoning). If the symptom is present, check for other signs of concussion or skull fracture (see below). If none are found, look for any source of poisoning. Remove it and ensure that the casualty is supplied with fresh air.

If you are alone, find shelter from the wind. Lie down, if possible, with your head lower than your feet. Arrest any bleeding as soon as practicable and do what you can to keep warm. Then rest for a minimum of 24 hours before attempting anything further.

FRACTURES

A bone fracture should be suspected if any or all of these signs are present:

- difficulty in normal movement of any part of the body.
- increased pain when movement is attempted.
- swelling or bruising accompanied by tenderness in the area of an injury.
- deformity or shortening of the injured part.
- grating of bone heard during examination or attempted movement.
- signs of shock.
- the survivor having heard or felt a bone break.

The only treatment available in a survival situation is immobilisation of the fracture. Unless some other immediate danger threatens, splint the casualty before moving him. In any case, handle him with the greatest care to avoid further pain or additional injury. If there is a wound associated with the fracture, remove the clothing in the immediate area and treat the wound before fitting splints.

Splints can be improvised from sticks, branches, suitable pieces of wreckage or equipment – even a tight roll of clothing or bedding. Pad the splint and fasten it so that it supports the joints above and below the fracture. A fractured leg can be partially immobilised by tying it to the good leg if nothing else is available. A fractured leg may be deformed, shortened or twisted unnaturally. In such cases re-alignment should be attempted before immobilisation **if the casualty is prepared to allow it.** Carefully and gently pull the end of the limb and reset or straighten it. When all that is possible has been done, apply the splints.

The only further help that can be given is to raise the injured part to cut down swelling and discomfort, and to treat any symptoms of shock. The casualty then needs rest.

CONCUSSION/SKULL FRACTURE

If a survivor is even briefly unconscious, if clear or blood-tinged fluid is coming from the ears or nose, or if the pupils of his eyes are unequal or unresponsive, then skull fracture or concussion should be suspected. If he is unconscious, his breathing and pulse should be monitored. If they are normal, he should be placed in the coma position. If he is conscious, place him in a reclining position with head and shoulders supported. In either case, keep him warm and handle gently.

BURNS

The immediate aim when treating any burn is to lessen the ill-effects of the excessive heat. Do this by gently immersing the injured part in cold water or slowly pouring cold water over it. Persist with this treatment for 10 minutes, or longer if the pain is not relieved. Cooling in this way will stop further damage, relieve pain, and reduce the possibilities of swelling or shock. Offer reassurance to the survivor.

A burn opens the way for infection to enter the body, which means that a dressing should be applied. A sterile non-fluffy dressing is best, but any suitable piece of clean material will do. Dressings and bandages can be made fairly sterile by boiling, or steaming them in a lidded container. Scorching of material will also kill most germs.

A solution of tannic acid will assist in the healing of burns. Tree bark, boiled for as long as possible, will provide this. Oak bark is the best source, but chestnut or hemlock are good alternatives. Any bark will yield some tannic acid. As the water boils away, replace it with more, adding extra bark if possible. A strong tea solution will provide the same assistance. Do not use either solution until cold.

If any restricting clothing or other item is being worn near the burned area, remove it before any swelling develops. Do not touch the burn, nor use any form of adhesive dressing. If any blisters form, do not break or drain them. They are a natural protective cover for the injury and should themselves be protected. If burns or scalds are severe, lay the survivor in a comfortable position a soon as possible. If he is unconscious, place him in the coma position.

The most likely type of burn to be encountered will be sunburn. Over-exposure to direct sunlight – especially when combined with persistent wind – can produce serious burning. Skin, wet with seawater or sweat, is similarly at risk. If it does occur, protect the survivor from further exposure. Treat the area with tannic acid solution (or ointment if available), or cool it with water. Then cover with a dressing. Keep the dressing in place unless is is essential that it be removed. Provide the survivor with plenty of fluids (or as much as possible) and rest the burned area.

FROSTBITE AND HYPOTHERMIA

Exposure to temperatures below freezing – especially if it is windy and/or wet – involves continual risk of Hypothermia and/or Frostbite.

Windy conditions increase the risk of Frostbite and Hypothermia because the cooling effects of cold air are markedly increased by its movement. Air moving at 48 k.p.h. (30 m.p.h.) and having a temperature of − 20 degs.C. has the same chilling effect as air at − 40 degs.C. moving at only 8 k.p.h. (5 m.p.h.). Wet conditions increase danger because wet cold air is a better conductor of heat, and can therefore carry more away from the body. In addition, many of the insulating properties of clothing are lost if garments are wet or damp. Both are serious conditions, and everything possible must be done to avoid them.

1. Make the most efficient use of all available clothing. Remember that a number of thinner layers are more effective than one or two thick, heavy garments in preventing loss of body heat. The aim is to maintain a layer of unchanging air close to your body. Tight clothing should therefore be avoided.

2. Adjust your clothing so as to reduce sweating. Too much perspiration would lower the insulating efficiency of clothing as well as cool the skin as the sweat evaporated. Remove layers of clothing and/or open garments at the front, wrist or neck to get the right balance.

3. Do everything possible to prevent clothing getting wet, and do all you can to dry it if it **does** get wet.

4. Take special care of hands and feet. They are at the limits of circulation and can lose heat very rapidly. Do everything possible to ensure that the fastenings at wrists, ankles, neck and around the waist are efficient without restricting the circulation of blood. Keep hands under cover whenever possible, warming them under the armpits or between the thighs when necessary. If toes are nipped by frost, warm them against a companion if possible. If alone, warm them by wriggling, moving the feet and massage.

5. Make every endeavour to keep your feet dry. If spare socks are available, keep some next to your body so that a change into a dry pair can be made at least once a day. Periodically remove footwear and rub your feet for up to ten minutes. Try to improvise over-boots to ensure extra insulation against cold and wet.

6. Any contact with bare metals or exceptionally cold liquids presents a particular risk to fingers and hands, and should be avoided. Examples of liquids in this category are petrol and anti-freeze solution.

FROSTBITE

Besides being a dangerous condition in itself – it can lead to gangrene – the risk of frostbite demands particular vigilance, since it can occur without your being aware of it. There may be a feeling of pins and needles in an affected part. Stiffness and numbness are equally likely to be the only symptoms. But either of these will be followed by a greyish or whitish colouring of the skin in the affected area.

It is important to check exposed skin areas frequently – in particular the ears and nose. Other high risk areas include ankles and wrists, which may be inadequately protected. If you have companions, pair off to watch each other for symptoms. If any are found, the frostbitten area should be slowly and naturally warmed. The best method is by skin to skin contact e.g. hands in armpits. Warm water (use the baby-bath test – you should be able to keep your elbow in it) can be used to provide **gentle** warming. Provide shelter as soon as possible, but in any case, insulate the survivor against further loss of body heat using blankets, extra clothing, etc. Provide hot food and drink as soon as practicable.

If frostbite is detected:—

> **DO NOT** rub or massage the area affected.
> **DO NOT** apply snow or ice. This treatment is dangerous.
> **DO NOT** employ hot stones or expose to a fire.
> **DO NOT** give alcohol to drink.
> **DO NOT** allow a survivor to walk, using a foot recently frostbitten.
> **DO NOT** break or open any blisters which may appear.

HYPOTHERMIA

This general condition of the body is caused when it loses heat more quickly than that heat can be replaced. Among the conditions likely to produce an increased risk of Hypothermia are cold, wet weather, wet clothing, immersion in cold water, exhaustion, inadequate clothing and shortage of food or drink. Hypothermia is not an easily diagnosed condition. It is important, therefore, to keep a special look-out if you are subject to any of these conditions.

Signs of hypothermia include:

- paleness and severe uncontrollable shivering
- being sub-normally cold to the touch
- muscular weakness and fatigue
- drowsiness and dimming of sight
- diminishing heartbeat and breathing

– eventual collapse and unconsciousness (extremely serious)

In addition to the signs listed, perhaps the most striking sign of the onset of hypothermia is that of a marked change in personality of the sufferer. An extrovert may become an introvert. Aggressiveness may change to submissiveness, or vice-versa. What is certain is that hypothermia is deadly unless treated.

The treatment of hypothermia is centred on stopping the loss of body heat and replacing lost warmth.

1. Provide shelter from the wind and cold as soon as possible.

2. If dry clothing/covering is available use it to replace any wet clothing. Replace wet clothing in stages, uncovering as little of the body as possible at any one time. Allow even that part to remain uncovered for as brief a period as practicable.

3. If no dry clothing is available, leave any wet garments on and cover them with additional insulation against the cold. Add a final waterproof layer. A metallised emergency blanket is ideal for this purpose. It is wind and water-proof as well as being reflective of radiated body heat.

4. Provide body warmth – another healthy survivor is a good source. If the casualty is conscious, give hot food and drink.

There are two other actions to remember if hypothermia is encountered.

(a) Proceed with treatment even if breathing and heartbeat are undetectable. If this is the case, assisted breathing and chest compression will be necessary. Do not assume death from hypothermia unless normal body temperature has been achieved and the casualty still does not revive.

(b) Handle the survivor gently. Frozen skin and flesh are very easily damaged.

If hypothermia is detected:—

DO NOT rub or massage to stimulate circulation.
DO NOT warm the casualty too quickly.
DO NOT permit the casualty further exertion.
DO NO give the casualty alcohol.

IMMERSION (TRENCH) FOOT

This condition occurs when the feet are immersed in cold water for prolonged periods. The feet swell, become white and numb, and the skin can become broken and the flesh ulcerated. It should be kept in mind that this condition does not only develop in extremely cold water. It can happen in water which is below 15 degrees Centigrade (or 59 degs. Fahrenheit). This is well above freezing. If the feet are wet for any lengthy period, check their condition frequently.

Immersion Foot can be prevented by keeping the feet out of contact with water. Wear sea-boots if available. If socks are wet, remove and empty the boots. Wring out the socks and replace them as quickly as possible. Rub the feet for 5 to 10 minutes periodically, or keep the feet and toes moving. If the condition does arise it should be treated as follows:—

1. Dry the feet very gently. **DO NOT** rub the skin.
2. Apply an antiseptic cream to any area where the skin is broken.
3. Protect the feet with bandages loosely applied.
4. Keep the body warm, but allow the feet to warm up as slowly as possible and elevate the legs.
5. **DO NOT** allow the casualty to walk on damaged feet.

BITES AND STINGS

No survivor should make the mistake of thinking that the greatest danger comes from the biggest animals. The vast majority of big game, snakes and other reptiles want to avoid you at least as much as you want to avoid them. The major – and very grave – threats are presented by some of the smallest forms of wild life. They can be carriers of debilitating and often fatal diseases, and can convey the infection when they bite. Every survivor has several lines of defence against disease germs and must make the best use of every single one.

1. IMMUNISATION

Be sure that you are immunised against as many diseases as possible – and that your immunisation record is kept up to date. Typhoid, Paratyphoid, Yellow Fever, Typhus, Tetanus, Smallpox and Cholera are among the preventable diseases. Seek medical advice regarding any special precautions needed for the areas in which you may be involved.

2. PERSONAL HYGIENE

Bodily cleanliness is a major protection against disease germs and infestations. A daily wash with warm water and soap is the ideal. If this if this is not possible, concentrate on keeping the hands clean, and wash and sponge the face, armpits, crotch and feet at least once a day. Clothing – especially underclothing – must be kept as clean and dry as possible. At the very least, shake out clothing and expose it to the sun and air each day. Check for and remove ticks, lice and fleas regularly.

3. PRECAUTIONS AGAINST INSECT BITES

Any insect bite is potentially dangerous. Mosquitoes, while not particularly dangerous in the Arctic and Temperate Regions, can be deadly in the Tropics. There they can carry malaria, yellow fever and filariasis. Do everything possible to gain protection against their bites.

(i) Use mosquito netting or repellant constantly if it is available. If not, cover any exposed skin with handkerchiefs, parachute material or anything else to hand. Even large leaves will help.

(ii) Wear full clothing – especially at night. Keep trouser legs tucked into the tops of socks and shirt sleeves into gloves or other improvised hand covering.

(iii) Smear the face and other exposed skin with mud before bedding down for the night.

(iv) Select rest-sites or camps which are clear of and higher than swampy ground or stagnant or sluggish water, since this is where mosquitoes breed.

(v) Establish a slow smoky fire to windward of the campsite. Keep it burning to drive insects away.

(vi) A ring of wood ash around your bed space will deter most crawling insects.

(vii) There is no immunisation against malaria, so any anti-malarial drugs must be used as directed for as long as they last.

Other small creeping, crawling and flying hazards include:—

Sandflies. These carry and transmit sandfly fever, which has to be treated in the same way as malaria. They are too small for ordinary netting to be effective – but they rarely rise above 3 metres from the ground or fly in moving air.

Flies. There are many species, varying widely in the diseases they can transmit. Protective measures employed against mosquitoes usually work against flies also.

Bees, Wasps and Hornets. All are very dangerous if aroused. Nests are generally brownish oval or oblong masses, on tree trunks or branches between 3 and 10 metres above ground. Avoid them if possible. If a swarm is disturbed, and you are a few metres distant, sit still for 5 minutes or so, and then crawl away slowly and carefully. Should you be attacked, run through the bushiest undergrowth to be found. This will beat off the insects as it springs back. Immersion in water is another defence.

Ticks. Carriers of typhus, these oval, flat insects should never be pulled off the skin or squashed while biting, or the heads may remain embedded and become sources of infection. Smoke, iodine, petrol or paraffin put on the bodies will relax their grip.

Ants. Tropical ants can bite severely and in great numbers. They and their nests are best avoided and left undisturbed.

Lice. Lice can also carry typhus. Check your clothing frequently for these pests. Remove them with anti-louse powder if it is available. If not, then boiling or a few hours' exposure to direct sunlight will remove them. If bitten, wash with strong soap or a weak antiseptic solution. Do NOT scratch louse bites. Doing so will infect the bites with louse faeces – which can lead to typhus. As a general rule, the less scratching the better – even though it may be difficult to restrain yourself.

Scorpions and Centipedes. These animals are seldom seen, even though common, since they shelter under fallen trunks, stones or rocks. They may also seek alternative shelter in discarded bedding, clothing or boots. This is when they are most dangerous. Always shake out bedding, clothing and boots before use. They will not normally attack unless disturbed, so use care when moving rocks or stones or handling dead logs. Their stings are painful, but only the larger species are likely to be fatal. Cold compresses will lessen the pain from a sting. If you brush or knock the animal away – do it in the direction of the animal's movement.

Spiders. Only the black widow spider and its tropical relatives present any life-threatening danger to the survivor. All of them are dark in colour and carry red, white or yellow spots. A bite from any poisonous spider should be treated in the same way as a snake bite (see below).

Leeches. Lowland forests, tropical and sub-tropical, are infested with leeches – especially after rain. Their bites cause discomfort and loss of blood. They also open possible entries for infection. In such conditions, or when wading through swamps or sluggish waters, check for these pests every few minutes, for you may not feel the bites. Flick off any which has not yet got a hold, but never pull a leech off, as its jaws will remain in the wound, causing irritation and infection. Salt, ash or a glowing ember or cigarette will make them drop off. If smoking, collect all the unburnt tobacco and wrap it in a piece of cloth. When moistened, the pack can be squeezed, and it will produce a nicotine solution which is an effective de-leeching agent.

Treat a bite by gently squeezing to ensure that the wound is clean. When left alone, the bleeding will soon stop. Leave the blood clot on the bite as long as possible. It is worth emphasising that trousers tucked into tightly laced boots offer good protection against leeches, especially when wading. Otherwise leggings should be improvised if at all possible.

Never put your face into water to drink, or a small leech may get into your mouth, nostrils or throat. If this happens, gargle or sniff up very salty water to get rid of them, for they can cause serious infections.

Flukes and Hookworms. These are found in many tropical areas in sluggish, stagnant or polluted water. Do not drink from such sources (unless the water is boiled), for they can penetrate the skin on contact. Even paddling or bathing in infested water can be dangerous. Once in the bloodstream, they can cause serious disease, e.g. Bilharzia. They are not found in salt water.

The sea also contains its share of dangerous animals which can threaten the survivor.

Sharks. Sharks are universally feared, but in fact they are unlikely to attack unless provoked. They are curious, however, and will investigate any objects in their vicinity.

If you find yourself forced to swim through shark-infested water, try to follow these recommendations to avoid stimulating their curiosity:

1. Be as quiet as possible.

2. Remove any bright or shiny objects such as jewellery or a watch. They may look like small fish to a shark.

3. Swim smoothly, with as little disturbance as possible. Avoid any splashing. A steady breast stroke is much better than the crawl in this situation.

The true danger arises if a survivor is losing blood, for then sharks will attack.

Baraccuda. These are likely to attack without provocation. They are found in tropical and sub-tropical waters in and around reefs.

Jellyfish. The Portuguese Man-of-War is one of the largest of the species, but all can inflict stings which are painful. Their major threat, however, is that their stings can induce cramp – dangerous even to the strongest swimmer. It is sensible to wear clothing while swimming to gain some protection.

Sting Rays. These flat fish, which can exceed a metre in length, inhabit warm coastal shallows. A poisonous spine on the tail can inflict a painful wound, which may be fatal if the fish is mature. If wading in such waters use a stick to sweep the water ahead.

Other Fish. There are many other species which can deliver severely poisonous stings – mainly from external spines. The Stone Fish, Toad Fish and Scorpion Fish are three examples. They are to be found among coral and in other shallows. The Weaver Fish can be mentioned as a European example. General advice would be to look out for and avoid all spiny, odd-shaped or box-like fish, whether for touching or eating. Treat everything found in tropical waters, along reefs or in lagoons with suspicion and care until you are assured it is harmless. Any stings received from a spiny aquatic animal should be treated as for snake bite (see below).

SNAKES

Most survivors are afraid of snakes – or at least the idea of snakes. In fact, our fears are very much exaggerated. Less than 10% of all snakes are dangerous – and almost all of those will do their best to get out of your way if they can. Nevertheless it is essential to avoid alarming, trapping or cornering a snake unintentionally, for, when provoked many can strike with lightning speed. Normally they move slowly, and can be outrun by a man. If you are in any area, temperate to tropical, which has a snake population, treat them with respect by taking these precautions:

1. Walk with care, checking the ground for each step.
2. If moving among rocks or climbing cliffs check that each handhold is clear.
3. Check the immediate area before you pick anything up from the ground.
4. Move slowly if hand or foot is near a possible snake hide.
5. Carry a stout stick, forked at the lower end.

6. Wear strong boots if possible. If not, loose leg coverings offer some protection.

7. Read all available literature concerning snakes inhabiting area(s) you may be involved in.

SNAKE BITE TREATMENT

If you, or another survivor, suffers a snake bite, your reaction must be rapid, but WITHOUT PANIC. The widespread, unreasoning fear of snakes makes a large contribution to the threat they offer. This fear has been known to throw victims of snake-bite into terrified panic, to which the only reaction has been to run wildly about. The first-aider's opening treatment in these cases, has actually been to catch the casualty!

The two major aims of snake bite treatment are:

1. To reduce the amount of venom entering the body, keeping it below a non-fatal dose if possible.

2. To reduce the speed with which any venom circulates through the system, so that the body has its best chance to deal with it as it is absorbed.

A moment's consideration will make it clear that any form of fear or panic – especially if violent exertion is involved – will instantly increase the rate of heartbeat, and therefore the speed of the circulating blood. It cannot be too strongly stressed that rest and reassurance are high on the list of priority actions. While this is being given, the site of the puncture should be located and copiously washed with water. This is important because, even if the fangs have penetrated the skin, there will be a large proportion of the venom discharged by the snake lying on the skin around the puncture. If not removed, some will seep into the wound.

Do not cut the wound in any way, as this will merely open further channels through which venom can enter the body. Do not attempt to suck the venom out of the wound, because the lining of the mouth is able to absorb many substances with ease. Use a restrictive bandage. Apply it from above the bite, wrapping it downwards towards the puncture site. It should be applied tightly enough to stop the return of venous blood, since this is what will carry the venom into and around the body. But it must not stop the arterial blood supply to the area.

The correct tightness of the restrictive bandage can be checked by ensuring that,

(a) there is still a feelable pulse below the bandage,

and

(b) that the veins below the bandage are distended.

The bite will bleed after the bandage has been applied, but this is no cause for alarm. The escaping blood will very probably carry out with it some of the venom from the wound.

The next step is to make sure that the bite is as low as possible compared with the rest of the body. If practicable, put a splint on the limb. Immobilising it will lessen the possibility of any muscle movement having a pump-like action on the veins. Then immerse the part in water – the colder the better – which further slows down the return of blood.

Reassurance should be constantly maintained, and the fear of death dispersed as far as possible. This will not only help in the manner already mentioned. It will also lower the risk, and therefore the seriousness of shock. How reassurance is given, or how confidence is built up is immaterial – as long as both are effectively done. Facts can help, and it is an actuarial fact that anyone in the tropics is statistically more likely to suffer death by being hit by a falling coconut than he is to die from snake bite.

If 15 minutes pass, and no pain or swelling of the bitten area is felt, nor headache or dryness of the mouth, then the bite was not poisonous. However, treat every snake-bite as potentially venomous, for it may well be too late if you wait for the appearance of symptoms before acting.

Any survivor who wears spectacles may be involved in a particular difficulty – the loss or breakage of his glasses. For many this could be a serious blow. It could render him unable to perform any task requiring sharp close vision e.g. tying on a fish-hook. It could rob him of the ability to read most printed instructions. This would be particularly serious if the use of a first aid kit was involved.

There is a partial answer available in most circumstances. It is one which makes use of the principle on which the pin-hole camera works. Pierce a tiny hole in any small piece of reasonably rigid material. Card is very suitable, stiff paper will work – even a thin disc of dried clay can be used. If this is held close to the eye, and the print to be read is held close, it will be seen to be in clear focus. Good light is necessary, and it may be that only one word at a time can be read. But with patience and a little experiment, reading is once more possible. If your aid is used as a monocle, both hands will be free to perform the required task. Like all Survival Techniques, this one works best when it has been tried and practised.

Every survivor must remember, always, that his first aid equipment is only as good as he is. His first aid techniques are only as effective as he makes them. His first aid results will depend on the confidence he is able to instil – in himself and in others. **All these can grow – if they are fed with knowledge and practice.**

CHAPTER FIVE

FIRE LIGHTING

Fire is one of the essential aids to survival, and the ability to light a fire in difficult circumstances is a survival technique of inestimable value. The discovery of fire was one of humanity's great advances, since, with the provision of shelter, it allowed man to modify his environment – enabling him to survive in otherwise unsuitable climatic conditions.

It is because fire has been such a vital part of man's history that it also plays an important psychological role in survival efforts. It is a source of comfort. The lighting of a fire is a proof that a survivor can control some, at least, of the dangers which face him. It also provides a sense of achievement in that the survivor has replaced, in his emergency situation, one of the major elements which contribute to his normal life. Even more important, of course, are the varying practical uses of fire.

Fire will provide heat and light, together with the ability to cook food. With fire, water can be purified and medical equipment sterilised. Clothing can be dried. Signals can be generated seeking help.

Fire – the essentials

Any fire requires three elements. They are: Heat; Fuel; and Oxygen. If any one element is missing, a fire will not burn.

Fuel

When considering the supply of fuel it is helpful to recall that fire is a form of chain reaction. Part of the heat generated by the combustion of any fuel is required to ignite the succeeding supply. The initial supply of heat available to start any fire is usually small – a match flame, for instance, which lasts for only a few seconds. It follows that the starting fuel, which must be set alight by such a brief, small heat supply, must be material which ignites very easily. It must be some form of TINDER. In the original Tinder-boxes, where fire was created by sparks from flint, charred or scorched linen was used. A wide variety of different sources of tinder are listed later in the chapter.

Tinder **must** be dry. It will ignite more readily if it is reduced to fibres, threads or shreds. It follows that any material which is suitable for use as tinder will burn quickly. It is therefore essential that, BEFORE attempting to set light to the tinder, you make certain that there is ready to hand a supply of the next category of fuel – KINDLING.

Kindling will consist of small, dry twigs, followed by dry sticks, which will enable a small, hot fire to be built. You may then gradually add larger sticks until you have a fire which will burn long enough to ignite small logs. When such a fire has been established, even green logs can be added, since the heat available will boil out the sap before the logs burn. At first, however, the wood you gather should be dead, and as dry as possible.

Standing dead wood provides the best material for the early stages of the fire, since it is nearly always dry. Even during rain, it is possible to obtain dry fuel from standing dead wood. The outside may be wet, but there will be dry material on the inside. You can get at this fairly simply with a knife. But even without a blade, the sticks can be broken, split or crushed, by pounding with stones, and the inner wood selected.

Before you attempt to light your fire, it is **ESSENTIAL** to collect, grade and stack the fuel into TINDER, KINDLING, and HEAVY FUEL. Be sure to gather sufficient quantities to build and establish your fire.

It is also very important not to fall into the common error of piling kindling and other wood on to the fire too soon. Doing so will probably limit the supply of oxygen and the fire will die. If you ensure that the fire is well-ventilated, it will burn efficiently, and the smaller wood will produce less smoke. Most wood-fire smoke is the result of incomplete combustion, which generates less heat, and so slows the development of your fire.

It can also be very easy to under-estimate the amount of tinder required to ignite the kindling. If too much kindling has been put on too early, you may find that it is impossible to add more tinder where it is needed without disturbing the whole structure. Once again, the fire will die.

Heat

The heat required to start a fire can be generated in a number of ways. The easiest to use is an open flame, as from a match or lighter.

Sparks from flint and steel, or from an electrical source, can be used to ignite tinder. A magnifying glass, or parabolic reflector, in sunny conditions, can do the same.

Friction is a good source of heat, but is the least preferable of these methods owing to the amount of effort and time involved. Details of the various heat-sources are given later in the chapter.

Lighting the fire

It is well worth-while to take some care when choosing the site for your fire. If you have – or are going to build – a shelter, you will not want it to be filled with smoke. On the other hand, heat from the fire should be available within the cover.

Check the wind direction, and the dryness of the location. Look at the availability of fuel – especially if you have decided to stay put and await rescue, or for the arrival of improved weather conditions. The search will be for a dry, clear space – with bare earth as the best choice for the fire site. You may have to clear an area and perhaps line it with wreckage metal, rocks or green logs.

If conditions are windy, some form of shield from the wind must be erected or provided before attempting to light your fire. Although the fire will need good ventilation once it is started, the wind can blow out the first tiny flames, or even blow away the tinder. If no other wind-shelter is available, make all the preparations with the wind at your back – using your body as a wind-screen. Begin with a small amount of tinder, having more ready at hand.

If you are using an open flame, hold it steady under the tinder so that the heat builds up at one point, dries the tinder if needs be, and then ignites it. As the initial tinder catches, add further small quantities above the new flames so that the heat builds up even more, so repeating the process on a larger scale. Once the tinder is well alight, add kindling from your graded stack, slowly building the kind of fire you need.

If anything other than an open flame is being used to start the fire, it may not be possible to induce flames into the tinder immediately. You may achieve only smouldering combustion, in which the tinder glows without flame. Gentle blowing or fanning of the tinder will brighten and intensify the glow by increasing the supply of oxygen until the heat produced is enough to ignite the tinder completely.

Once the fire is established, it is often useful to enclose it in a circle of stones, if they are readily available. This will define the size of the fire and lessen the danger of its spreading. If larger stones are used on the windward side, the fire will be able to burn more steadily than if it were entirely open to the wind. This is important, because a continually fanned fire consumes much more fuel than one which is sheltered. Gathering wood for a roaring fire can use up a great deal of time and energy.

It is worth bearing in mind that a well established fire will burn almost any kind of fuel. Green logs or wet dead wood will burn more slowly and so economise on consumption.

A circle of stones will also retain the ashes and embers of the fire. A fire may appear to have burned out overnight. If so, check the ashes and embers, for they will often retain enough heat for you to be able to relight your fire from them. If the ash-bed feels warm, gently push some tinder down into the ashes, almost covering them. Use a twig to do this or a burned finger could be the result. After a little while, the tinder may start smoking. Then use gentle blowing or fanning and added tinder to relight the fire.

Partial damping down at night, using earth or water, will slow the rate of burning, leaving a revivable fire in the morning. A star fire will serve the same purpose.

Always keep a good supply of fuel on hand, and prepare an adequate amount of earth, sand or water to control the flames if necessary.

STEPS TO REMEMBER

1. Choose and prepare the site for your fire.
2. Gather your fuel supply: sort it into categories (Tinder, kindling, heavy fuel).
3. Prepare the tinder.
4. Light and build the fire – slowly. Do not smother.
5. Check fuel stocks – kindling and heavy fuel.

SOURCES OF TINDER FOR USE IN FIRE LIGHTING

A. WOOD OR PLANTS

Decayed or powdered wood.

Catface. (Resinous scab found on many evergreens where bark has been damaged.)

Pulverised outer bark (cypress; cedar; birch.)

Pulverised inner bark (red elm; chestnut.)

Coconut Palm frond (fabric-like material at base.)

Bamboo – membrane lining of cavity.

Pussy Willow – fuzz from seed clusters (late spring.)

Elderberry – pith from insides of shoots.

Chaff from Cat's Tail.

Cones from evergreen trees.

Arctic Cotton Grass or Sedge (eriophorium) – Aug/Sept.

Down from Bullrush.

Termite Nest material.

Ferns, Moss, Grass. Evergreen Needles and Fungi. All will provide tinder if dead and dry.

Any fine dried vegetable fibres.

Dead leaves – especially those retained by the beech and oak throughout the winter.

B. CLOTH

Scorched or charred cloth – especially linen.

Pulverised cloth (lint). Scrape to a fine, loosely piled fuzz. Do not use WOOL itself, though cotton "wool" is ideal.

C. LIQUIDS

Petrol or jet fuel.

Insect repellent.

Oil.

(These are all best used in conjunction with some solid form of tinder.)

D. MISCELLANEOUS SOURCES

Matted body hair.

Birds' nests.

Nests of rats or mice.

Gunpowder (obtainable, with care, from ammunition.)

Bat droppings (powdery, dry.)

Some photographic film.

Charred rope, lint from twine, canvas, bandages, etc.

All tinder obtained from solids is most effective if it is reduced to shreds, threads, or fibres and loosely piled to ensure good ventilation with enhanced combustibility.

HEAT SOURCES

Matches

A supply of matches should be carried as a matter of course on all outdoor trips, for they are the easiest and most obvious means of generating flame. They are, however, vulnerable to the effects of damp. Matches can be protected from water by dipping each separate match into molten wax, covering the head and half the stick. The outside of the box can be protected by spraying it with hair lacquer.

Even better protection can be gained by carrying the damp-proofed matches in a container such as a 35mm film holder. Place the matches head down in the holder so that a scrap of emery cloth can be carried with the matches but kept away from their heads. Sticking the emery cloth to the inside of lid will keep it safe.

There are many different makes of windproof and waterproof matches available commercially. These will light in even the worst of storms. It is, however, of prime importance to remember that the quality of the matches or their packaging is valueless unless each produces a fire. Waste of matches – or of any other resource – could be fatal in your survival situation.

The aim must be – a fire for every match.

Lighters

A lighter can be a life-saver. It must be used sparingly. One of the ways to economise in its use, when having built a fire, is to use that fire to prepare and dry kindling for the next. This is particularly valid if you are on the move and cannot take your fire with you. With tinder prepared in this way, the lighter flame is needed for the minimum time, and its fuel is conserved. If the lighter fuel is eventually exhausted, do not forget that sparks from the flint can be used, with tinder, to light a fire.

Of course, any available fire-lighting items would benefit in the same way from tinder preparation.

Igniting damp tinder with a candle.

Candles

A candle, however small, will prolong the active life of your lighter, besides helping the achievement of the aim, "One match – one fire." With the one match or single lighter flick, a candle can be lit immediately. There is then a constant naked flame to ignite the tinder – even if it is slightly damp. To put this technique to use, cut a small hole in the ground or build a small shield of stones around the candle. Pile the tinder over the hole or shield, and slide the lighted candle underneath. As soon as the tinder starts burning, remove the candle keeping it for the next fire-lighting.

Any hot wax should not be wasted. Make use of it to waterproof something, or keep it to use with your next tinder. Wax itself can be conserved if the candle is set in a small metal container (e.g. a metal 35mm. film can), so that it operates like a nightlight – which, of course, it can be.

The Burning Glass

The use of burning glass is restricted to reasonably bright conditions, but in such conditions it is a valuable and effective aid to fire-lighting. A glass may be specially made, or might be improvised from a lens from binoculars, a camera, spectacles or a compass. An efficient size would be about 5 cms. in diameter.

Flint and Striker

These are commercially available, and consist of a manufactured flint with an attached serrated steel striker. The flint, struck rapidly downwards, will provide sparks to fall and ignite the tinder. Natural flint is relatively hard to find, but it is possible to buy it from gunsmiths dealing in weapons using black powder.

Magnesium Fire Starter

This is one of the better items on the market. It consists of an aluminium block impregnated with magnesium and having a bar of flint along one edge. Any sharp edge will produce shavings from the block. They can be ignited with ease by sparks struck from the flint bar. The magnesium content burns at a heat in excess of 5,000 degrees F. and will set light to tinder – even if it is damp. This item of fire-lighting equipment is highly recommended for inclusion in any Survival Kit.

Magnesium Fire Starter in use.

The Electric Torch

Any torch with a focussing reflector, or which uses batteries with more than one cell, is a possible source of heat for fire-lighting. There are two possibilities.

The first makes use of the batteries, removed from the torch, but held together as they are normally in operation one above the other. Wire wool is used to connect the negative of the lower cell to the positive of the upper. It is possible to make a short circuit and so produce a spark. Even better, one can create, through the overheating of one of the wire wool strands, a burning glow which will run through the wire wool. Tinder mixed with the wire wool will ignite from the heat produced. Cotton wool is ideal for this particular use.

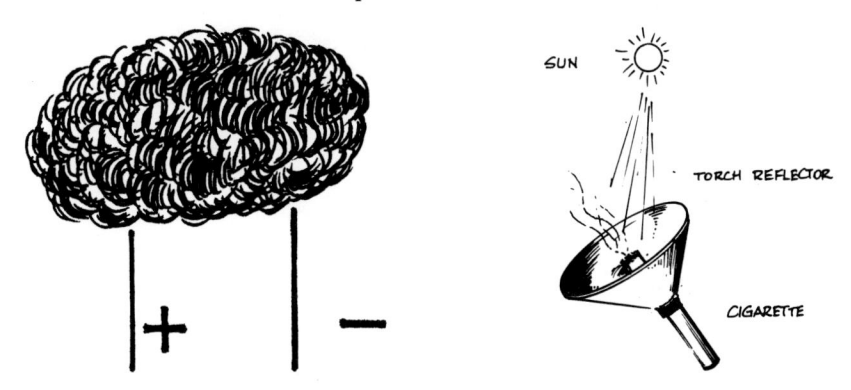

The second method is possible in any hot, sunny location. Remove the bulb holder and reflector, and position some very dry tinder in place of the bulb. Aim the reflector directly at the sun and it will concentrate the sun's rays at its focal point. It is possible to achieve ignition with the right choice of tinder. A dry cigarette might be suitable, and once glowing, could be used to ignite other tinder by gentle blowing or fanning.

If batteries of larger capacities are available – as from a wrecked or failed vehicle – another application of electricity for fire-lighting is possible.

A wire directly connecting positive and negative terminals will cause a short circuit and will heat up very quickly. The thinner the wire, the more quickly it will heat up, so some care is necessary. If a short length of thin wire – of one or two strands – can be connected up to the battery by a thicker wire at each end, the heating is likely to be confined to the thin length. This can be used to attempt tinder ignition. Alternatively, sparks can be produced over a pile of tinder by brushing the ends of the wire together, and the tinder can be set alight in this way.

Using a multicell battery for fire lighting. (Keep sparks away from top of battery).

Spontaneous Combustion

This may seem an unlikely method of fire-lighting in a survival situation, but circumstances might make it possible – particularly if a vehicle with a water-cooled engine is in any way involved. The radiator may contain an anti-freeze solution. Potassium permanganate is a mild antiseptic, and so might be included in a survival pack in this role. When anti-freeze, even if diluted to a degree, is added to potassium permanganate, spontaneous combustion can be caused by the heat generated by rapid oxidisation.

To employ this technique, a teaspoonful of potassium permanganate is placed on a sheet of paper or other inflammable material. Two drops of anti-freeze are added. The sheet is then rolled up tightly and placed on the ground with tinder laid above. Combustion will occur within a couple of minutes. Too much liquid will slow the rate of heating, and the paper will only smoulder, needing to be fanned or blown into flames. (The tight rolling is necessary to ensure that the heat is not allowed to dissipate and so be ineffective in raising the temperature to the necessary 451 degrees F. – the flash-point of paper).

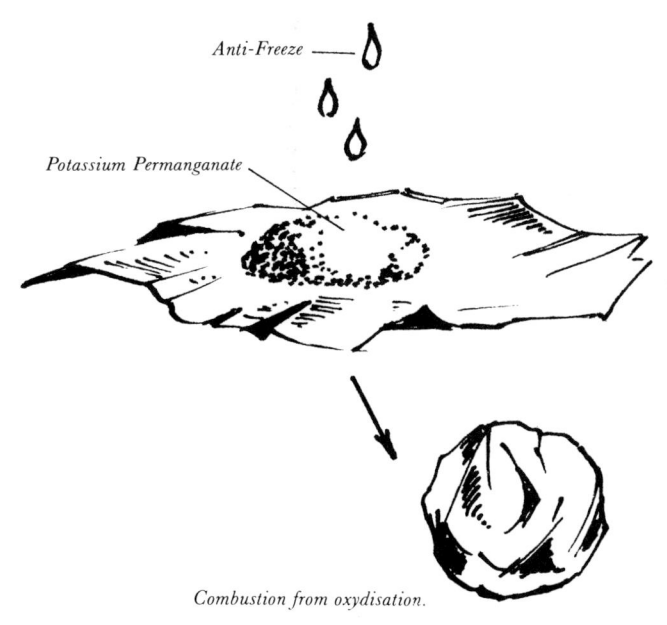

Combustion from oxydisation.

Highly Inflammable Materials

There are many highly inflammable materials which will serve as very effective tinder. Always examine your resources with great care to check if any such materials are available. Gunpowder has already been mentioned, and is available from small arms or shotgun cartridges. TAKE CARE if trying to extract it. It is a mixture of potassium nitrate, sulphur and charcoal in equal parts. Another mixture, equal parts of sugar and sodium chlorate, will give a high heat output, and would be of great assistance with efforts to light a fire with damp materials.

IT IS VITAL TO REMEMBER that many man-made materials produce poisonous gases when they are burned. NEVER burn them in any constricted space – such as a cave – and avoid breathing in any smoke if they are being used as tinder.

FIRE FROM FRICTION

The survivor must be able to create a fire, if it is humanly possible, with what he has. Even if the survivor has some means of making a fire – matches, for instance – they are consumable. The time may well come when some other, non-exhaustible method has to be found.

To solve the problem, it is worth looking back at what man did in the early days of his use of fire. Primitive people reveal the answer. They created fire from friction – and many still do. Any survivor with realistic intentions will familiarise himself with the process.

The fact that friction creates heat is well-known, and can be simply demonstrated by rubbing the hands together. What follows are techniques to employ this principle to generate and concentrate sufficient heat to ignite tinder. Skilled primitive man is able to perform this feat with, literally, no more than two sticks to rub together. By moving the palms of his hands rapidly back and forth, while holding a thin stick between them, he causes the stick to rotate at speed. The point of the stick is in contact with a second stick, and the resulting friction generates the heat required. Although the process looks simple, it requires long practice. The Bow-Drill is a means of putting this method into operation more easily and quickly. A minimum of resources is required to make it.

The Bow

Any pliant stick, between 65 and 85cms. long and about 2cms thick, can be used as the basis of the bow. It must be springy enough to tauten the bow-string so that it will grip the drill when operated. Use a length of leather thong or cord to bend the bowstick by about 15cms. There should be enough slack to enable the string to be looped once around the drill.

The Drill

A sound, dry length of medium-hard wood is needed for making the drill. Cedar, elm, willow, balsam fir, cottonwood or cypress are good examples of the type of wood required. Choose a piece from which a straight shaft, between 30 and 40cms. long, and about 2cms thick can be cut. If possible, shape the shaft so that it has an octagonal cross-section rather than round. This will allow the bowstring a better grip when in use. Sharpen to a blunt 60 degree point on one end, and a sharper 30 degree point on the other.

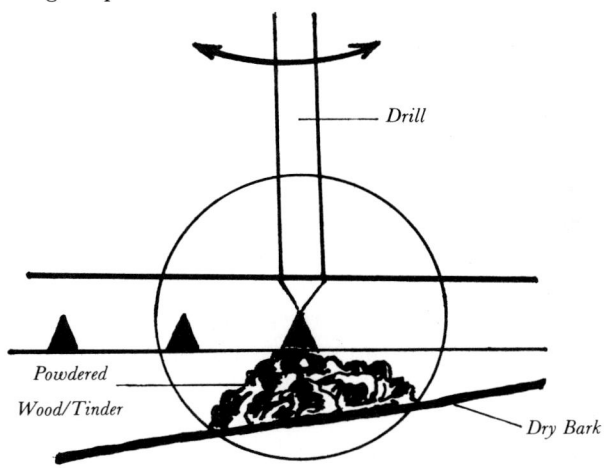

Drill

Powdered Wood/Tinder

Dry Bark

The Fire Block

Select wood as described for the drill (employ the same species, if possible), using a piece about 20cms. long, 10cms. wide and 2cms. thick. At the centre of one edge, cut a vee-shaped notch. The notch should be about 2cms. wide at the edge of the block, opening a little wider on the underside. Its point should extend about 2.5cms. towards the centre. At the point of the vee, cut a little rounded hollow or pit, so that the vee-point is at its centre.

The Socket

This is required to enable the upper end of the drill to be supported during use. Any piece of reasonably hard wood which will fit the hand will do. A pine or hemlock knot is very suitable. Cut a hollow 1cm. across and 1cm. deep in the flatter side. Shape the other side to fit the palm of the hand. If possible, lubricate the hollow with candle grease, animal fat, or soap.

Tinder

Good tinder can be made of many things. See list. A wad of fine, soft, very dry dead grass mixed with shredded cedar or birch bark is excellent for use with the Bow Drill.

Operation

Place the block on the ground with a piece of dry bark, or thin flat wood under the notch. Place a small amount of tinder rubbed into a loose ball on the bark near the notch.

Loop the bowstring once around the drill, and fit the blunt end of the drill into the pit on the block. Hold the block firm with the left foot. Fit the socket over the upper end of the drill with your left hand, and steady the hand (not the wrist), against the left shin. Hold the bow in the right hand, string side towards the leg, the bowstick curving away. Draw the bow back and forth with the right hand, using the full length of the bow. As the drill spins in the pit, fragments of wood are ground to powder. This powder, heated by the friction, falls through the notch, and gathers on the bark below.

When a considerable volume of smoke is rising from the notch, check the pile of powder. As that begins to smoke, also, carefully lift the block clear of the bark. Gently fan or blow the pile until it glows. Then add the small ball of tinder. Continue blowing/fanning until it ignites. It goes without saying that a survivor attempting to light a fire by this or any

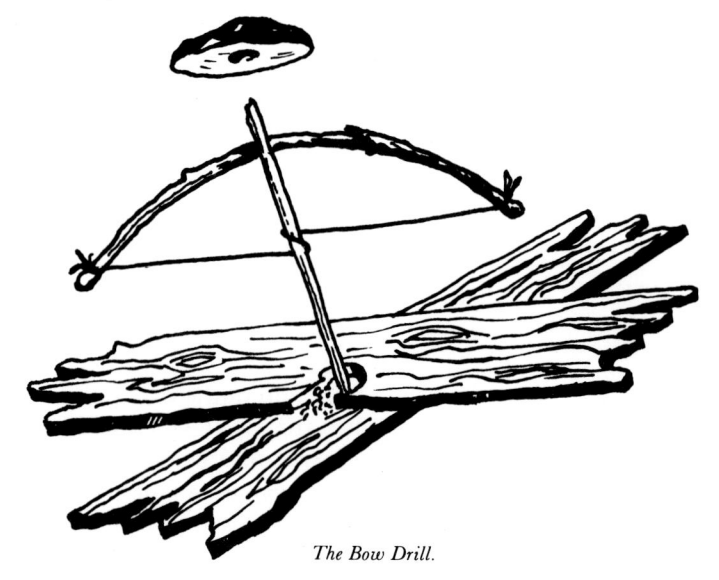

The Bow Drill.

other means will have prepared sufficient tinder, kindling and wood to build the fire securely.

Some hints on operation. The drill must be held steadily upright. This cannot be done unless the upper hand is braced firmly against the shin. The drill must not joggle, and the block must not be allowed to move. Saw as quickly as possible when smoke begins to rise. If any sand is available, a pinch sprinkled into the pit will increase friction.

This is a skill which, like all the others, requires practice for proficiency. It may take 10 to 15 minutes to produce your first glowing coal. That length of time can be very much reduced by improvement of technique and equipment through experience.

TAKE YOUR TIME. DO NOT BE FRUSTRATED. IT WILL WORK.

The Fire Thong

A stout thong, 60-80cms. long – is required for this method of fire lighting. It can be leather, or natural fibre. Split open one end of a dry stake or small log. Hold the split open with a stone. Insert the thong near the closed end of the split. Lightly pack dry tinder around the thong.

The split stake should be held as still as possible. This can be helped if the split end is propped up on a rock. Work the thong back and forth, tensioning it against the upper side of the split. The friction will generate heat. When the tinder begins to smoke, gently fan or blow it into life.

The Fire Thong.

Summary

Once your fire is alight, be sure to employ it to the maximum effect. Cook or heat your food and drink to supply inner warmth to your body. Dry any wet clothing or equipment. Add extra stones to the circle around the fire. If you have no sleeping bag, they will act as body warmers for up to two hours. Prepare and store tinder and kindling for your next fire.

Even if the situation appears desperate, and it seems impossible to produce a fire, a calm, thoughtful approach to the problem, based on these simple steps, will give you your best chance of success:—

    (a) create a shelter

    (b) create a flame

    (c) use the driest tinder and kindling possible

    (d) build your fire slowly until it supports itself

    (e) maximise its use

CHAPTER SIX

SURVIVAL SHELTER CONSTRUCTION

From your assessment of the situation, you will have decided an order of priorities, and where the need for shelter lies in that order. In most circumstances the need will be fairly pressing. Even in a temperate area of the world it will most certainly be urgent. In a cold area it will be absolutely and immediately vital. Generally, obtaining shelter and warmth come second only to first aid.

The most dangerous conditions include cold, wind, rain or snow. It is essential to protect yourself against these, as each of them is a factor which hastens hypothermia. Exposure to any combination of them can rapidly produce deadly results long before any shortage of food or water would take effect.

Even in summery conditions or hot climates, shelter is needed from the sun so as to avoid hyperthermia (overheating of the body). It may not affect the survivor as rapidly as loss of body heat, but it can still produce deadly results. It will very quickly lead to a loss of body fluids. Shelter and protection may also be needed against insects and other unpleasant or harmful forms of life.

Another positive benefit to be gained from a good shelter is that it allows rest and sound sleep. This is invaluable since it makes possible the maintenance of a high level of physical and mental response to the many challenges which may confront you.

There may be temporary shelter to be found among the natural features surrounding you. Seek it in or around trees, thick bushes or natural hollows. If safe, make use of caves, rock overhangs or any available wreckage. Do not overlook any possibility offered by a parachute, any packing materials available – or even a life-raft. This last item may be available even if a forced landing or crash has occurred on land. Never waste time and energy constructing a temporary shelter or wind-break if nature or circumstance already provide it.

The climate and terrain, together with personal circumstances, will always influence the siting of a shelter and the type of construction involved. There are, however, some general points worth keeping in mind when approaching the job. Choose the site using to the full any natural cover from the wind. If no such cover is available, remember to angle the shelter so that its entrance or open side is away from the wind. Paradoxically, a hillside is usually warmer than a valley floor, even though it may be windier. Build the shelter as near as possible to a fresh water supply, to sources of building materials and, very important, firewood. Any spot in a forest and near a fast-flowing stream can be the site of a very desirable residence.

In lowlands, recognise the danger of floods. On the coast keep the tides in mind. In mountainous areas make sure that the chosen site is not in the path of possible avalanches or rock-falls. If in the forest, look around for fallen trees which may indicate that this is an area of shallow soil. If the wind can blow one tree over, it could do the same to others nearby. In the same way, isolated single trees are best avoided. Remember the old adage about never sheltering under a tree during a thunderstorm. On the other hand, the branches of an isolated tree which has already fallen could well provide a ready-made framework for a sound shelter.

Choice of shelter type will depend on the materials that are at hand. If a groundsheet, poncho or any other weather-proof piece of material is available you are halfway there as far as immediate shelter is concerned. If you have only one piece of wind- or water-proof material, and it is used as part of the shelter, aim to replace it by natural materials as soon as possible. You can then wrap it around your body. This will provide the most efficient protection. It will be a ''shelter within a shelter''. In most cases, shelters will have to be built with natural materials. There can sometimes be considerable difficulties, but it is possible to create some form of shelter almost anywhere.

The Sanga

This is simply a wind-break, built of any materials available – stones, branches, snow, wreckage – anything. In the absence of any better possibility its value lies in the way it reduces exposure to the chilling effects of the wind. Prehistoric man realised its value, for it is one of the earliest forms of man-made shelter. Use any survival blanket, poncho, plastic sheet, etc., as a roof to give shade during the day and as a blanket at night, unless it is needed for protection against rain or snow.

The Lean-To

The lean-to frame is the standard shelter pattern – probably because it is one of the simplest. When setting up the frame, make sure that the roof slopes down into the prevailing wind. The covering can be almost anything from foliage to plastic sacks, a groundsheet to wreckage panels. Even turf blocks can be used. It is certain that a firm mud or turf layer on top of foliage will harden, prevent the shelter cover from being blown away AND make it more wind and water-proof.

The sides of the shelter can be filled in using a similar foliage and mud method or could be walled with turf blocks.

If there is a supply of usable cord, a variation of the lean-to can be built especially suitable in any area covered with short bushy vegetation. Cut four or five stakes of the greatest length possible. Force their ends into the ground, then bend the tops over and tie them down at an angle of 45 degrees. It may be possible to find a spot where two or three can be incorporated into the framework without being cut – i.e. leaving them rooted in the ground. This will give the shelter much better stability.

Twigs and branches can then be interwoven as lattice-work to provide a firm hard frame. More foliage is added until complete cover is formed. A layer of light turf or mud will complete the roof.

Wooded Areas

In any forested area there may be large fallen logs to be used. A trough dug between two such logs, covered with a roof of branches and foliage, provides a shelter which is fairly cheap in effort. In the same way, a single log can be supplemented with a low earth wall or used as the basis of a small lean-to.

Layered Tree Bivouac

A small shelter can be made quite quickly using any small tree. Cut partially through the trunk at a point about shoulder-height until you are able to push the upper portion over so that its top rests on the ground. The stem is left attached to the butt.

Cut away the branches on the underside and break the upstanding branches on the outside so that they hang down. Thatch the shelter using the foliage cut from below.

Grasslands

If you have to make a shelter in an area covered with grass, with trees either scarce or non-existent, it is possible to cut turf bricks and build as below.

Making the roof will be easier if you can find any small sticks or boughs to support a turf roofing layer. An alternative would be any kind of sheet material which could be anchored by the top row of turf bricks. If nothing but turf is at hand, make the shelter small and narrow enough for longer turf strips to be used in pairs, supporting each other.

If the grass is long enough, bundles might be suitable for a thatched covering for the shelter – but in this case, try to pitch the roof as near to 45 degrees as practicable to provide a run-off for any water.

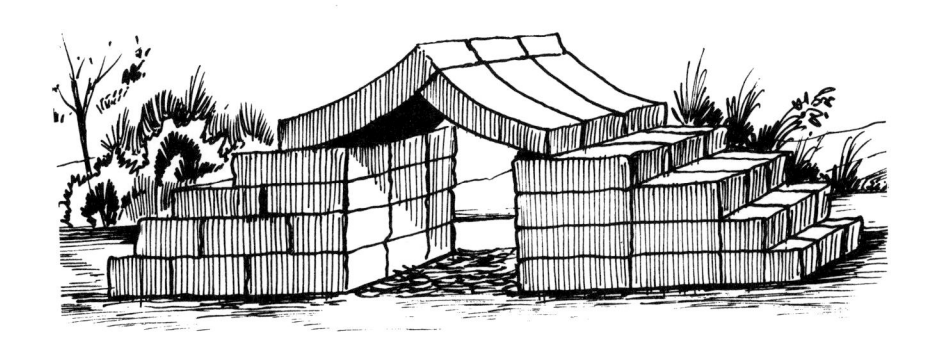

If the ground is suitable – i.e. soft but not wet – it may be possible to combine the effort of digging or cutting the turf with building a low wall along the edge of the slit trench produced. The effective height of the wind-break is then increased for about the same amount of effort.

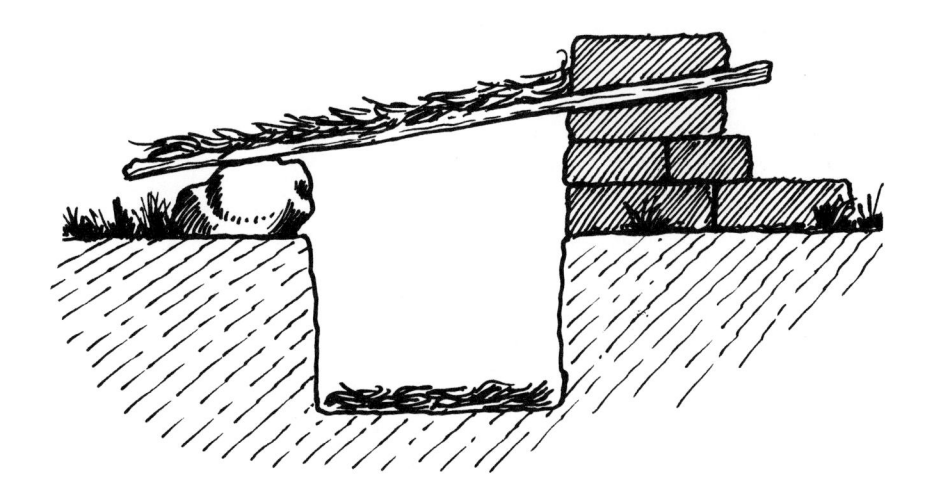

It is essential to make sure, however, that any rain will drain away from the trench and not into it. Going below ground level can also be very helpful in hot conditions, although the hardness of the ground too often renders this difficult.

All these shelters, and especially the lean-to varieties, can be improved by the addition of a fire and fire reflector. The fire is best set on a base of green logs. The reflector is made of interwoven green sticks. Large stones stacked around the back of the fire will also reflect heat. The hot stones can be taken into the shelter at night. With care they can be placed or buried beneath your bed-space where they will emit warmth during the night.

The Parachute Tent

If you are lucky enough to have a parachute it is a simple matter to fashion a bell tent from it. First remove all the valuable paracord rigging lines. Tie a good length of cord to the centre of the parachute canopy. Tie a suitable log or stone to the other end and lob the cord over a convenient tree branch. Pull the parachute to its full height and secure the cord to the trunk. It is then a simple matter of pulling out the parachute skirt and pegging it in a circle.

Para-tent on Teepee frame.

The tent can be improved by cutting one side of a panel to form a door – on the lee side. The making of the Yukon Stove will be described later, and it can be used inside this type of shelter. Parachute material is wind resistant, and showerproof as long as it is not touched, but it does not protect against heavy rain.

SNOW SHELTERS

There are a number of different types of snow shelter. Some of them suffer from significant drawbacks. One may demand too much time and energy in its construction, especially for a solitary survivor. Another might require a greater depth of snow than is available. Very cold, hardpacked snow may not be available for the cutting of snow blocks.

The Snow Trench

Even a hole in the snow provides temporary shelter as an emergency measure, and it can be improved to make a simple shelter for one man.

If the snow is soft, branches or sheeting of some kind would be needed for the roof.

The Fir Tree Snow Shelter

If in a wooded area, by far the simplest shelter is to be found under a

large fir tree. There will often be a natural hollow in the snow around the base of the trunk to give you a good start. Dig away the snow from the base, using it to build up and improve the protection on either side of your shelter area. Cut the low branches on the side away from the shelter to use either as bedding or to interweave with the branches on your side to improve the overhead cover. You can build a fire under the tree, but make sure it is at least part of the way around the trunk from your shelter. This is because the heat will melt the snow in the branches above the fire.

This type of shelter can be readily made in forests during the winter. The basis provided by nature only needs improving to make it warm and comfortable.

The Snow Cave

This type of shelter requires a depth of snow of two metres or more. The simplest approach would be to build into a snow drift or cornice. To improve the snow cave, aim for as many of the features shown in the cross-section illustrated as you can achieve.

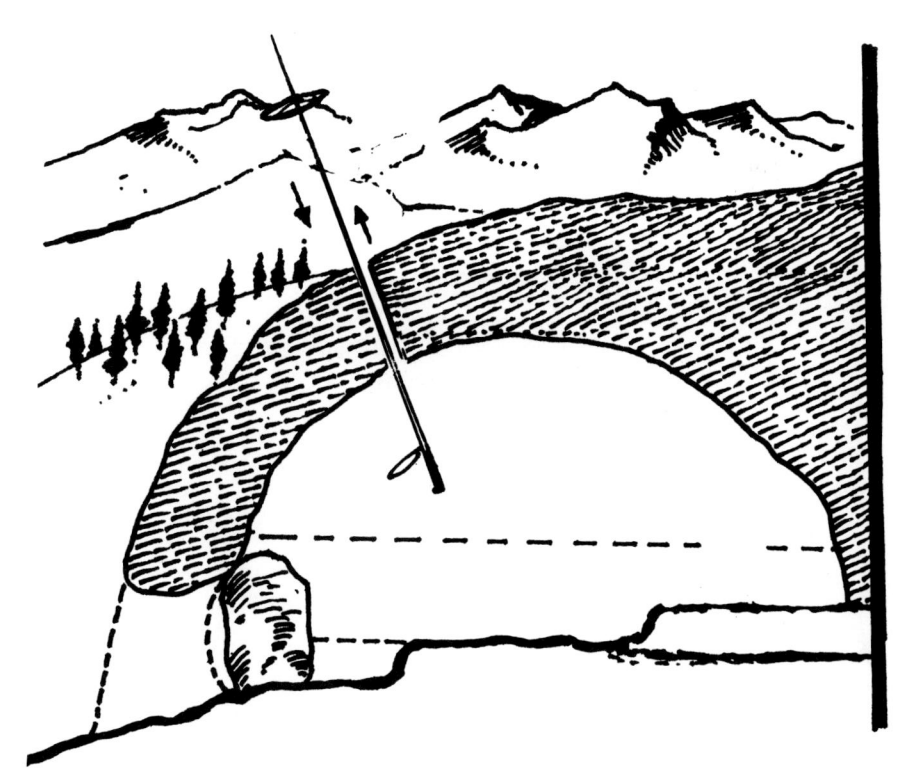

The Snow Cave. Note ventilation hole in dome-shaped roof and raised sleeping platform.

Sometimes this type of shelter is more difficult to make than it appears, because of the hardness of the packed snow. Without some tools it may be next to impossible. Make sure that the inside roof is always dome shaped.

The Snow Igloo

An igloo built of snow blocks can be a good refuge for two or more survivors, if the plan is to remain in one location for any length of time. It requires tools for its construction – an axe, a knife, a saw or a spade. It also takes time and effort, as well as care and thought in placing the blocks. Two or three working together can reduce the difficulty, however. Cold compacted snow is necessary for block-cutting. Build up from the base in a spiral form that is angled upwards.

Take care to lay out the entrance tunnel on the lee side of the shelter. In any snow shelter, build your bed on a raised platform, so as to avoid the coldest air, which will gather at the lowest level.

DESERT AREAS

The problem of obtaining shelter in desert areas is complicated and difficult, but the possibilities are worth some thought – since roughly one fifth of the earth's surface falls into this category.

The first complication is that deserts are places of extreme conditions – extreme heat during the day, and biting cold at night. They also vary greatly in their composition from being entirely made up of either rock, sand or salt – or of any combination of these. Some deserts are plains, some mountainous, some depressions. Some are totally barren, some have scanty vegetation, while others have a variety of plants. All these variations can occur in combinations which make desert shelter difficult to achieve if you are entirely without some material resource.

It is highly unlikely that you, either as an individual or as one of a group, would be lost in the desert on foot. Any serious survival situation in such areas would almost certainly be due to some form of transport failure. Having regard to the peculiar difficulties of the desert environment, your situation assessment will probably favour the choice of remaining where you are to await rescue. The factors favouring this choice would include.

(1) The availability of survival resources for shelter construction and other purposes from the vehicle or wreckage.

(2) The fact that rescuers could see the vehicle or wreckage much more clearly than they would spot people. In addition, they would be searching during the hours of day-light. Since travelling in the early morning, late evening, or at night, would be your only sensible options you would be sheltering when the searchers were looking for you.

Of course, your particular situation may require that you take the option of moving. You may know, or be reasonably sure, that help lies within walking distance, either through pre-knowledge of the area or from observation before the transport failure.

If this is your decision, remember that water will be your prime need in desert survival. Take as much as you have, or can carry – even if you have to discard other things. But do not discard any effective clothing. You will need it during the cold nights, as well as for protection against the sun, the risk of sunburn and attention of insects. It is also essential to help minimise loss of body fluids through excessive sweating.

Still air is the best protection against excessive heat – as it is against extreme cold. If you can hold a layer around your body it will help throughout the 24 hours of the desert day. Loose clothing serves best in the daytime, while as many layers as you can manage provide best protection during the night.

Shelter from the sun and heat is the main aim when in the desert. Use a groundsheet (or any alternative) to cover a depression scooped out of the ground. If there are any rocks or vegetation, drape the sheet over the rocks or plants. If you have no material help, look for shade or shelter from natural desert features – rocks, rock cairns, caves or ledges. Dry stream beds may offer shelter. These wadi-banks, or the sides of ravines or valleys, are worth looking over for crevices or caves.

There is some disagreement about the value of burrowing into the sand to protect your body from the sun, as there is about whether it is an effective method of reducing loss of body-fluid. It is reasonable to suppose that if you could burrow deep enough to find cool or damp sand, then this would provide some relief.

If you cannot find or make any fixed shelter from the sun, remember that your clothing can give you considerable help. Keep your head and body well covered throughout the day. Long trousers and long sleeves are needed, as well as a neckerchief hanging down to shade the back of your neck. Wear your clothing loosely, but do not open it while still in the sun. Even reflected sunlight can produce sunburn. Keep the upper surfaces of your feet covered at all times. Sunburn blisters on this area can immobilise you. If it is possible – using rocks, piled stones, wreckage, etc. – always sit a few inches up above the ground when resting. The temperature is appreciably lower even this short distance above the sand.

Whichever type of shelter you set out to build, remember that your aim is to protect yourself against those aspects of the environment which can threaten your safety.

In all areas with hot climates, insects are likely to be a problem. You can gain some protection against the winged species if you can erect your shelter on any site which receives some breeze – a hillside or ridge, for instance, or a place which gets an on-shore wind.

JUNGLE AREAS

In jungle conditions, on the other hand, there is usually an abundance of troublesome and unpleasant insects – not to mention reptiles – on the ground. This means that a good basis for any shelter would be a raised platform. Even if your resources do not make it possible to build a platform big enough to support the entire shelter, it is certainly very important to avoid sleeping directly on the jungle floor. A bed of bamboo or any small branches covered with palm leaves or other foliage is a real necessity.

Obtain ground cover of some kind – even dead tree bark would be better than nothing. You may be able to consider making a hammock. A parachute provides almost the ideal materials for this.

Any shelter in temperate or arctic conditions, on the other hand, must fulfil the main purpose of keeping warmth around you, whether from a fire or your own body, so that you are protected against the cold. Still air is your best protection. To get it, make your shelter small, snug and windproof. Ensure that you are insulated against heat loss through the ground. Consider the possibility of building a fire on your sleeping area so as to warm and dry it before you make a bed.

A bed can be made of small branches. Push the lower ends into the ground, making all of them slope in one direction. Cover this "mattress" with small twigs and tips of other branches. Alternatively, make use of small twigs, foliage, dried leaves, bracken, etc., to prevent direct contact with the ground.

Finally, remember that when you are wet, cold, and maybe miserable – **every hour spent building your shelter and your fire is worth many hours sleep.**

CHAPTER SEVEN

TYPES OF FIRE, STOVES AND COOKING

Once your fire is alight, (see chapter "Fire Lighting"), you should make sure that you are getting the best out of it. You can begin, if your fire has to be lit on the surface of the snow, on ice or wet ground, by making up a solid platform of logs or stones for use as a firebase.

If you want a fire to warm yourself, you will find that a small fire is good for this purpose. It uses less fuel, is more easily controlled, and not so hot as to make it impossible to crouch near it so as to gain the most benefit. Some form of reflector behind the fire will increase your profit from the fire's heat. You will get more heat from a number of small fires in a line alongside you, or in a pattern around you, than you will from one big fire.

One of the types of fire you need to consider fairly soon is a **Pyramid Fire.**

Pyramid Fire.

The purpose of this fire is to dry out wood for future use. You may need dry wood to re-generate your fire if it has died down, or has been banked down overnight. You will certainly need dry wood to prepare one of the most important types of fire – your **Signal Fire.**

This must be prepared so as to be ready for instant use. It will consist of a fresh pile of very dry tinder, together with dried or partly burned twigs. Over these you construct your pyramid of dry logs – some of these may also be partly burned.

You need to be sure that your Signal Fire will ignite quickly, which means it **must** be kept dry. You may well have to build a shelter over the prepared fire if rain threatens. Clear the ground immediately around the site so that when the fire is lit, it will not spread out of control. If it is possible, prepare three such fires in a triangle with 100 foot sides. If you have any additional fuel – oil, petrol, etc., – you can use it to speed up ignition.

Signal Fire.

When the blaze develops, try to produce some contrast with the background. On a clear day, burn vegetation to make white smoke. If overcast, make black smoke by burning oil or rubber, if available. At night, build up the fire to get tall, bright flames. The over-riding need is to have your Signal Fire ready to burn as quickly and fiercely as possible, so as to make the utmost of any possible chance of being seen – and surviving.

The **Star Fire** is a simple but effective fire. It can easily be controlled by pulling the logs outward, when the flames will die down, leaving the embers undisturbed.

You can leave this fire unattended for up to a couple of hours – to go hunting, for example – without the fear that a flare-up from the fire will burn down your shelter. On your return, simply push the logs inwards to bring their ends together over the embers. Fanning or blowing on the centre will soon re-ignite them. If the weather is wet, a large flat rock placed over the charred ends will protect your fire.

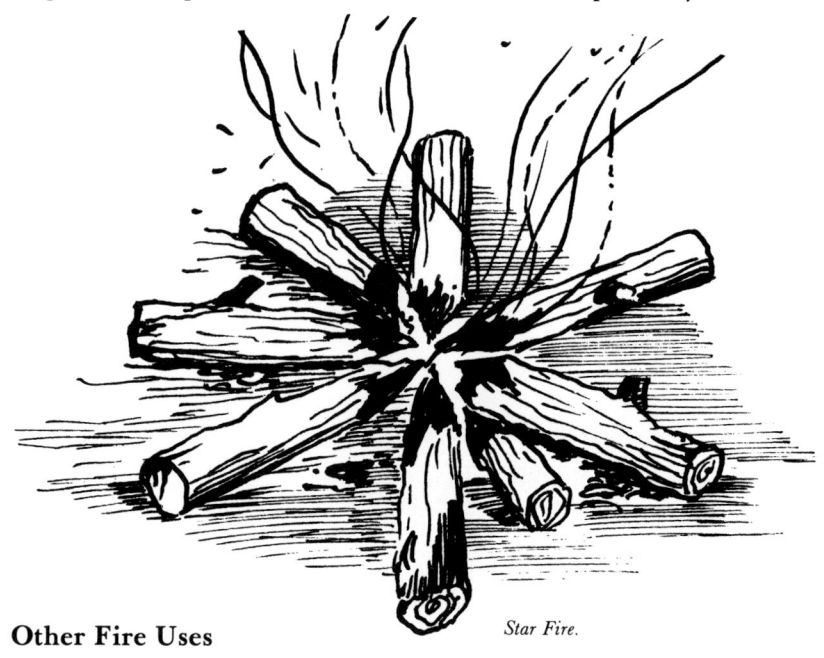

Star Fire.

Other Fire Uses

Two other uses of fire are the boiling of water and cooking. The boiling of water is often a necessary precaution to ensure that it is purified of any harmful organisms. Water-borne diseases are among the greatest hazards which face survivors. (See "Water Procurement.") In addition, of course, hot or warm drinks are a valuable source of body heat. Cooking is important because it can produce food that is safer to eat. It does this by destroying bacteria as well as **some** toxic materials and harmful products contained in animals and plants. It also makes most food more palatable.

A small fire, used with some kind of stove is the best combination for cooking purposes. A bed of glowing hot coals is the ideal source of heat for cooking. Logs laid in two layers at right angles to each other will settle into a level bed of coals. The easiest way to utilise such a fire is to build it between two logs, two rows of stones, or in a narrow trench. Any of these will support a cooking vessel or hot plate over the fire.

Cooking Fire.

An improvement on this simple set-up would be an improvised stove using any available metal can or box. This is economical as far as fuel is concerned, and is well-suited to colder conditions, since, **with care,** it could be used inside a shelter.

An Improvised Stove.

A cooking pot can be suspended over a fire using a simple arm, made from a stick, either cantilevered or supported by a second, forked stick.

Less fuel will be needed if the fire is enclosed by logs, stones, or the sides of a shallow trench.

A fire for roasting is best made in a pit, and built so that a good bed of glowing embers is formed. The meat, fowl or fish can be spitted above the pit as shown below.

The Hangi is a development of the fire pit. It is particularly useful (i), if cooking for a group of survivors and (ii), if no food containers are available.

Prepare a pit of suitable size for the number of survivors to be fed. A hole 60cms. deep and of similar diameter would accommodate enough food for a small group. Set tinder and kindling on the floor of the pit. Prepare a pyramid fire of about six layers of logs – each layer at right angles to the layer beneath. Incorporate stones into the pyramid as illustrated. Fist-sized stones are suitable, but **AVOID** soft or flaking stones. These may well explode when heated.

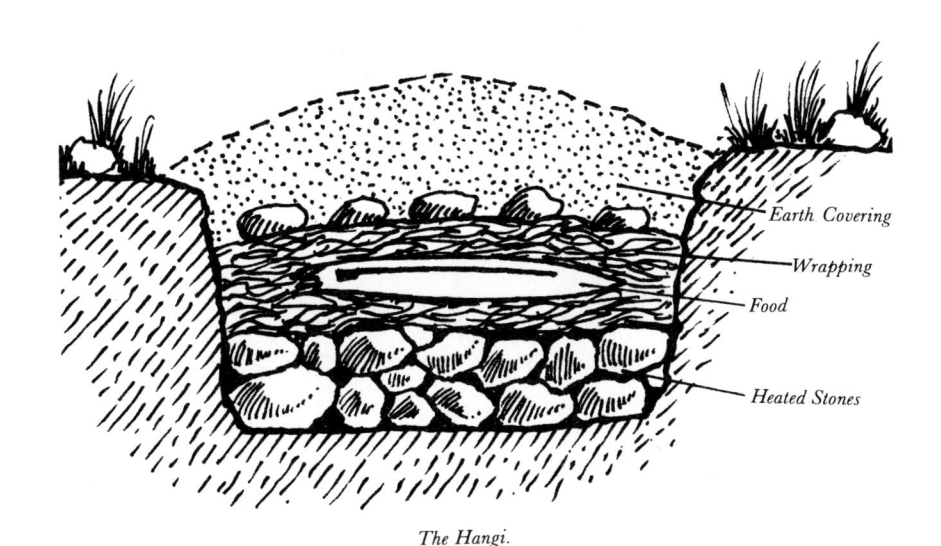

The Hangi.

Light the fire in the pit, and tend it until it ignites the log pyramid. Eventually the heated stones will fall to the bottom of the hole. Any burning embers remaining must be removed and the ash cleared from the layer of hot stones. If no food containers are to hand, wrap the food in large clean leaves from a safe source. Lay the wrapped food on the hot stones, putting what needs most cooking (e.g. meat), at the centre. Vegetable foods should be located further from the centre in order of their cooking requirements (i.e. roots; fruit; flour cakes; leaf dishes; etc.). Keep all food clear of the sides of the pit.

Now cover the pit using branches, foliage etc. to support the final covering of the earth dug from the pit itself. This will retain the heat in the hangi, and during the next 1 to 2 hours or so the food will be cooked.

By far the best use of fire for cooking and other purposes is obtained from the Yukon Stove. If you are in one location for more than 24 hours you should certainly consider seriously the possibility of building this type of stove.

Rocks, stones and mud are used in its construction, with the tortoise-shell as the basic pattern. At one side you must leave a hole for the intake of fuel and air, with another at the top as a chimney. Two further refinements are very desirable. The first is the building in of a metal box or large can into the back wall. This will provide an excellent oven. You must remember, however, that food placed in the oven will be burned unless it is separated from the metal by small sticks or stones. If twigs are used they will turn into charcoal after a day or two. You should keep them for use in de-odourising boiled water if necessary, and other medicinal purposes.

The second improvement possible is to use a large flat rock as part of the top of the stove. It can be used as a griddle for making oatcakes, drying leaves for tea, parching grain, etc. and even frying birds' eggs.

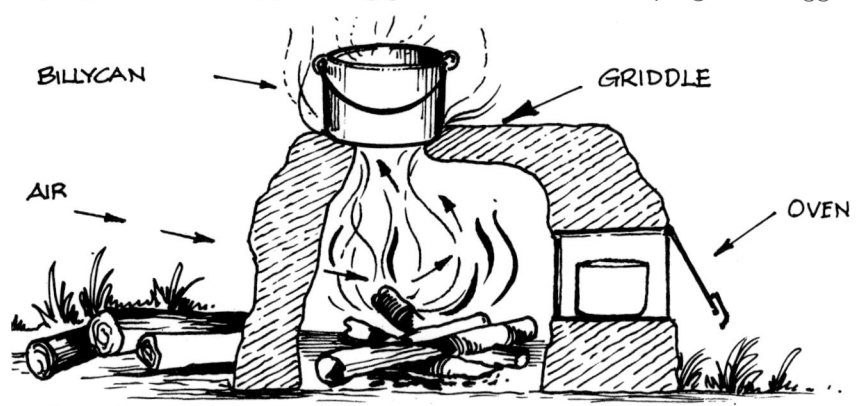

One of the Yukon's major advantages is that it can be left unattended while you are working at other activities, and you can return to a warm fire and a hot meal. By covering the fuel/air intake with another stone the rate of burning can be partly controlled. In wet weather the oven enables fuel to be dried. Clothing can be laid over the outside of the stove and will dry without burning. You can warm yourself without risk of being burned.

Another use for a small fire is the drying and curing of meat and fish. This is easily done by constructing a small triangular pyramid frame with a drying/smoking platform, made of lattice-work, halfway up it. In the summer it may be left open if not too breezy, but in windy or wet conditions it should be covered over in teepee form.

An alternative method uses a fire built in a smoking pit.

Fire, although it can be a life-saver, should never be used in a casual or careless manner. If not handled with care and foresight, it can destroy your equipment, your shelter and you, yourself. Never allow familiarity to breed contempt.

Any survivor who is undergoing extremely cold conditions is in danger of allowing his desire to get warm and stay warm to overcome his normal common sense. The use of a fire or heater of any type inside a closed shelter produces a very real risk of suffocation by carbon monoxide – one of the great Arctic hazards – unless proper ventilation is assured. Any sort of fuel burning in a confined, poorly ventilated shelter can produce a dangerous amount of this gas in as short time as thirty minutes. The gas is doubly dangerous as it is odourless.

You **must** provide effective ventilation if you intend using a stove or heater inside your shelter. This means two openings – one at the top of your shelter as a chimney, with another close to ground level to admit fresh air. If you are in a heated shelter and begin to feel drowsy – look out for the danger of carbon monoxide poisoning. Get out into the fresh air, moving slowly and breathing easily and evenly. Most important, find and remove the cause of the fumes. If a group are sleeping in a heated, closed shelter, one of their number should stay awake on carbon monoxide guard duty.

It is better to rely on your clothing and other insulation to keep you warm. Reserve the use of stoves or heaters inside the shelter solely for cooking. Only if you are sure of safety to the point of being positive should you extend their use to heating.

Preparing Wild Food

Most forms of animal food require cleaning and skinning, plucking or scaling before being cooked.

(i) Birds

These should generally be plucked and cleaned before cooking. The skin should be left in place as it will help retain the food value. It is easier to pluck a fowl after plunging it into boiling water, although water-fowl are best plucked dry. After plucking, cut the neck off near to the body. Draw the insides out through this hole. Wash the carcase inside and out with fresh clean water. The neck, liver and heart can become the ingredients of a stew.

If time is short, it is quicker to skin a bird than to pluck it. Skinning is best done after gutting and cleaning the carcase. Small birds, after gutting and cleaning, can be baked in a clay case. The feathers will then come away when the case is opened.

All scavengers – vultures, buzzards, carrion crow etc., first need to be boiled for at least 20 minutes to kill any parasites that may be present. Only then should you proceed with other traditional methods of cooking. The clean feathers are worth saving for use as insulation in clothing or bedding.

(ii) **Fish**

As soon as a fish is caught, bleed it by cutting out the gills and other large blood vessels which will be found next to the backbone. Scrape off the scales. Some fish like catfish and sturgeon have none. These should be skinned. Gut the fish by cutting open its stomach and scraping it clean, washing out any particles remaining. Fish below four inches in length do not require gutting, but will need scaling or skinning. Remove the head, unless you intend cooking the fish on a spit.

(iii) **Animals**

The sooner you can skin and dress a carcase after death, the easier your job will be. Small and medium sized animals should be hung head downwards with throats cut to allow blood to drain into any available container. The blood, boiled thoroughly, is valuable for its salts and food value.

Cut the skin right around the knee and elbow joints. Continue down the front of each hind leg, joining the cuts and extending down the belly in a Y pattern. Cut from the belly to each elbow joint. Make a complete circular cut around the sex organs. Then from each knee downwards, start peeling back the skin until it is removed entirely. Next, cut open the belly, using wooden skewers to pin the flesh back. Remove the guts from the windpipe upwards. Clear the entire mass using a deep circular sweep of the knife to remove the sex organs.

Throw away the entrails, and the glands in the anal and reproductive area. (Unless they are to be used as bait: see "Animal Food".) Make use of the kidneys, liver and heart, and the fat surrounding the intestines. The meaty parts of the skull are all edible, including the brain, tongue and eyes. The skin should be kept, to be cleaned and dried for later use.

Larger animals are dealt with in the same way, except that their size and weight may be too great to allow you to hang the carcase.

Rabbits are relatively easy to trap and kill, and can be very tasty though they do lack fat. To skin, make a cut behind the head large enough to allow two fingers to be inserted. Peel the skin back, and sever the head and lower limbs. Cleaning is carried out by cutting down the belly and opening the body. A sharp shake will cause most of the intestines to fall out. Remaining pieces should be scraped out and washed away.

Rats and mice should not be overlooked, for they provide edible meat – especially when stewed with dandelion leaves or other vegetables. They must be skinned, gutted and washed, and then boiled for about ten minutes before being added to the stew. Their livers are good food and should always be included.

Other edible animals include dogs, cats, hedgehogs, porcupines and badgers. All must be skinned and gutted before cooking – again best done as a stew with edible leaves (see "Plants as Food"). The livers of the first two are particularly valuable. Another good option for small animals is that of baking in a casing of clay. Carcases cooked this way must still be gutted and cleaned, but the clay, when it is removed, will take with it the hedgehog's spines or the small bird's feathers. Many reptiles – snakes, lizards, frogs, alligators and turtles – are edible. The head and skin should be removed before cooking. Roast or fry their meat.

Methods of Cooking

A. Meat

(i) **Roasting (or broiling)** is a quick and simple way to cook reasonably tender meat. Roasting can be done by spitting meat on a stick and holding it over or near hot embers. An arm or crane as shown earlier is a handy way of doing this. Roasting forms a "crust" on the outside of the meat which helps retain the juices.

(ii) **Boiling**

If meat is tough, it needs to be cooked slowly by boiling and finished off with later roasting, baking or frying. Boiling, because it retains most of the food value in the surrounding water, is usually the most effective cooking method. Remember, however, that the boiling-point of water decreases with altitude, due to diminished air pressure. The higher you are, therefore, the harder it is to cook by boiling, until above 12,000 feet (4000 metres) it becomes impractical.

If you have no metal container for water-boiling, there are some other alternatives to consider.

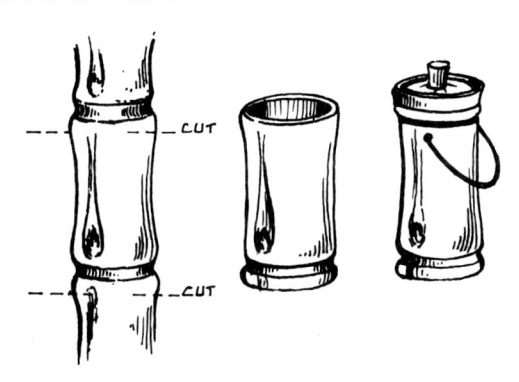

A section of bamboo, cut just below each of two joints, will provide a container for the boiling water – as will half a green coconut. Both will remain unburnt until after the water has boiled. Containers made from large single leaves (e.g. banana) or birchbark will also hold water for boiling if they are kept moist and the fire kept low. A square or rectangle can be folded in the manner shown to produce a water-tight container.

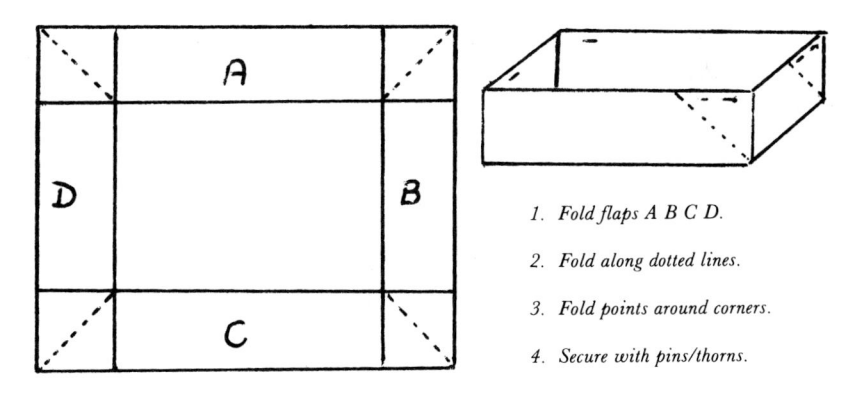

1. Fold flaps A B C D.
2. Fold along dotted lines.
3. Fold points around corners.
4. Secure with pins/thorns.

Folded Water Container.

Thorns can be used to secure the folded corner points. Do not overlook other container possibilities – such as shells.

(iii) Baking

Food to be baked must be enclosed and then subjected to constant medium heat. The enclosure may be either an oven, a pit beneath the fire, any closed container, or even a wrapping of leaves or clay. Any of these is best used with glowing coals.

A fire pit is more efficient if it can be lined with stones to hold or reflect the heat. Half-fill the pit with coals, place the food container among them, and add a further layer of coals above. Cover the whole with a layer of earth. Cooking in this manner produces evenly done food, which will have been protected from any kind of pest.

(iv) Steaming

If you have no container and wish to prepare food requiring little or minimum cooking, steaming is a method that can be used. A pit is prepared by putting in a thick layer of heated stones which are covered with leaves on which the food is placed. More leaves are used to cover the food, and a stick is pushed down into the food space. Now pack an earth layer over the leaves and around the stick. The stick is now withdrawn, and leaves a hole down into the food space. Pour water down this hole, and your food will cook slowly but effectively.

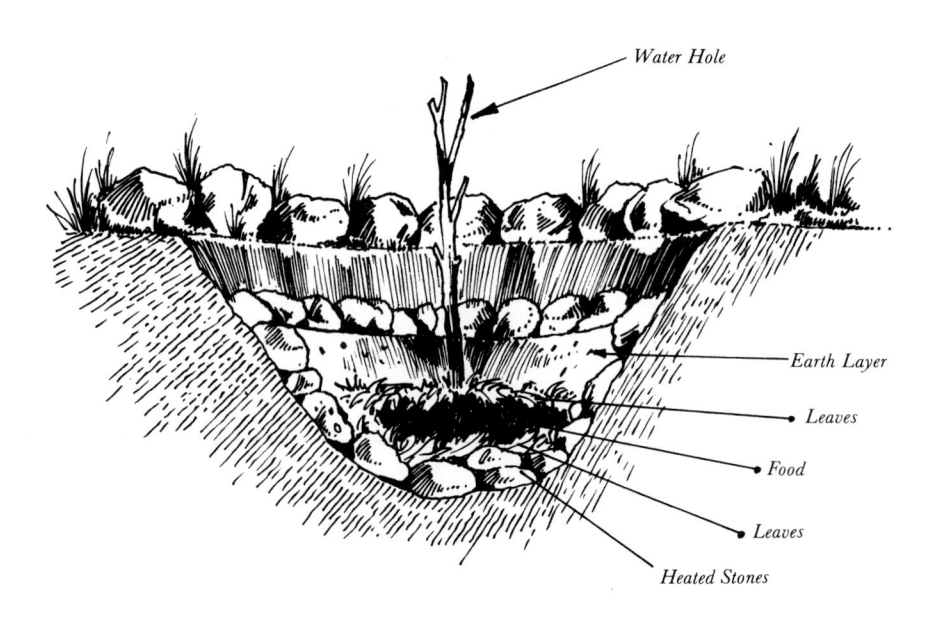

The Steaming Pit.

Animal Food

Small Game

Small mammals and birds may be cooked complete or in parts. They can be roasted, baked or boiled. Smaller game is best boiled so as to lessen waste. **All** entrails and reproductive organs must be removed before cooking. Carcasses – especially birds – can be made tasty by stuffing them with edible berries, grains, roots, greens or nuts.

Fish

May be roasted by direct heat, baked using an oven or other wrapping, or they can be fried. Never eat fish raw if there is any means of cooking it.

Amphibians and Reptiles

Small snakes, lizards and frogs can be spitted on a stick and roasted. Larger eels and snakes are better if they are boiled before roasting. Turtles should be boiled until the shell comes off. The meat is then cut up and used to make a soup with any edible plants available. Salamanders are edible if spit-roasted, but all frogs and snakes must be skinned prior to cooking, since the skins may contain poison.

Molluscs

Shellfish may be boiled, steamed or baked in the shell. They are an excellent basis for a soup with green vegetables.

Crustaceans

Crayfish, crabs, shrimps and prawns must be cooked so as to destroy the organisms they contain which are capable of inducing diseases in humans. Cook them alive by dropping them into boiling water. Carry this out at the very earliest moment possible after catching, since they spoil very quickly.

General Hints

Animals larger than the domestic cat should be boiled before roasting or baking. Roasting, unlike boiling, should be done as quickly as possible, since a slow fire's direct heat will toughen the meat. Particularly tough meat is best stewed with vegetables. Larger animals will need to be cut into manageable pieces before cooking. When roasting or baking any kind of meat, fat should be used if available. Place the fat at the top of the meat so that it will run down over the outside. Try to catch dripping fat to baste as cooking continues.

Plant Foods

(i) **Roots and Tubers**

These are more easily baked or roasted, although they can be boiled.

(ii) **Herbs**

Leaves, stems and buds must be boiled until they are tender. Any bitter taste can be diminished by replacing the water several times.

(iii) **Nuts, Grains and Seeds**

Most can be eaten raw, but many are better if they are parched. Parching involves slow heating until the food is well scorched. This is best done in a metal container, but can be achieved on a hot flat stone – the top of a Yukon Stove would be ideal. Some nuts – such as acorns – are better crushed than parched. Chestnuts are excellent whether roasted, steamed, baked or raw.

(iv) **Fruit**

Any fruits which are tough, or have heavy skins should be baked or roasted, while succulent fruits can be boiled. Many fruits are valuable food when eaten raw.

(v) **Bread**

Flour and water can be used to make bread. Use sea water, if available, so as to include salt, and knead the dough well. Baking can be carried out in an oven, or by laying thin sheets of dough on hot flat stones. A stick with the bark removed can have dough twisted around it, to be held over the fire. Check that the stick does not contain bitter sap which could affect the bread's taste.

The loaf can be improved if you add a little leaven to the dough. Leaven is simply dough which has been allowed to go sour.

(vi) **Eggs**

These are one of the most convenient and safe foods. They may be eaten even during the development of the embryo. If hard-boiled, they provide a convenient and easily portable food-reserve, which will keep for several days.

Food Preservation

No survivor can count on a regular supply of wild food in any survival situation. One or two days' good hunting or gathering may be succeeded by a period when food is harder to find, catch or trap.

The weather may make food gathering – or any other activity – difficult. It is important, therefore, to know how to preserve food. This will allow regular supplies to be maintained – or a portable reserve to be built up if you plan to move. You must do all that you can to avoid food wastage through deterioration.

In cold climates surplus food can be easily and quickly preserved by freezing. Cut it into strips or small pieces and spread it on the ground outside your shelter. Guard it against animals while it freezes. Then store it safely above ground level – at a minimum height of six feet.

In temperate climates or during the summer, meat, game or fish should be stored in the coolest, shadiest place available. Food surplus to immediate requirements can be preserved by drying. This can be done naturally, in the sun and the wind, but is probably better achieved if a fire and its smoke are used, as in a smoke teepee.

Meat to be smoked or dried should be cut into thin slices – approximately 1cm. thick – across the grain. These are then laid on the smoking platform and left until brittle. Do not use wood containing pitch (e.g. pine or fir) as its acrid smoke can taint the meat. Remember, once your fire is going, to add green wood or foliage to make smoke. If you have a tent or teepee, this can be used for smoking/drying food, but take care to avoid damage to the shelter. Any ventilation flaps should be closed while smoking is in progress. Another alternative is to use the smoke-pit method, which, although it takes more effort to construct will produce results more quickly.

Fish are prepared for smoking/drying by removal of the heads and tails so that they can be spread flat. Thin twigs can be used as skewers to hold them so.

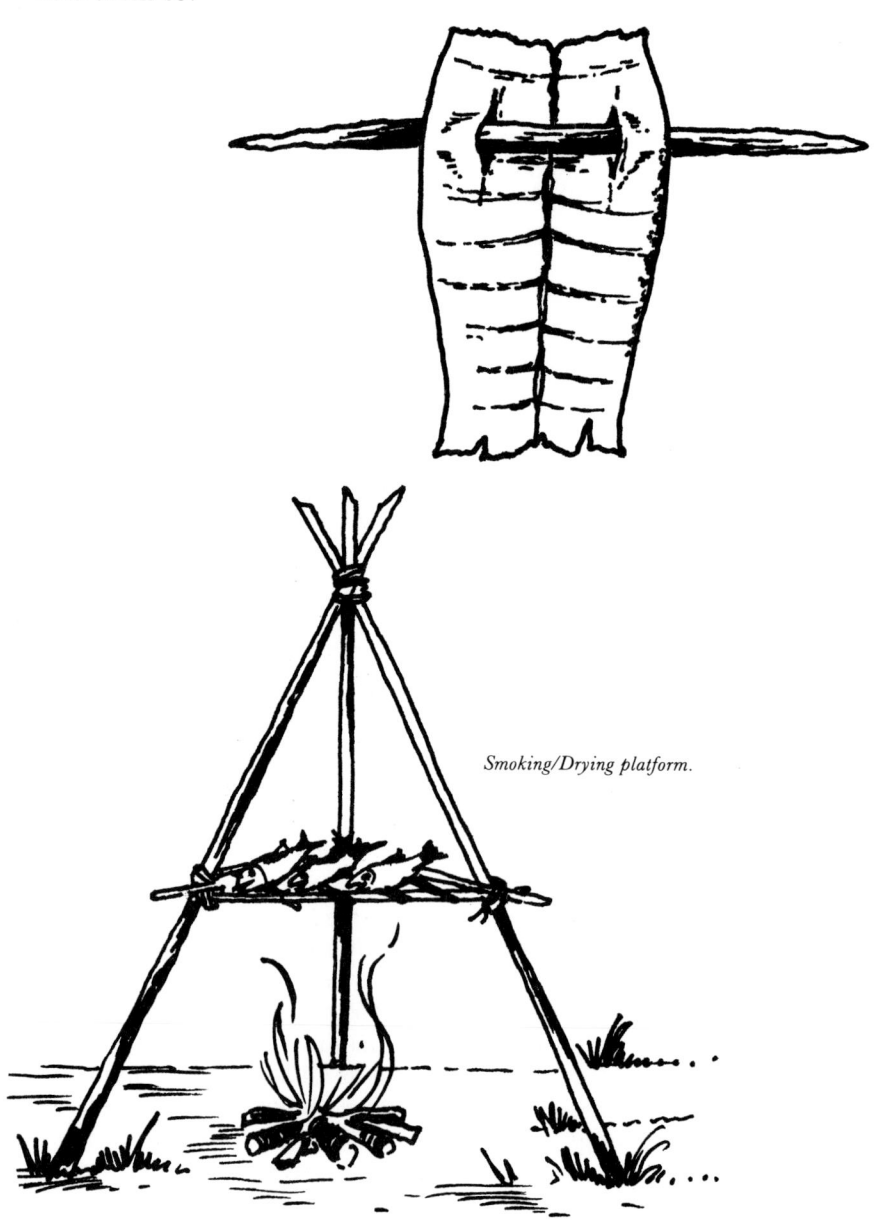

Smoking/Drying platform.

Plant food can also be dried using any of these methods. Fruits are best cut into thin slices to speed drying, in the sun or by the fire. Mushrooms dry easily and keep well. They need to be soaked in water before they are used.

SUMMARY

1. Fire will supply personal warmth and can be used for cooking. Both these purposes are best served by a small fire rather than a big one. In very cold conditions, two or more small fires will provide you with more warmth than even a very large fire. These fires will be enhanced if some form of reflector is employed.

2. The Pyramid Fire is used to dry and prepare fuel for future fires. In particular, it allows preparation of Signal Fires ready for immediate use.

3. The Star Fire is a simple fire which is economical. It can be left alone with safety when necessary.

4. Any cooking fire is most effective when used with some form of stove, even if improvised. If possible the stove should include an oven. The Yukon Stove is the best pattern.

5. Cooking fires can also be employed with various types of pit. The simple Fire Pit assists roasting and baking. The Hangi cooks in quantity and without containers. The Steaming Pit is self explanatory.

6. Fire can be employed for food preservation via drying or smoking.

7. Fire can be used to make charcoal. This is wood which is subjected to heat without being completely burned. It can be made by leaving twigs in an oven for a period. It can be obtained from incompletely burned logs. It serves many purposes. These include filtration and removal of unpleasant tastes from water, use as secondary fuel for fire-lighting and in limited amounts, as treatment for stomach upsets. It is always worthwhile taking advantage of this by-product of your fire.

It is all-important to take care of your fire and to use it with caution. Ensure its supply of fuel. Bank it down when it is not in use. Above all – make sure it does not go out until **you** choose. Remember – always – your fire can be a major factor in your survival. It is easier and less dangerous to keep it going than to be forced to relight it.

CHAPTER EIGHT

SURVIVAL NAVIGATION

Your assessment and planning have led to the decision to move. The move might be limited to the gaining of a more favourable survival site – one which offers better shelter, or an increased availability of food, water or fuel. Your intention might be to walk all the way out to reach help and safety. Do not forget, however, that unless you tell them, any searching rescuers will not know what you are trying to do.

Be sure, therefore, to leave an indication of your plans, in the form of signs clearly visible from the air. (See "Location Signalling"). If you are starting from a crashed or broken-down vehicle of any kind, leave a message. This should include the day and time you left; your direction of movement, intended route and destination; the number of people in the group; a list of supplies – and any other relevant information. This message will help searchers to find you.

If your movement is towards a more favourable location, and that location is visible, there will be no problems of navigation. You will be able to see the direction in which to travel. (Remember, however, that the straight line is often **not** the quickest or easiest way between two points in rough country).

If the aim is to reach safety, you need a clear idea of your starting position, and of the position you will be heading for. Both are needed to decide upon the direction of travel. The more exactly you can establish these points, the more exact will be the calculation of the direction to follow.

If travelling on land you should have a reasonable idea of your position, as you would have been reading a map or following road signs before the emergency arose. In the event of an aircrash, try to find the navigator's chart, which should clearly show your route. If the chart cannot be found, then you must attempt an estimate of where you are.

Mentally, picture the aircraft's track from its departure point to its destination. You know how long it was airborne. Knowing what the flight time was to have been, work out what proportion of the route was flown before the crash. This will at least give an estimate of the area in which you are located.

It is, of course, only the roughest of estimations, because the aircraft might have been affected by unexpected head or tail winds – or may

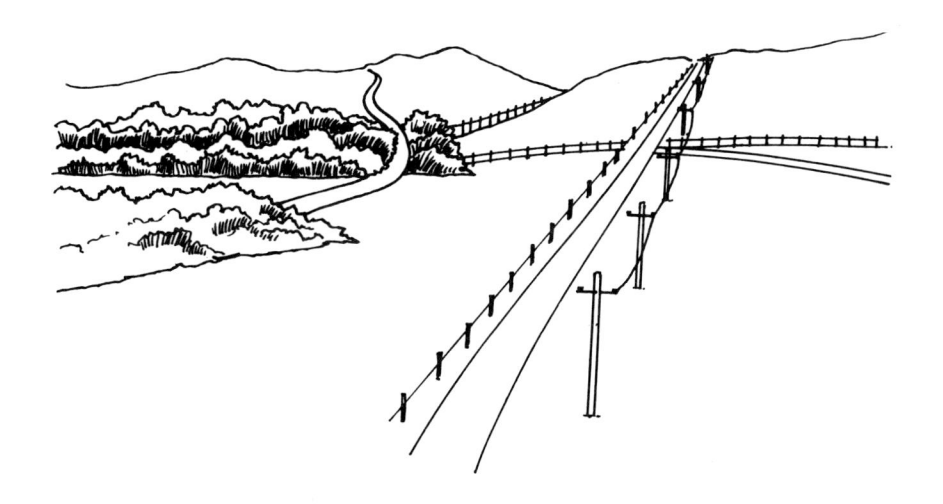

Orientating a Map.

have been off course. But however rough an estimate, it is still better than just plain guess-work, unsupported by any logic, or evidence.

Of course, the ideal starting point is a positive fix of position based on recognition of a prominent feature of the terrain that can also be identified on a map. From such a fix, you can calculate accurately the direction to follow.

In a serious survival situation involving an aircraft or boat, you should be able to find a compass. The transport will have been equipped with compasses, apart from which the survival dinghies or rafts will carry them. If engaged in an expedition on foot into any remote, wild area, it would be irresponsible not to carry one – even if familiar with the area.

Being able to use a compass in conjunction with a map is not only a survival skill, but can be beneficial throughout life, even in normal everyday situations. It is worthwhile acquiring and practising this technique. **Always** take particular care that the compass is unaffected by any metal in the vicinity – especially any on your person. Very small amounts can distort the compass reading if they are near to the pointer.

If you have a map, even without a compass, the chances of navigating the way to safety will be very greatly increased. A map will enable you to fix your position to within a few miles provided you can identify one prominent feature on the map and on the terrain. Two or more features identified with certainty will enable you to fix your position positively and accurately. Now the map itself can be used as a compass. To do this you have to orient your map.

Spread your map on level ground. Rotate the sheet until the features on the map are in the same relative positions and directions as on the terrain. Your map is now orientated, and lies on the ground depicting the area as it would be seen from above. The Grid Lines will now be indicating True North to within one degree, depending upon the accuracy of the orientation.

You can orient your map without recognition of any physical features – as when visibility is poor – if you have a compass.

The map should be spread flat as before, and the compass placed on it so that the North and South points correspond with the Grid Lines on the map. The map should be clear of any source of metallic influence. Slowly rotate the map with the compass on it so that the compass needle lines up with the Grid Lines and the North/South points. Next, check the magnetic variation as shown on the map.

Carefully rotate the map until the compass needle shows the same variation. Over most of Britain, for example, the magnetic variation is approximately six degrees west. This means that your compass needle will now be indicating 354 degrees instead of 360.

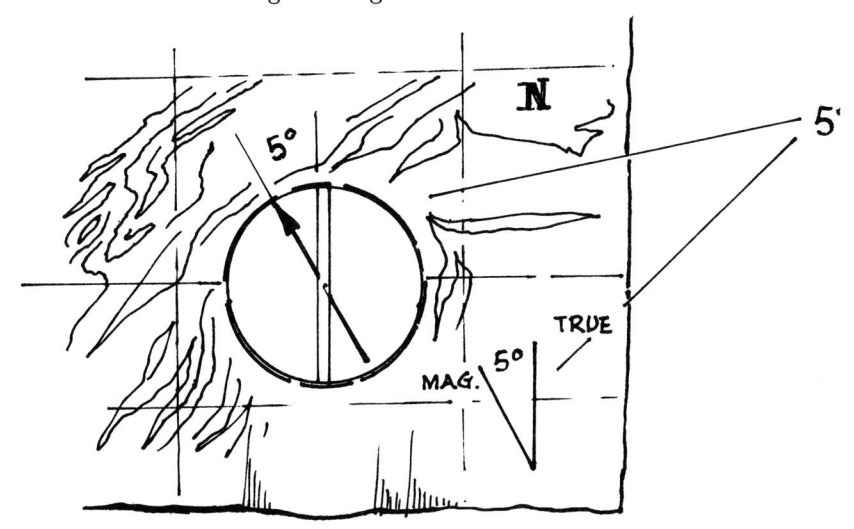

With the map oriented in this way, it is a simple matter to calculate the compass bearing to follow. When you have decided what the course is to be, selected some object or feature at the limit of visibility. Use this as an aiming point, and move towards it. This will obviate the need to make continual reference to the compass. In poor visibility, or on featureless terrain, however, there is little choice but to make frequent checks on direction with your compass.

If you have both map and compass, and can identify two or more features in the area, a more exact positional fix is possible.

Take a compass bearing on the first feature. Add 180 degrees to the bearing. This gives a "reverse bearing". Use it to plot a line from the feature back through your locality. Repeat this procedure for the remaining feature(s). Your position will be at the intersection of lines of "reverse bearing." Sometimes, due to the difficulty of obtaining exact compass readings the lines will form a small triangle where they intersect. Take the centre of this triangle as being your position.

Your map will also show if there is any habitation in the area, as well as indicating any roads or railways. It will show the easiest and safest route towards help. If used with care and thought, a map can also lead to the nearest water (or chance of water), shelter, and the areas offering the best chance of obtaining food from the wild.

DIRECTION FINDING WITHOUT A COMPASS

Although a compass provides the simplest and most fool-proof way of finding direction, there are many other methods you can employ if you are without one.

1. **The Sun**

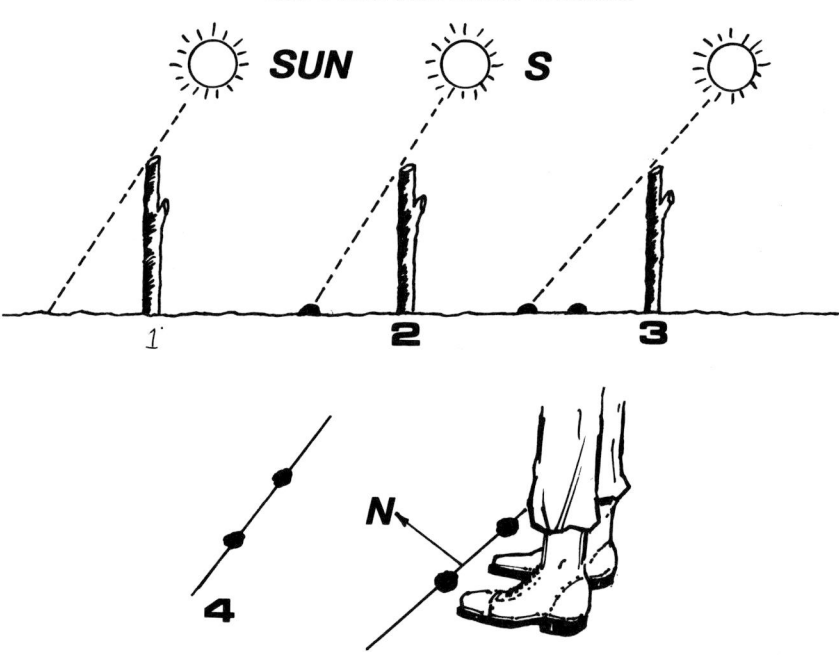

The Stick and Stone Method

a) Cut a stick about 1 metre long and push it upright into the ground. Choose a level spot where a shadow will be cast.
b) Mark the very end of the shadow as accurately as possible, using a small stone.
c) Wait for 15/20 minutes. You will observe that the shadow has moved. Mark the tip of this shadow with another stone.
d) Draw a line on the earth, running through the first stone and on through the second. This line will run from West to East.
e) Now stand with the toe of your LEFT foot against the line and close to the FIRST stone. Bring the toe of your **RIGHT** foot to the line near to the **SECOND** stone.

YOU ARE NOW FACING NORTH

Note that the accuracy of your direction finding will depend on the accuracy with which the shadow tips are marked, and the care taken in placing your toes to the line. A line drawn at right angles to your East/West line will produce a North/South indicator. From these Cardinal Points it will be a simple matter to calculate any other desired direction.

This method will indicate North whether used in the Northern or Southern Hemisphere.

If you carry out this method of direction-finding before the middle of the day, you will be able to use it for the additional purpose of ascertaining real time – that is, local time by the sun. This knowledge is valuable if you have a non-digital watch since, if the watch is set to real time, it can itself be used as a compass, in conjunction with the sun, and later, the moon.

To find real time, set up your stick and stone method before midday. Extend the West/East line so that you can run a line at right angles from it to the base of the stick. This will be a North/South indicator. It will also mark local noon when the shadow of the stick falls along it – and you can then set your watch.

2. **The Watch**

Northern Hemisphere

Having checked that your watch is set to local time, point the hour hand towards the sun. Greater accuracy of aim can be achieved by

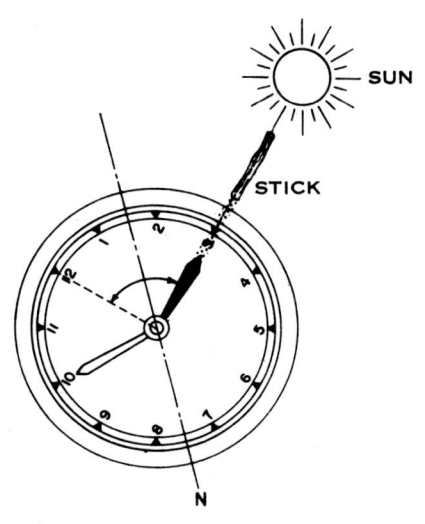

The Watch as Compass – (Northern Hemisphere).

using a blade of grass or thin twig to cast its shadow along the hour hand. A North/South line will now run from the centre of the watch face through the point on the dial edge which is mid-way between the hour hand and twelve o'clock. The Northern indicator will be the end of the line further from the sun.

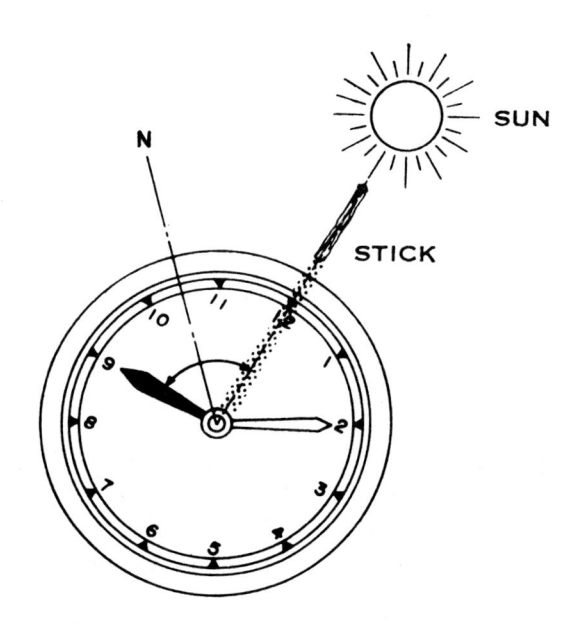

The Watch as Compass – (Southern Hemisphere).

Southern Hemisphere

In the Southern Hemisphere the number 12 must be pointed at the sun. The North/South line will run from the centre of the dial to a point on its edge which lies mid-way betwen 12 and the hour hand. The North indicator will be the end of the line nearer the sun. Real time setting is again important.

Should you be in any doubt as to which end of the line is pointing North, remember that the sun is in the eastern part of the sky before noon, and in the western part in the afternoon. The morning sun will be on the right-hand side if looking North. The afternoon sun will be on the left.

3. The Stars

The stars have been used as aids to navigation for many centuries. They still have an important role to play, and are also used in map-making. Any knowledge of the stars is worthwhile in itself, but for the survivalist this knowledge will be a most valuable acquisition.

The brightest stars appear to be set in fixed patterns, or constellations. It is true that the individual constellations do not vary, either in their particular patterns or in their relationship to each other. But a brief observation of the sky will reveal that the whole body of stars seems, because of the Earth's rotation, to be wheeling around a central point.

The Northern Hemisphere

In the Northern Hemisphere the central point of this wheel is marked by Polaris – also called the Pole Star or North Star. Because of its central position it shows no apparent movement, remaining static in the sky above the North Pole. It follows, therefore, that if you can locate Polaris, you have an accurate indication of true North.

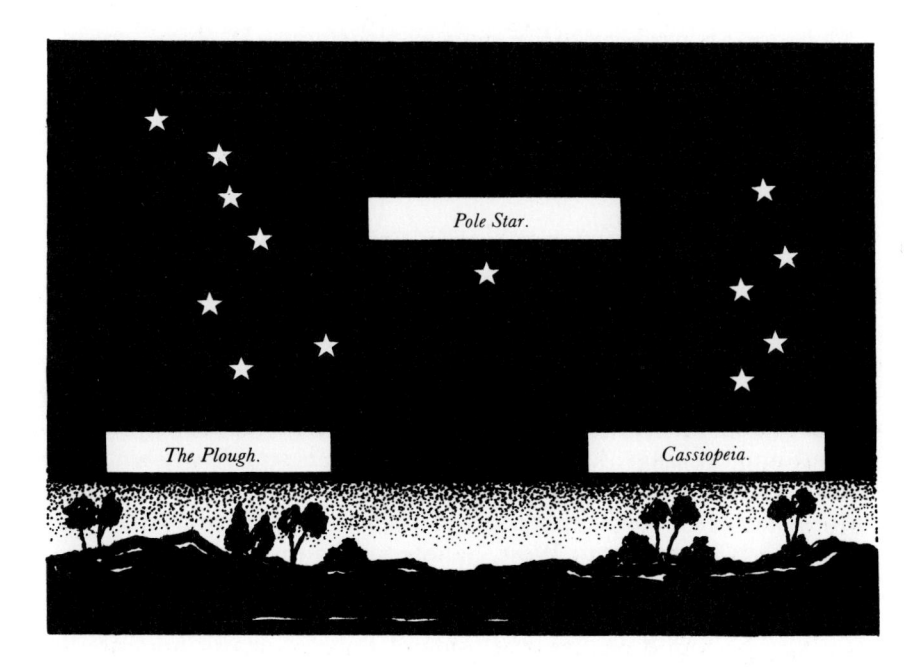

Pole Star.

The Plough.

Cassiopeia.

The rest of the stars appear to rise and set during the night, so that the constellations slowly change their positions in the sky. Regardless of these changes, however, they remain in the same situations relative to each other and from Polaris – much as the spokes of a wheel do in relation to the hub, even though the wheel is turning. If you can identify two or three constellations, they will guide you to Polaris and you will be able to establish your direction.

The best guide to Polaris is the constellation known as the Plough, or Big Dipper. It is made up of seven main stars.

The two stars furthest from the "handle" always point towards Polaris. If you follow their line for about six times the distance between them, you will find Polaris, even though it is not a particularly bright star.

You can check your star identification if you know that Polaris lies halfway between the Plough and another constellation called Cassiopeia.

Cassiopeia is made up of five main stars forming a W shape, one half of which is slightly more flattened than the other. It appears on the other side of Polaris, almost opposite the Plough, as if the two constellations balance each other. Neither the Plough or Cassiopeia ever set if they are seen from any country North of 40 degrees N. latitude.

There is an interesting – and significant – difference between the sun's apparent movement around the sky and that of the stars.

The sun's complete movement takes 24 hours – but the stars take 4 minutes less. This means that they rise a little earlier each day. The daily difference is small, but over a few weeks it adds up to produce a considerable variation in the location of the constellations in the sky. On autumn evenings, for instance, the Plough is seen low down in the North, under Polaris. On winter evenings it is in the North East with the handle turned down. In the spring it is nearly overhead, while in the summer it is in the North West, handle turned up.

Cassiopeia, of course, moves in exactly the same way, and so is always to be found on the other side of Polaris, nearly opposite the Plough.

The Southern Hemisphere

In the Southern Hemisphere there is, unfortunately, no star that corresponds to Polaris – that is, which remains fixed above the South Pole. Look, instead for the Southern Cross. It is made up of four main stars, with the fifth, a fainter star, showing a little off the centre of the cross. Follow a line through the longer of the Cross members for four and a half times its length. This brings you to the point where such a south pole star would be. Note a landmark directly below this point – and it will indicate South.

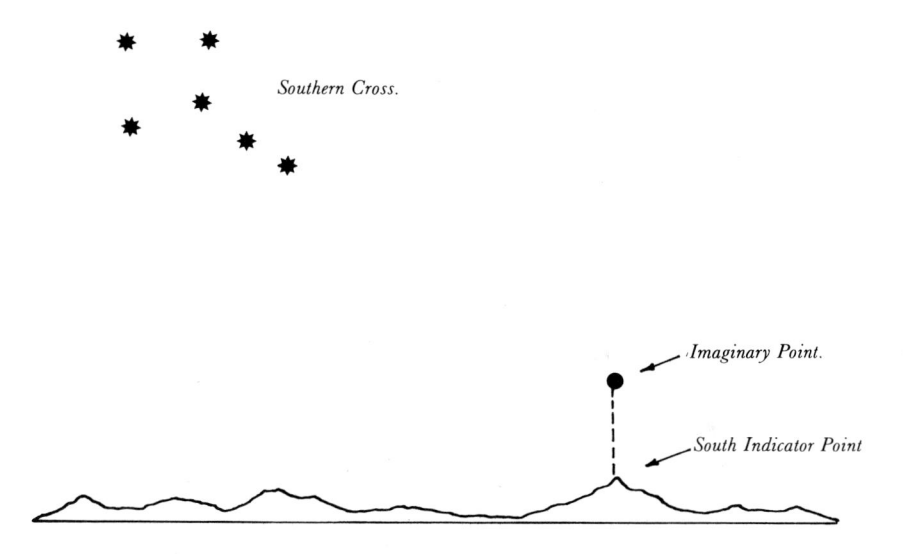

Southern Cross.

Imaginary Point.

South Indicator Point

To check that your line is extended in the correct direction, note that it should pass through a group of four faint stars soon after leaving the Southern Cross.

If determining your direction ready for the next day's march, take the bearing using a stick laid on the ground as a pointer. This will continue to show the required line of march in the morning.

The Star Movement Method

If the sky is partly obscured and you are unable to locate and identify individual constellations, the stars can still be employed for navigation. You can get a general indication of direction by making use of the knowledge that they appear to be wheeling around the sky. Detect which way any star is moving and you will know roughly which direction you are facing. Two fixed reference points are needed to detect star movement. One way of getting these is to set up two sticks in the ground so that they are like the sights of a gun aimed at any prominent star you can see.

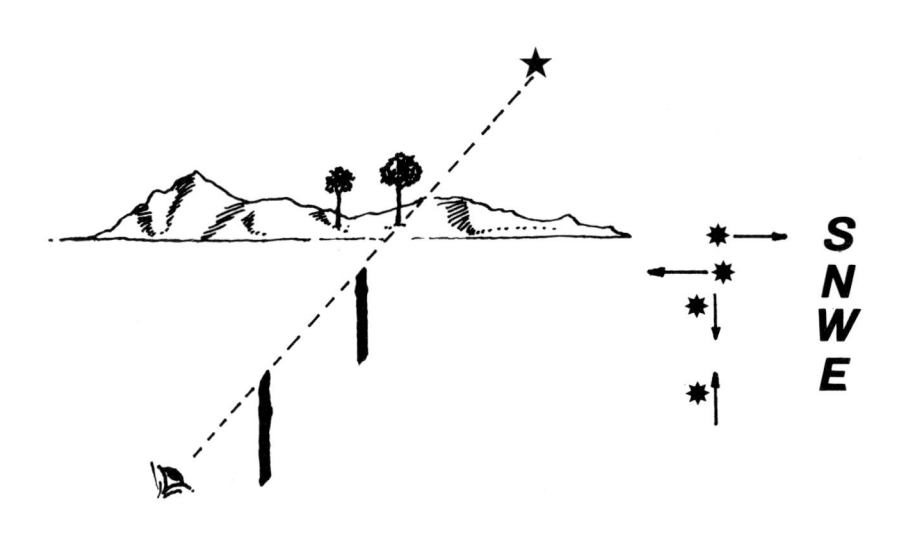

If the star appears to be:

a) Looping flatly towards the **RIGHT,** you are facing **SOUTH** (approximately).

b) Looping flatly towards the **LEFT,** you are facing approximately **NORTH.**

c) **RISING,** you are facing approximately **EAST.**

d) **DESCENDING,** you are facing approximately **WEST.**

If you are able to steady your head against some fixed object, this can be done using only one other fixed reference point, since your eye can be the first. It is important, if this method is used, not to spend too long staring at the chosen star. If you do, it will appear to wander – or maybe not move at all. Use a series of glances as your guide. Practice will help a great deal in star movement detection.

4. The Moon

There are two methods you can use to navigate by the moon which will produce reasonable results.

1. The Quarter Moons

Produce a line through the horns of either of the quarter moons down to the horizon. Where it meets the horizon it will indicate South, if you are in the Northern Hemisphere. It will indicate North if you are in the Southern Hemisphere. Tests have demonstrated that this can provide a rough but very ready guide when moving at night.

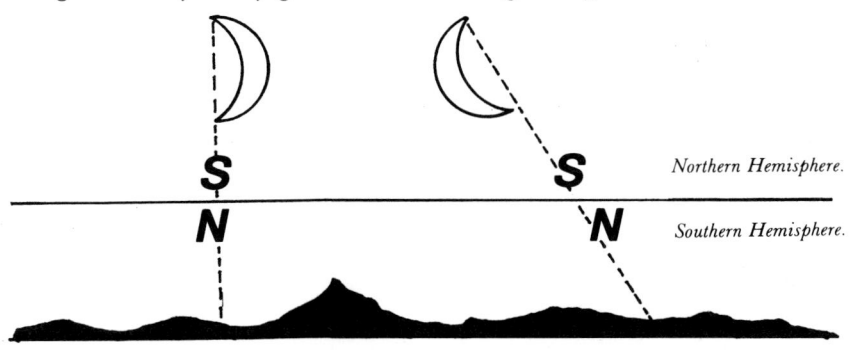

2. The Quarter Moons and the Full Moon

If you have been able to set your watch to local real time, or check that it is already correct, you can obtain a good indication of direction from these phases of the moon. Use it in conjunction with the following table.

Local Time	Direction Indicated		
	1st Quarter	Full Moon	Last Quarter
1800	South	East	
2100	South-West	South-East	
Midnight	West	South	East
0300		South-West	South-East
0600		West	South

5. **Vegetation**

If you find yourself in an area which supports much vegetation, there are most probably many navigational clues at hand. They will not provide very accurate directions, but they will, if you look for them, give general indications of direction.

Many perennial plants – trees, shrubs, etc. – have more prolific vegetation on their sunny sides (i.e. the side nearer the equator). There are exceptions – such as trees or bushes which have been affected by the prevailing wind. You will need to use your powers of observation now – as part of your long-term preparation for survival – so that you can differentiate between these effects.

Coniferous trees are more bushy on their sun-facing sides, while willows, alders and poplar trees tend to lean towards the sun. No reference has been made to plant growth indicating North or South – only that it can point out the sunny, or Equatorial side of the plants. Of course, the Equator is to the South if you are in the Northern Hemisphere, but lies to the North if you are in the Southern Hemisphere.

In either hemisphere therefore, plant growth will help to indicate – roughly – the opposite Pole.

The major exception to this general rule is the family of moss plants. Preferring damp conditions, they grow best on the aspects of trees, rocks, etc. which receive the least sun. These will be found on the sides facing towards the Poles. Remember that MOSSES give an opposite indication of direction to the rest of the plants.

There are other, more localised, species of plants which will provide navigational clues. Add to your survival preparation by reading more about those which grow in any area of particular personal interest.

It may be difficult to get accurate directions from plant growth, but keep your eyes open and practise careful observation. The vegetation will then become another factor in developing a keen sense of direction to a level where it becomes a valuable survival skill – as well as a convenient everyday talent. Remember, also, that many of the plant growth indications can be used by night as well as by day.

6. **Prevailing Winds**

These are probably of greatest assistance in desert areas, where local aids to navigation are often very sparse. The prevailing winds will shape the sand dunes.

If you know, or can observe, the prevailing wind direction, the shape of the dunes will provide a very rough indication of direction.

In other areas, particularly the interiors of great land masses, prevailing winds can only be taken into account when they have been constant for a few days. You must allow time for local temporary variations to dissipate.

It can be useful to remember that in coastal areas the local winds follow a pattern. They blow onshore during the evening and offshore during the morning.

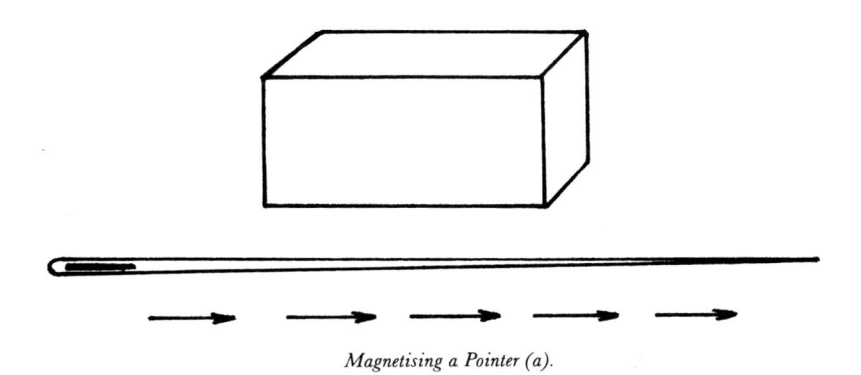

Magnetising a Pointer (a).

The Improvised Compass

We have looked at some of the methods the survivor can use to find direction if he has no compass. It may, however, be possible to improvise a simple working version.

a) It is possible to make a compass by magnetising a needle, nail, pin, razor blade – or any suitable metal object (i.e. something that will react to a magnet) – provided it can be suspended so as to swing freely as a pointer. The metal indicator can be magnetised by stroking it with one pole of a magnet. The pointer will require re-magnetising from time to time. Stroke the metal pointer in the same direction each time, using the same end of the magnet.

Sometimes, suspending the pointer can present difficulties, especially if the thread is stiff or has been twisted. This will inhibit free movement of the pointer. If using a small object such as a needle or a scalpel blade, the problem can be overcome by pushing the pointer through a small piece of cork, two or three matchsticks, or a small piece of twig. It can then be floated in still water. Take great care that the water container itself is not made of any metal that affects the pointer magnetically. The pointer will now swing freely.

It is worth recalling that every radio set — down to the smallest transistor receiver — has a permanent magnet as part of its loudspeaker. It can therefore be of use in compass-making. **The successful Survivor will always be on the look-out for ways in which things can be used for original and sometimes unexpected purposes** — like, for instance, the generator mentioned in "Situation Assessment and Planning," — which also contains a permanent magnet.

b) It is also possible to magnetise a steel pointer using electricity, if you have a battery producing more than 6 volts and a length of

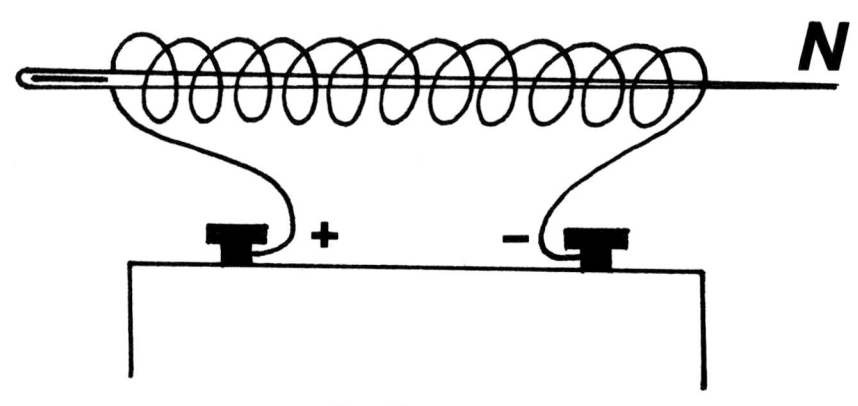

Magnetising a Pointer (b).

insulated copper wire. For low voltages like these, the insulation will often be a coat of varnish only. Wire of this type will be found in the coils inside radios, generators and other electrical equipment fitted to most types of transport.

Wrap the wire around the pointer, making as many turns as your wire allows. Connect up to the battery and allow the current to flow for 15 to 30 minutes. Be sure that the ends connected to the battery are free of insulation, or the current will not flow. The coil you have made around the pointer may begin to heat up if it is too short. If this happens, disconnect it, allow it to cool down and re-connect. Repeat the procedure if necessary. The North indicator will be the end of the pointer nearer to the negative battery terminal. (Remember — N for Negative and North.).

c) Hammering can magnetise a piece of iron if it is hammered while lying on known North/South line. Such a line could be established by taking a bearing on the Pole Star and marking it on the ground. Keeping the pointer lying on the line, hammer it for some time. It will become magnetised. When properly suspended it will indicate North and South.

Any doubt about which end of a pointer is showing North is easily resolved if you recall the check using the sun's situation in the sky before noon and after.

These are some of the techniques you can use to help navigate your way to safety in a survival situation. Some of them depend upon observation, some on recognition and location of stars, and others on a knowledge of a particular skill. But for effective use, **all** rely upon familiarity – the familiarity which only comes from repeated practice. Use every reasonable opportunity to check directions, landmarks, and the position of constellations. Look at vegetation for signs of significant uneven growth. Watch the moon's progress through its phases and use it frequently to check direction. Practice star movement direction until it becomes easy. This kind of preparation will gradually give you an awareness of direction as second nature. It will always be of value.

CHAPTER NINE

WATER PROCUREMENT

Nothing is more important to your survival than your water supply. The human body – itself about 90% water – cannot maintain its efficiency without a regular minimum intake. The amount required varies according to climate and the level of activity being carried out. In this context, eating is an activity. Even in a temperate climate the daily requirement is 2.5 litres. If your efficiency is to be maintained – along with the chance of survival – this requirement has to be met. In addition, everything possible must be done to make certain that the water is pure. Water procurement involves two factors: Quality and Quantity.

This constant need for water arises from the fact that the body is continually releasing its liquids during its normal functions, i.e. breathing, urination, excretion and sweating. The last of these increases greatly in hot climates or conditions. It follows, therefore, that in any situation where water might be in short supply, the first step is to protect and conserve the water already in the body. The basic rules have been touched upon in "Shelter Construction", but they are of such vital importance that they bear repetition in greater detail.

1. Cover any exposed skin as soon as possible. This will not only give protection against sunburn. It will help to slow down the evaporation of sweat – and so lessen the need for its replacement by further body-fluid. Loose clothing is the best option since it traps a layer of relatively still air around the body. This air acquires increased humidity from evaporated perspiration, and so slows down the evaporation rate.

2. Sit or lie in the shade to reduce dehydration caused by direct sunlight. In hot conditions, sit or lie a little way above the surface, if this is possible. Use rocks, wreckage, or anything else available. Even a few inches is helpful. The temperature will be appreciably lower, even this short distance off the ground.

3. Avoid energetic work during the heat of the day and, when it is necessary to move, do it without hurry. In this way you will generate the minimum of body heat and retain the body fluid which would have been needed to dissipate it.

4. Suck small pebbles or chew grass or string to help allay thirst

Breathe through the nose to avoid loss of fluid through evaporation of saliva. Talk only when necessary.

5. Drink in the cool of the evening or at night – and then in small sips. Don't swallow hurried mouthfuls.

6. If sea-water or other waste water is available, use it to wet your clothes. This will cool them and you, and reduce sweating. If you have built a survival still, (see later in Chapter), you will have an alternative use for this water.

7. You may well have to ration your water supply – but whatever water you have will last longer if you do the utmost to control sweating and other body fluid losses.

All these actions, however effective they may be, are only short-term responses to the main problem. Long term survival demands a good supply of drinkable water. Without it, your survival prospects are non-existent unless rescue intervenes. Without water, anything else you have – food, equipment, shelter, fire, etc. are worth nothing.

If you have any choice of water sources, on the other hand, always use water from a fast-flowing stream or river – preferably from as near the centre of the stream as practicable. In temperate regions, away from human or other sources of pollution, spring water is usually reliable. Rain, directly collected in any manner, is usable.

It is essential to remember that much surface water, especially if stagnant or muddy, will be contaminated with water-borne diseases and will be extremely dangerous to drink unless purified.

Do not underestimate this risk. The disease-inducing and other harmful organisms contained in impure water constitute one of the greatest enemies of survival.

If your only source of water is impure – or even suspect – do not drink any until it has been filtered and purified.

Filtering

The first step towards making water fit to drink is filtration. This will remove any creatures of any size as well as mud particles, leaves, or other foreign matter. There are water filters available which are most suitable for use in the survival situation. One example is the Aquafilter. If none are available, clean sand held in a shirt sleeve, sock, or cloth can be used effectively. A bamboo section plugged with grass makes a good sand filter.

Another option with muddy water is to let it stand for 12 hours so that all but the most minute particles settle to the bottom. Draw the water off, or pour it out slowly and with care to avoid disturbing the sediment.

If the source of water is a flowing, but muddy stream, such as occurs after heavy rainfall somewhere along the stream's course, it might be possible to scoop out a hollow a short way from the stream bank. If this is taken down below the level of the flowing water, it is likely that the hollow will gradually fill with water seeping through the soil from the stream into the hollow. The water will undergo some degree of filtration during this process. If possible, supplement this natural filtration by passing the water through sand as described. After filtration purify the water in one of the following ways:—

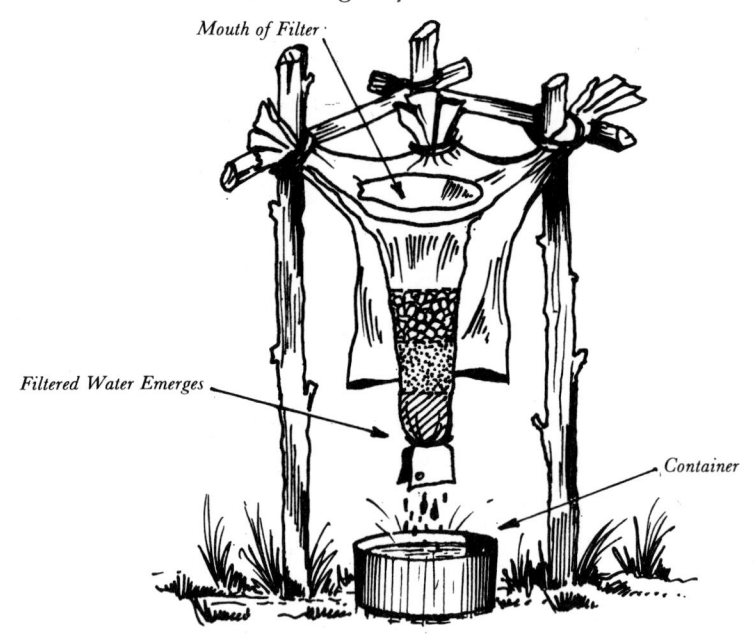

(a) Use purification tablets if available. Follow the instruction for use with care.

(b) Boil the water for five minutes. Try to obtain fast enough boiling to agitate the water, so ensuring equal distribution of heat. Do not forget to lengthen this time as altitude increases, since the boiling point of water gets lower as you go higher. Do not boil for too long, however, or water will be lost through evaporation.

(c) Add controlled amounts of iodine or potassium permanganate.

(d) Use an Osmoration Kit. This may also be used to purify sea water.

(e) If the climate is hot and sunny, consider the possibility of setting up a survival still. It can be employed to purify water in the same way that it obtains it from the ground or vegetation.

Charcoal added to any purified water will help remove unpleasant tastes or smells if added an hour before drinking. Don't worry about any small pieces of charcoal left in the water when drinking it. A small amount will do good rather than harm. An alternative way of taking filtered water with an unpleasant taste is via rectal infusion.

Water Location

There are many places where surface water cannot be found. In such places you have to be able to reach the water table – the depth at which the level of ground water lies below the surface. Ground water is the

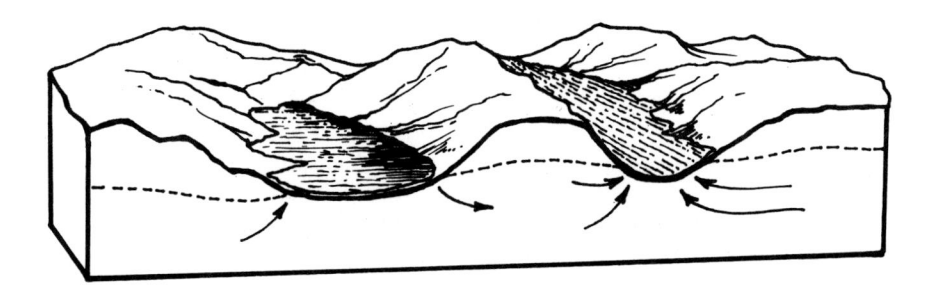

The Water Table – Likely Spring Locations.

result of rain which has soaked into the earth. It is usually pure. The land contours and the rock or soil types will determine how easy or difficult it will be to reach this water. The other major factor, of course, is the amount and frequency of rainfall.

Rocky Areas

In any area of varying rock strata, look for water seeping out wherever different types of rock overlie or intersect each other. Water will soak through porous rock (e.g. sandstone) but be contained by rocks such as granite. Where the end or edge of a layer of non-porous rock emerges from or is near to the surface, ground water is likely to appear as a spring. Limestone is water-soluble and frequently contains waterworn channels and caves. Look carefully among these for springs or underground water. On rocky hillsides, check carefully for any green area.

Choosing the greenest of these, dig narrow sloping furrows along their lower edges. Water will probably collect slowly in the downhill ends of the furrows.

Earthy Areas

Where the surface is soil-covered there is usually a greater likelihood of being able to find water. In undulating country always look for ground water along the lower hill slopes and on valley floors. These are the areas where the water table will either reach the surface or lie not far below. On the lower slopes there is also a good chance of water emerging near any rock-layer outcrop. Try to picture, in your mind's eye, the rock "skeleton" underlying the visible surface. This picture, if you can "see" it, will help in understanding the water pattern of your location.

Always look for the best indicators that water is present – green or luscious vegetation is good evidence – before digging for water. If no outstanding signs are visible, look for soil markings. They may be from animals or plants, and would show the spots where water has gathered or emerged during wetter periods of the year. They might be animal track marks, showing a place where animals gathered to drink at some earlier time. There might be an isolated patch of dessicated vegetation. These signs would pinpoint the best chance of finding water within digging distance of the surface, in that area. If no such signs are to be found, look at the lie of the land and dig in the valley floor, preferably beneath a steep slope.

In river valleys and plains the water table is generally near the surface, and a reasonable amount of digging will give you access to a plentiful water supply. In this situation, do not allow the availability of plenty of water to cloud your judgement regarding the imperative need to check for purity and lack of contamination.

The Sea Shore

Near the sea, the nature of the shore will dictate where best to look for water. On a rocky shore, examine the cliffs for differences in rock strata, for rock faults (i.e. displacement or slippage of rock layers), or green vegetation. Check all these points for water. If the rock layers are not lying level, water is most likely to emerge where they dip.

The Coconut Palm.

On a sandy shore the problem, when digging for water, is likely to be the difficulty of avoiding contamination by sea-water. Choose a spot at least 100 metres horizontally (or 3 to 4 metres vertically if the beach is steep) above the high tide line. Dig down until there are signs of moisture. Continue until the sand is damp. Then wait to see if water seeps into the hole. If it does, do not go any deeper, or the increased depth may be adding salt water to the supply.

On a beach backed by dunes there is a good chance of finding ground water in the hollow on the landward side of the dune nearest to the sea. But again, if you have to dig for it, don't go too deep. Water in such a location is probably safe to drink – as long as there are no signs of recent habitation or pollution. Filtration and the addition of charcoal will make it more pleasant to drink. If you have the means, it is always better to purify it.

On a sandy beach backed by rocks or cliffs it is always worthwhile looking for signs of ground water emerging below sand surface level. At low tide, look for any signs of water-flow on or under the sand, or from the seaward side of any sand banked up on the beach. Trace the flow back up the beach to the cliff or rock and dig there.

You must never drink sea-water. It contains so much salt that the kidneys are unable to cope with it, and will ultimately fail. For similar reasons, urine should never be drunk, for the body wastes it carries will cause illness. Both these liquids, however, can be utilised in the solar or survival still which is described later in this chapter.

DRINKING SEA WATER WILL BRING DEATH MORE QUICKLY THAN NO DRINKING AT ALL

Cold Weather Areas

These areas include high mountains and plateaux as well as the Arctic and Antarctic regions. Water supply may seem a minor problem if you are surrounded by snow and ice, but in reality it can present considerable difficulties. The extreme cold does assist the survivor by ensuring that most of the rain or snow-fall remains available on the ground instead of running away or soaking down into it. This same cold then presents him with a demand for a considerable amount of heat to melt the snow or ice to obtain his daily water supply.

Surface snow, in particular, takes much time and a great deal of heat to melt. This is because air is trapped among the flakes, and acts as an insulator. To discover just how much air **is** present, fill a vessel with loose snow packed reasonably tight. Note the little amount of water which actually melts out. The empty space in the vesesel represents the volume of the trapped air.

[A quick diversion back to Chap. on Shelter Construction. It may be easier to grasp that a shelter made of snow can offer a chance of warmth to a survivor inside, when the insulating properties of a snow-block are borne in mind.]

If you must eat snow to quench your thirst, compress it in the hands until water drips from the snowball into your mouth. Do not eat loose snow as it can cause dehydration and lead to hypothermia.

Ice is a better source of water, for it will melt more quickly as it contains little or no air. Crushing the ice into the smallest possible pieces will further reduce the amount of fuel needed to melt it.

Blue ice, from glacier or iceberg, will be free of salt and will provide good drinking water. As soon as any snow or ice has been melted, use it as quickly as possible. Make up hot drinks or cook food. Be sure to consume all the water, as there is no point in burning valuable fuel just to allow the water to freeze again. Remember that freezing does not purify water, so that melted ice or snow should be purified before drinking.

In a cold mountainous region there is a good chance of finding water even if the landscape appears arid. Look into cracks and crevices, or under overhanging ledges. Water frequently collects – or is trapped – in such places. Dig at the lowest point of any dry stream bed which may be discovered, for a seasonally reduced flow of water often continues beneath the stones and gravel.

In high mountain snowfields, consider an improvised snow melter, using the warmth of the sun. A black plastic bin-liner or similar sheet provides an excellent basis. Open it up, and use it to make a gently sloping trough, supporting it a few inches off the ground with pebbles, rocks, sticks, etc. When the plastic has warmed, loose snow scattered on it will melt and run down into your container.

Improvised Snow Melter.

If no plastic sheet is available, a large flat rock of convenient shape will operate, provided it is placed so as to catch the sun's rays. There may be an existing sloping rock surface ready for use.

Desert or Other Arid Areas

These are the regions where the survivor will be brought face to face with the importance of water. Life is impossible without it. Ample food supplies will be worthless. In hot deserts an absolute minimum of 5 litres a day are required. If less than this is available, the process of dehydration will begin. Whatever water is drunk will slow down the process, but as long as body fluid losses are greater than the water intake, dehydration continues.

The first effects are feelings of thirst and discomfort, followed by loss of appetite. Next comes a general slowing down and an increase in body temperature. Continued dehydration leads fairly quickly to death. The greatest danger during the early stages of dehydration does not arise from the physical symptoms, however. The real peril lies in the fact that your ability to think logically and to make sound decisions is among the first of the things to suffer.

The net result is that, in any hot, dry area, a shortage of water may mean that the time available to you may be short. This makes correct decisions and prompt action all-important. The survivor will be the one who has thought out his responses to such a situation BEFORE that situation arises. He will have planned his Survival Routine in advance. The following are some of the guide-lines and techniques upon which the Routine could be based.

Whatever water you have must be used to the greatest advantage. Having taken the steps described earlier to conserve body fluids, remember now that the body uses water for digestion and assimilation of food, as well as for the excretion of wastes. So, if you have no water you must not eat. In any case, do not eat or drink for the first 24 hours, and then drink only planned amounts at planned intervals. Note the amount of urine passed and drink that amount of water plus an extra half litre a day. Increase the extra amount cautiously if the early effects of dehydration are detected. Do not be alarmed if the urine is thick and you are constipated. These are two of the body's natural reactions to help conserve its own fluids.

Your real need is to obtain further water supplies. Never wait until you are without water before you begin locating, collecting and storing it. When a survival situation arises in the desert or any similar location start looking immediately for signs of water.

1. Look for any trails – animal or human – that may lead to water. The best supplies come from wells or oases. If anywhere near either, you may find a trail leading to it.

2. Dry river or stream beds may still have water under the surface. It finally goes underground at the lowest points on the bed – and these will usually be found on the outer edges of bends. These are the best places to dig.

3. Keep a sharp watch for any natural cisterns, which may be found under cliffs, behind projecting rocks or in rock gullies. The presence of animal droppings may be an indicator of such a place.

4. Bird flight can be a pointer to water. It is worth watching for, especially at dawn and dusk. Parrots, the zebra bird, the asian sand-grouse, crested larks and pigeons must all live near water or visit its source every day. Birds will also circle water holes in the desert.

5. Any green vegetation shows that there is some water in the ground. Some – willows, elder, cat tail – will only grow where it is near the surface. Any of these plants would mark a good spot to dig.

6. Dig anywhere there is damp sand, or where animals have scratched. Flies often hover over places where water has lain recently. Look for moisture under the surface by digging at the base of the STEEP sides of dunes.

7. The desert people will usually know of any locations where water will linger, either briefly or for longer periods. They will often cover such places in various ways in order to protect the source from fouling or pollution from any cause. Investigate any unusual piles of brush, etc., seen in low or sheltered places. A close look at a large suitcase found lying on the sand in a remote area once led to a surprising discovery. It was acting as the cover to a well. Further investigation revealed that the case held the bucket for drawing water!

The Dew Trap

A clear night is likely to produce dew. Cool stones (i.e. any which

The Dew Trap.

have been in the shade during the day) or bare metal surfaces will act as condensers for dew. Collect it by wiping or sponging it up with any clean piece of cloth. The supply can be almost certainly improved by the construction of a dew trap, if you have a foil blanket, plastic sheet or metal wreckage panel.

After scooping out the trough, scatter leaves, twigs or grass over the bottom to insulate the covering sheet from the ground warmth. Darkening the upper surface of the sheet will, if it is possible, improve its ability to radiate heat.

The aim is to produce a surface which is cooler than the surrouding air. If this can be done, condensation will occur as it does on the interior surface of a house window. Secure the sheet over the trough, ensuring that it is a few cms. clear of the ground. A small stone placed in the centre of the sheet will ensure that the water collecting on the underside will drip into a container.

The Survival Still

If no water can be found in any of these locations, or if any water found is impure, a drinkable supply can be obtained by the use of a survival still. This is a simple device which will produce water almost anywhere. To make it, a clear plastic sheet about 2 metres square is required, together with a water container. A plastic drinking tube about 1.5 metres long is desirable.

Dig or scoop out a hole in the ground, about a metre across and some 75cms. deep in the centre, where the container is placed. Fasten one end of the tube in the container. Spread the plastic sheet over the hole, bringing the other end of the tube out under its edge. Secure the edges of the sheet with spaced stones. Put a rock or weight on to the centre of the sheet so that it sags into an inverted cone. The centre should be allowed to drop about 35cms. below horizontal. Now put soil or sand all around the edge of the hole to secure the sheet and seal the hole off from the atmosphere.

What will happen is that the sun's rays will pass through the sheet, warm the ground underneath, and evaporate any water present. This will result in the air trapped below the sheet becoming saturated. The water vapour will begin to condense out on to the underside of the plastic. The droplets will run down along the sheet and fall into the container. The still will usually produce at least half a litre in 24 hours, though very dry desert conditions may yield less than this. In better conditions 1.5 litres may be expected.

There are some points which must be carefully observed during construction.

(a) Make sure that the sheet does not touch the sides of the hole at any point, or the water will be lost back into the ground.

(b) Make sure that the sheet is clear of the container also, or some water will be sure to run down its outside and be lost.

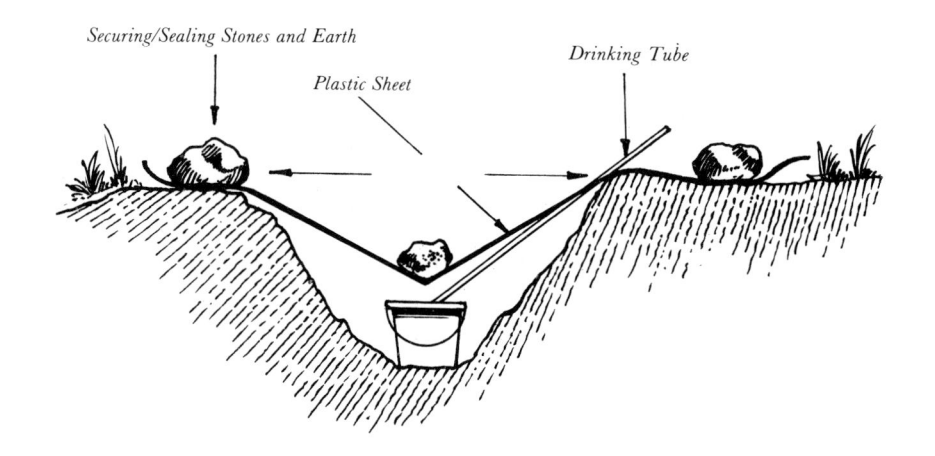

The Survival Still.

(c) Check that the seal around the edge of the hole is complete and airtight.

(d) Use a drinking tube if possible. Should no tube be available, disturb the sheet as few time as practicable. Each time the plastic is lifted all or some of the saturated air will be lost, and there will be a time-lag before the water starts collecting again.

There are one or two refinements possible which will improve the still's performance. Sea-water, urine or any other impure water can be poured into the hole for distillation. Take the greatest care that any such liquids have their own trough. Dig this trough into the side of the hole. It will prevent any impurities reaching and contaminating the collecting water or its container.

Production can also be increased if any fleshy plant material can be sliced or broken and used to line the hole. Daily output can be increased in this way to 2 litres – even in the desert.

Gradually the yield from any one hole will diminish. The still should then be re-sited. Choice of location depends on different factors.

If suitable vegetation (e.g. cacti), or impure water are available, the best location will be in the sunniest convenient spot. If you are using sea-water to prime your still, it will require re-location occasionally because of the salt accumulation in the hole. If the ground has to supply the water, site the still in the places you would choose to dig – low points, river beds, dried up water holes, etc.

Three final points remain:

1. A single still is unlikely to provide enough water to sustain one man indefinitely, though its yield will extend his survival time and increase his chances of rescue. Two stills, except in extreme conditions, could produce an adequate supply.

2. Although the still depends upon the sun's energy, this does not mean that the hours of darkness are unproductive. The plastic sheet cools more rapidly after sunset than the ground underneath. Evaporation and condensation continue, though at a reduced rate. Cloudy days affect the operation adversely.

3. Any clear plastic sheet will work to some extent, but most effective will be a sheet with the underside slightly roughened. It is commercially available in this form. Alternatively, scrubbing with scouring powder or careful application of fine emery cloth/sand paper will produce the minutely scratched surface required. The effect of this roughness is that the water droplets can cling to the under-surface more easily, and run down into the container before they become big enough to drop off on to the ground.

It may be necessary to use a piece of plastic, aluminium foil, etc. as your water container. If so, dig an additional hollow in the centre of the hole, shaping it to support the flexible material.

The survival still has one other advantage – it will act as a collector if rain should fall. In this connection, a survivor must prepare rain-traps in advance if conditions allow it, using any available or adaptable materials. Any material sheets or panels, large leaves, etc., should be positioned ready to divert rainfall into containers. A tree can be used as a collector if a cloth is tied around its trunk, with the knot at the lower side. Reinforce the loose ends with a small stick and set them to slope downwards and outwards. Rainwater running down the trunk will move into and along the cloth, dripping from the free ends into a container below.

The Vegetation Still

A plastic survival bag can be employed to erect a vegetation still. Cover a suitable green plant with a bag, the neck being tied around the plant base. Dig a small depression near the plant and press the plastic down into it. This will form a collecting point for the moisture transpired by the plant.

The Vegetation Still.

Plants as a Water Source

Some plants will yield water – or drinkable sap – and should be kept in mind in an emergency. Some examples are given here, but further detailed study of the plants common to the particular regions in which you have an interest would be well worthwhile. DO NOT drink milky or coloured plant juices. The only exceptions to this are:

1. Coconut milk.

2. The juice of the American barrel cactus.

Some trees – including alder, aspen, birch, maple and some cacti – have water which can be tapped by cutting a V in the bark. Insert a peg or nail, sloping out and down and catch the water that drips out.

Vines

It is always worth trying to get water from vines, as many will provide some drinkable supply. Cut the vine nearly through as high up as you can comfortably reach. Sever the vine close to the ground. Hold the cut end so that any water available will drip into your mouth or container. When the flow stops, repeat with another section of vine.

Palm Trees

The best known source of liquid from the palm tree is the coconut. Green nuts are the best choice. They hold more "milk" than the riper specimens, and are opened without difficulty using a knife. If no knife is available, the matted outer covering can be split if hit sharply against a sharp rock edge. The inner shell has to be broken carefully – to avoid loss of milk – by blows from rocks or heavy sticks.

A drinkable liquid is obtainable from the Coconut, Buri, Nipa and Sugar Palms. The first two require to be climbed for the flower stalks to be found. When the tips of the stalks are cut off and the stalks are bent down-wards, the sap will begin to flow.

Plants as Water Collectors or Holders

Some plants catch or hold water. Bamboo stems are an example. Try shaking old bamboo stems. If water is heard moving, pierce just above each joint in turn to release the water. Other trees which hold or will yield water include the Bromeliads of the pineapple family, found in tropical America; the Umbrella Tree of tropical Western Africa, and the Baobab Tree found in Africa and Northern Australia.

It is always worth while keeping a watch for old trees which may be holding water in trunk hollows or bough junctions. Many fleshy plants store water in their leaves or stems and are also worth investigation. Desert plants frequently have their roots running just below the surface

CUT TO RELEASE WATER

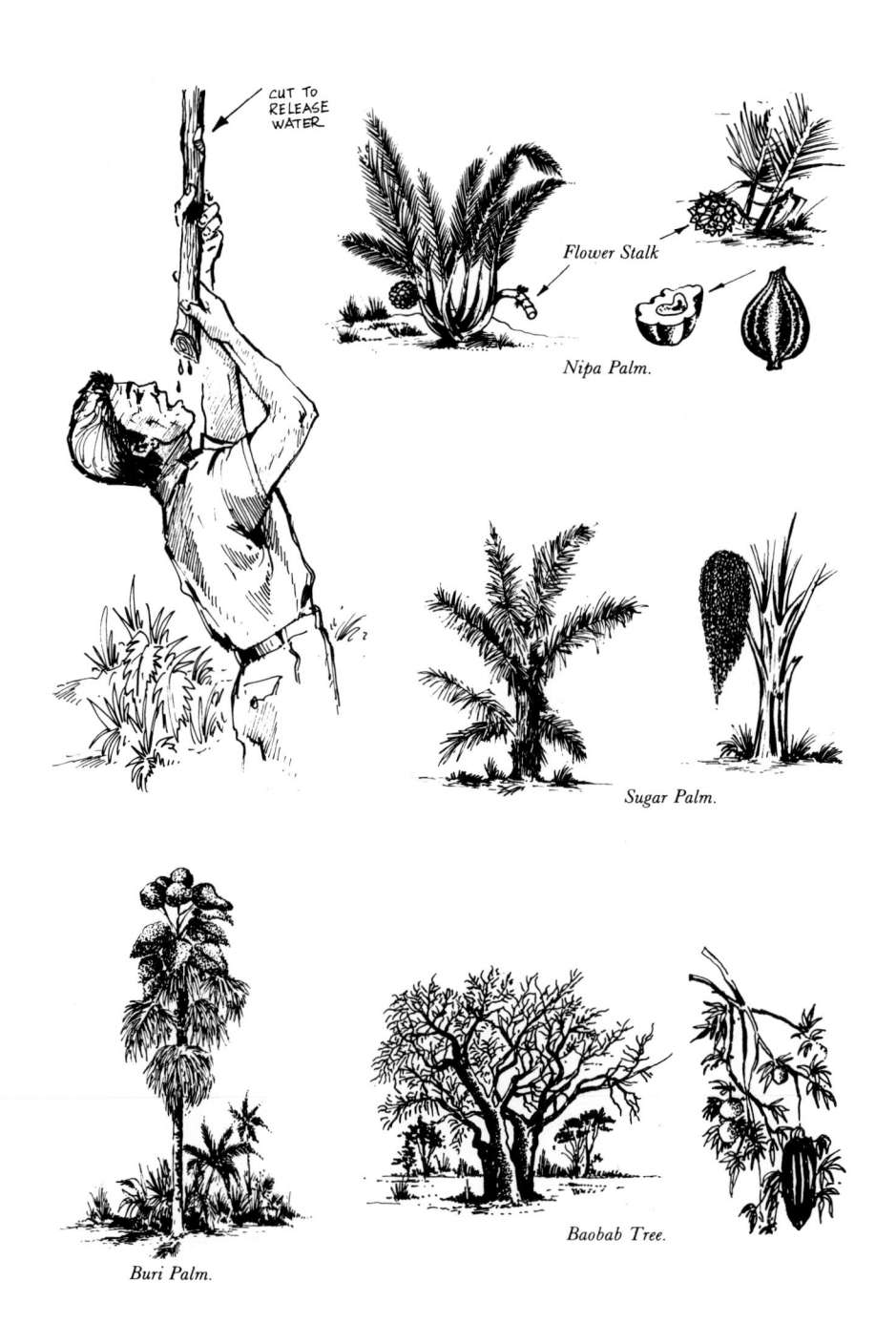

Flower Stalk

Nipa Palm.

Sugar Palm.

Buri Palm.

Baobab Tree.

– and some store water there. Dig them out of the ground, cut a metre or so length, strip the bark and try sucking for water.

Bromeliads.

At Sea

The first thing to remember if you are in a survival situation at sea is that **YOU MUST NOT DRINK SEA-WATER.** If you do, it will sharpen thirst instead of relieving it. The salt accumulating in the body will then lead to increased body-fluid loss and eventually to kidney failure.

Survival time with no water at all will vary according to conditions, but approximately four days will result in a deranged mind, with death following after seven to twelve days. It is all-important, therefore, to swing into your survival routine by doing everything to conserve existing body-fluids. Cover up and protect yourself from the sun and wind. Avoid unnecessary effort and keep calm. All these things will minimise sweating. In addition, wet your clothing occasionally to help with keeping cool.

If there is time before taking to the lifeboat or raft, drink as much as possible. Do not eat or drink during the first 24 hours. Eat later on only if you have sufficient water. There may be chemical or osmoration kits in the lifeboat or raft which will purify sea-water. If so, follow the instructions for use included. A Solar Still may be included. If so, put it into operation immediately. If not, consider your resources and the possibility of making your own.

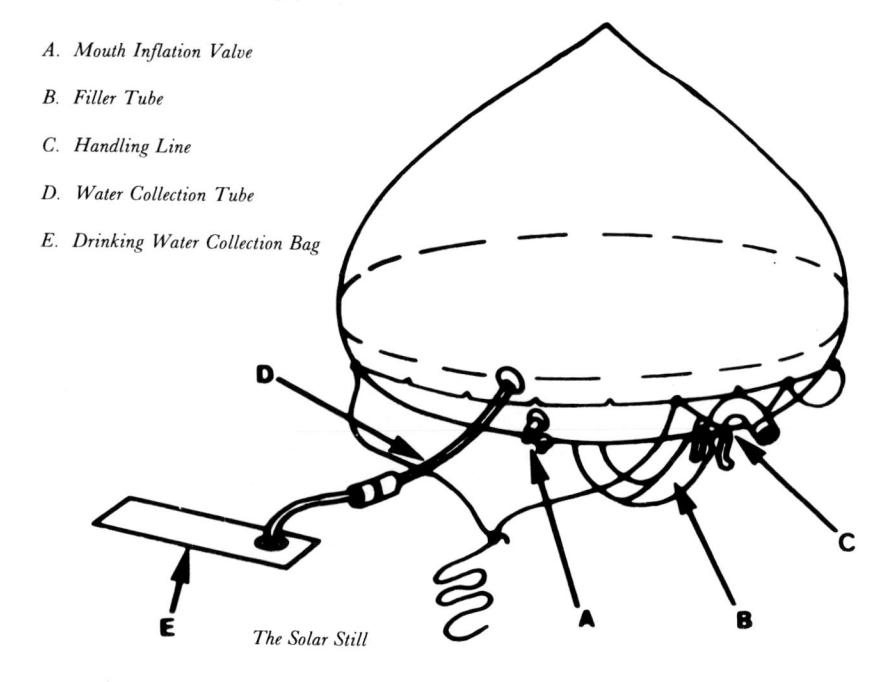

A. *Mouth Inflation Valve*

B. *Filler Tube*

C. *Handling Line*

D. *Water Collection Tube*

E. *Drinking Water Collection Bag*

The Solar Still

There are only four natural sources of drinkable water at sea.

1. **Rain Water**

As soon as any other priority actions have been taken – rescue, first aid, etc. – make your plans for rain water collection and storage. Include every item that can be pressed into service. Anything that will hold water should be checked for cleanliness and made ready for storage use. Anything that can be used to collect water should be prepared, and the method of collection decided. Any clean cloth can be used to mop up water so that it can be wrung into a container – or even sucked dry. Have a dry run of your collection set-up. It is imperative not to lose any water you could have collected. If all storage space is full, drink all you can, for your body is also a storage vessel.

If you have been at sea for any length of time, make sure that every part of your water collection and storage equipment is free as possible from contamination by salt behind by the evaporation of sea-water that

Water Collection and Storage.

may have splashed over it.

2. Ice

Sea-ice loses its salt after a year or so. It then takes on a blue tinge similar to glacial ice (e.g. icebergs). Both will provide drinkable water. Salt free sea ice usually has rounded corners – an aid to recognition.

3. Animal Body Fluids

All fish caught in the open sea have edible flesh, with the exception of jellyfish. The raw flesh is not salty and can provide both water and nourishment.

4. Sea-Water

As sea-water freezes it tends to concentrate much of its salt into that part which freezes last. Fill a container with sea-water and allow it to freeze. When the outside is frozen, there will be a salty slush in the centre. Dispose of this, and the ice left behind will have lowered salt content. It may be used to supplement the fresh water supply or will keep you alive if it is all you have.

Summary

Your chances of survival will be greatly increased if you understand fully the human body's need for water and the effects of an extended shortage in its daily requirement. This understanding will emphasise the importance of the survival techniques best able to make the most effective response to a shortage of water.

1. Conserve and protect your existing body fluids from the start and right through the situation.

2. Assess your supplies and initiate a planned and disciplined use of what you have.

3. Consider possible sources of water and make plans or take action to obtain it.

4. Check the purity of water from any source and take adequate measures to make supplies safe. Remember that, although thirst can kill quickly, contaminated water will bring about a slow death.

CHAPTER TEN

Location Signalling

In a survival situation one of the early decisions will be whether to remain in one place or to move towards help and safety. Whichever choice is made, communication and signalling to anyone who could help is important. But if you have elected to consolidate your position and await rescue, it becomes absolutely vital to use all possible methods to indicate where you are. Everything else done – building a shelter, making fire, obtaining water and food – while essential, are limited to being means of extending your survival time until rescuers arrive. Establishing communication or the display of successful signals, on the other hand, can attract your rescuers and bring the emergency to a safe end.

Recall some of the points considered during, "Situation Assessment and Planning."

1. Has an accurate plan of your movements been left with a responsible person? If you have remained on your intended route, it can be anticipated that the area will be searched. An immediate start must be made on location signals. If you have deviated from the plan, there are two options to consider.

(a) Is it possible to move far enough and fast enough to regain a position on your projected route? If this is practicable, your chances of being spotted will be greatly increased.

(b) It may be that such a move is not feasible, because someone in the group is unable to travel. In any case, survival and location probabilities might be assessed as higher by remaining with the vehicle, wreckage, etc. If this is so, consider the possibility of a return trip to the nearest convenient point on your planned route. The aim would be to leave a marker or signal to indicate the direction of your camp. A simple arrow would serve the purpose. (See International Ground to Air Signals listed below). If possible, leave a note giving your estimate of the distance involved. This would very greatly help the rescuers on the ground.

Location Signalling Equipment

1. If a radio distress beacon is included in the vehicle equipment it should be activated. Follow any instructions with care, and check its

operation with care. It should then be sited as high above ground or sea level as possible. It must be clear of obstacles. This is important because the radio signal generated will be on a frequency which operates on a line-of-sight basis. Anything in the way will prevent its signal being radiated in that direction.

Additionally – or alternatively – check your resources for the possibility of putting together even a crude radar reflector. Metal surfaces at right angles to each other – in three planes if possible – will produce good radar echoes.

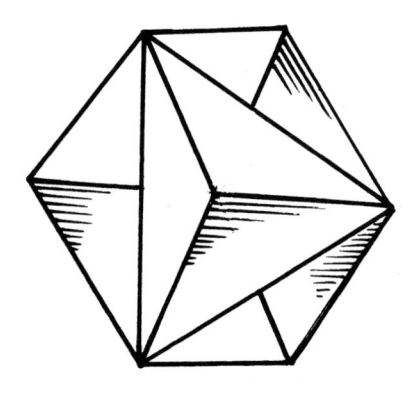

Radar Reflector

Wreckage panels, petrol cans cut open, etc., can provide usable raw material. The reflector should be sited as high as possible.

2. Any supply of flares, signal pistol, smoke canisters or distress lights must be inspected. Check first on their condition. Then make absolutely certain that the instructions on their operation are fully understood. Keep them safe, dry and ready for instant use. Do not use these signals unless you are sure there is a reasonable chance of their being seen, or you may not be able to seize a later and possibly better moment. But be equally sure that no worthwhile opportunity – and it may be fleeting – is missed because of unreadiness.

If you have any choice, a red flare signals distress, while a white flare acknowledges or warns. But any flare will achieve the main intention – which is to attract attention and show your rescuers where you are.

A torch can be a good means of signalling at night, or during dull weather if you have a target within sight or sound. Six flashes in one minute repeated after a further minute's interval signals distress. The acknowledgement to this signal is three flashes.

The Morse Code is given below:—

Letter	Character	Letter	Character	Letter	Character	Num'l.	Character
A	·—	J	·———	S	···	1	·————
B	—···	K	—·—	T	—	2	··———
C	—·—·	L	·—··	U	··—	3	···——
D	—··	M	——	V	···—	4	····—
E	·	N	—·	W	·——	5	·····
F	··—·	O	———	X	—··—	6	—····
G	——·	P	·——·	Y	—·——	7	——···
H	····	Q	——·—	Z	——··	8	———··
I	··	R	·—·			9	————·
						0	—————

A lantern is valuable both as a night light and as a location signal. Remember, however, that organised searches will normally operate during daylight hours only. Any ordinary traffic – by air or sea – may have been requested to keep a look-out in the area until you are found, so the sight or sound of any such traffic should stimulate some active response from you.

If you do not have a heliograph, any shiny reflective surface will provide a means of using sunlight for signalling. The only problem is the accurate aiming of the reflection at the target so that the flash is seen there. This can be overcome with practice. With the reflector in one hand, align the reflection on to the other palm at arm's length. Slowly move the extended arm to aim at the target, maintaining the reflection on the palm. When the target is seen between the fingers, the signal is directed correctly. Since this procedure takes a little time to operate even with practice, it may be worth giving serious consideration to the inclusion of a purpose-made heliograph in your survival kit. The need, with location signalling, can often be urgent, with only a momentary opportunity to grab the attention of possible rescuers.

It is also possible to sweep most of the horizon with accuracy using the signal from such a heliograph — especially if the sun is high. Since the mirror-flash can be seen many miles away, it is good practice to sweep the horizon at regular intervals even if no ship or plane is in sight.

Although visual signals are generally more effective, a whistle can be used to attract attention. At dusk, in fog, in an afforested area or in calm weather or sea, sounds can be heard over considerable distances. The distress signal is the same as that flashed with a torch — six blasts per minute with one minute intervals. Three blasts make the reply.

If you have no whistle, use your own natural whistle, or your voice by calling. Do not shout, as this will strain the voice. In still conditions, an improvised drum might be effective. A stout stick used to hit wreckage panels, empty fuel drums, trees, rocks, or another stick will produce a noise which will carry.

Most of the methods described so far might be classed as active, producing more or less temporary signals. There remain the signals

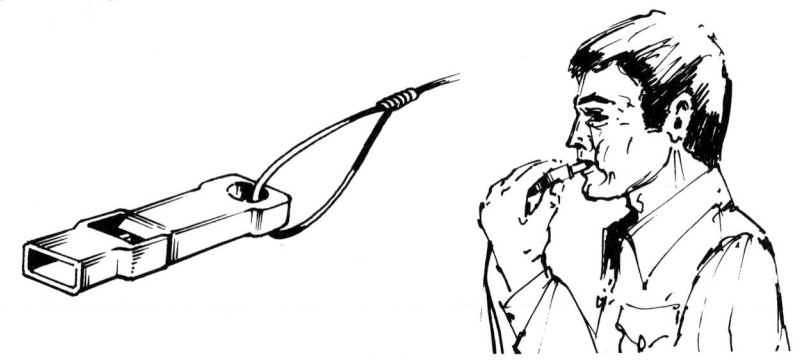

SIX BLASTS PER MINUTE
WITH ONE MINUTE INTERVALS
THREE BLASTS REPLY

you can produce which will give passive, but more permanent, indications of your locality. The key to effectiveness in such signals lies in creating contrast, and, where possible, movement.

Contrast is created by disrupting the normal pattern of the terrain. Do this by introducing regular shapes which do not naturally occur – circles, squares, letters or straight lines. A large circle, with minimum diameter of 3 metres can be made using stones, broken or trampled out in snow, but a trampled signal would be improved by the addition of some contrasting material – earth, campfire ashes – even marker dye if a dinghy is among the wreckage. On sand use rocks, sticks, cacti or seaweed. Choose the things which make the best contrast against the background surface. If you require specific help, form one or other of the signals given below:—

V	X	---->	Y	N
Require Assistance	Require Medical Assistance	Go/Going This Way	Yes	No

Another option is to spell out S O S. Make any Ground to Air signals as large as possible, and add extra shapes if space, time and energy permit.

Increased contrast is gained if you incorporate brightly coloured wreckage, clothing, blankets, etc., in your signals. Lay them out on the ground or hang them from trees. Anything shiny or brightly coloured which is moving will be even more eye-catching. A flag-pole will increase the distance over which signals can be seen from the ground.

If any possible rescuers are seen, or heard, use any available clothing or material as flags, and keep waving. If there is some suitable material that is not required for other uses during daylight hours, it is useful to have it ready, attached to the longest convenient pole you can easily handle, so that maximum signalling movement is available. Two men, holding a survival blanket, flag or other brightly coloured sheet, can, by keeping it taut, manipulate it to show flashes of light or colour. These will catch a searcher's eye more readily than the display of a passive sheet.

Besides these demonstrations of where you are, signal fires should always be kept in readiness. Details of Signal Fire preparation have been given in Chapter 7. If possible, prepare three fires set in a triangle with 30 metre sides. Keep them dry at all times. When the moment arrives to use them, remember that your need is to produce contrast. A clear day will call for white smoke, produced by green or damp vegetation added to the fire as soon as it is going well. Overcast conditions are best dealt with by producing black smoke – burn oil or rubber if you have it. If none is available then a bright fire is probably best. At night, too, large, bright flames give the clearest signal.

If your Situation Assessment led to the early decision to move towards help and safety, location signals are still very important, although there will probably not be as much time available for setting them up. Easily formed signals should be employed – letters or shapes tramped out in vegetation, snow or sand, or formed with stones, branches or other contrasting material. Lay out any coloured items not immediately required for use – securing them with stones to guard against loss. As always, keep any specific signalling equipment ready at hand. Never leave a camp or shelter site without a sign that you have been there. The direction-of-travel- arrow is probably the sign most helpful to searchers.

If travelling in the desert, location signals are doubly important. Since travel will generally only be possible at night, the location signals left at previous camps will be the searchers' main guide. In the same way, the need to seek shelter from the sun during the day will mean that all they are likely to find of your current location will be the signs you put out for them.

If you are at sea, in a dinghy or life-boat, many of the items mentioned above will probably be available – radio beacon, radar reflector, flares, whistles, lights and heliograph. Another possibility is a sea-water dye marker. The general approach to signalling will be the same. Set up the radio beacon and/or reflector as well as anything available as a signal flag. Make regular sweeps of the horizon with the heliograph whether or not any target is in sight. Save any consumable signalling devices until you are sure there is a good chance of their being seen or heard. If no signalling equipment is available when a possible rescuer is near, wave items of clothing or agitate the water as violently as possible with oars or paddles. If there are a group of survivors, watches should be organised. No watch should exceed two hours. The watch-keeper should be tied securely to the dinghy or life-boat.

Will Rogers is quoted as saying, "'You never have a second chance to make a good first impression''.

If you don't think about – and prepare – the best location signals possible, you may never have a second chance to make any impression at all.

Location signalling is important!

CHAPTER ELEVEN

WILD PLANTS AS FOOD

As soon as the more urgent aspects of your survival situation have been dealt with, it is time to assess, plan and act in relation to your food supplies. Food stocks may appear to be reasonable, the prospects of early rescue may seem good, but remember – the survivor is one who hopes for the best, but plans and prepares for the worst. Work on that basis. Within two days you should have:—

1. Taken stock of food and water supplies.

2. Divided your food stock into thirds. Make the best estimate possible of the time it will take your rescuers to arrive (or for you to walk to safety). Allocate two thirds for the first half of that time and one third for the remainder.

3. Begin, as soon as possible, to search for wild food to supplement your existing supplies.

There are some ways in which available food can be conserved, and used to the best advantage.

(a) Eat regularly. Aim for one good meal a day. Cook it if that is at all possible. This will make the food safer, more palatable and easier to digest. In addition, cooking can be a restful and relaxing activity.

(b) Do no unnecessary strenuous work – for this will require increased amounts of food and water.

(c) Remember that eating increases thirst. If the water supply is limited, the amount and type of food eaten must be strictly controlled. Eat less, and avoid all dry starchy food or salty meat. Go for foods high in carbo-hydrates. Wild plants can supply many of these.

There are two sources of food from the wild – plants and animals. Animals will usually supply richer food than plants, but it costs the survivor time, effort and energy to hunt or trap them. Food from plants, on the other hand, is usually available – except in extreme conditions or locations. Plant foods may not provide a fully balanced diet. They may be relatively low in food values. You may have to eat greater quantities than normal to meet your body's requirements. But they are sustaining – and they are widely available if you know where to look and what to look for.

Of course, obtaining food from wild plants is a survival technique to be learned and practised. Well under one half of all plants are edible – and most of them only in parts. The potato, for example, is a valuable food – but the plant itself is poisonous. Some plants are poisonous in their entirety. Eating wild plants carries its own inherent hazards. Knowledge and skill, therefore, are needed to take advantage of Nature's bounty. If you know what plants to look for in your location, you should normally be able to find enough food to keep yourself alive.

The sight of birds or other animals eating plants or berries does not guarantee that the plant concerned is either safe or suitable for human consumption. Rodents, for example, eat fungi which are poisonous to man, while many animals eat grass, which is totally indigestible to us. It is best to familiarise yourself with a number of plants which are easily recognisable and relatively abundant, and which can be eaten with confidence. To do this, studying this or any other book is not enough. Take the book into the field. Use every opportunity to find these plants in their natural habitat. Handle them. Taste them if they are edible raw (and are clean). Try cooking them if necessary. Only by personal, active study of the environment will you prepare yourself for finding food from plants if it is required of you in some other place at some other time.

Listed below are a selection of plants which are distributed over most Northern Temperate Regions. All have parts, at least, which can be eaten with confidence. Do not eat any plant unless it has been identified with certainty. If any doubt exists, follow the steps of the edibility test described later in the chapter.

Dandelion *(Taraxacum Officinale)*

Perennial, widespread throughout Northern Temperate Regions. Leaves shiny, bottle green, deepy toothed, 15cms, form rosette at plant base – inner leaves erect, outer leaves shorter, spreading. Flowers yellow, solitary on stems up to 30cms, March/August. Much milky sap. Young leaves may be eaten raw – their bitter taste alleviated if soaked for 2 hours in cold water. Developing shoots, before stems begins to grow, can be used like brussel sprouts. Older leaves, with tough centre vein removed, better boiled. Cleaned roots can be boiled like potatoes, having pleasant taste. Sun-dried roots, baked and crushed, provide coffee substitute. Valuable food source – leaves and roots available throughout year.

Great Plantain *(Plantago Major)*

Slightly hairy perennial widespread throughout Northern Temperate Regions. Large oval leaves forming loose basal rosette. Stem, 20-45cms, carries very small flowers in closely packed spike. Young leaves can be eaten raw: older leaves, with fibrous ribs removed, cooked as greens, though rather bitter. Best used as ingredients of stew.

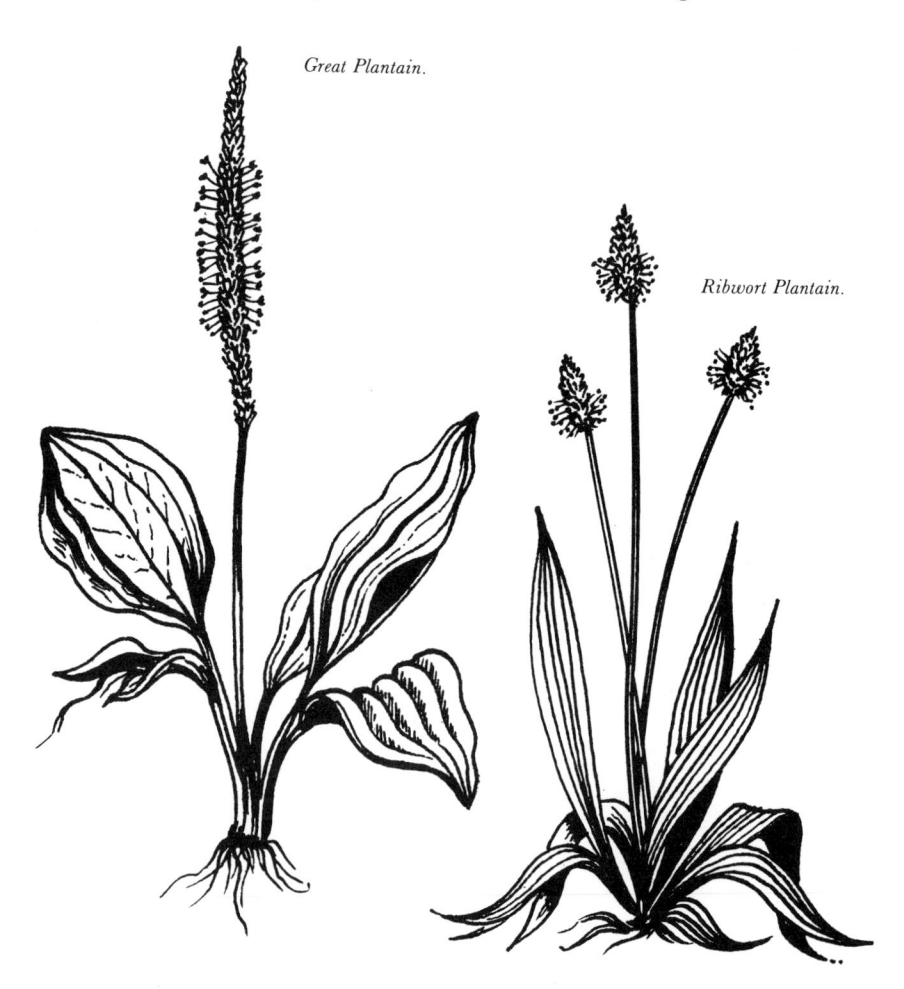

Great Plantain.

Ribwort Plantain.

Ribwort Plantain *(Plantago Lanceolata)*

Closely related to Great Plantain. Differs in having narrower pointed leaves, shorter flower spike (1-5cms) and deeply grooved stem. Distribution and edibility as for Great Plantain.

Bracken *(Pteridium Aquilinum)*

   Widely distributed throughout world. Perennial with large fronds 20-200cms (and can go up to 400cms), growing singly from base densely covered with short soft (felt like) rust brown hairs. Young fronds are coiled inwards, 3-pronged as they unfold. Older fronds clearly 3-pronged. Gather uncoiling young fronds, brush scales or fine hairs from stalks, wash, and boil until tender (approx 30 mins). The underground stems can be roasted and the inner portion eaten. AVOID the Male Fern which has single fronds, and is sometimes found in similar habitats.

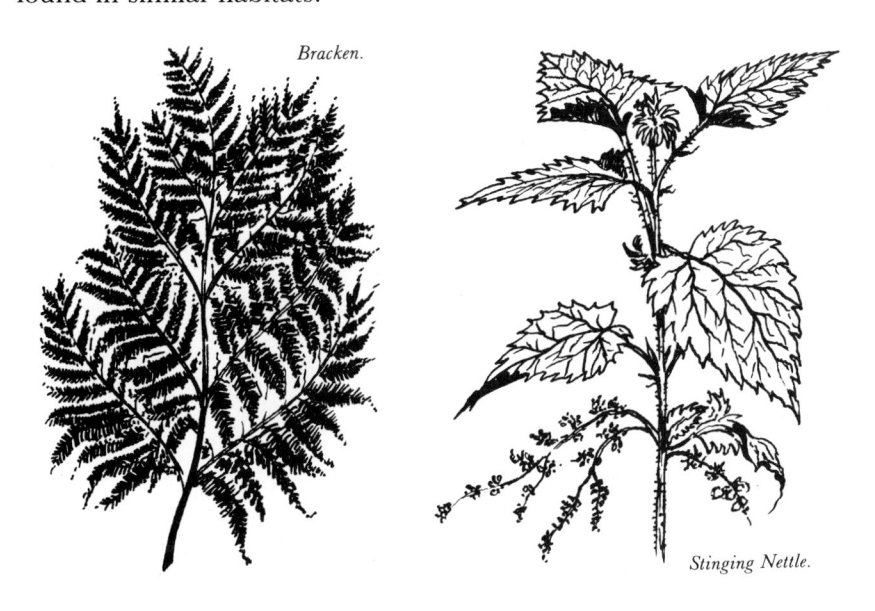

Bracken.

Stinging Nettle.

Stinging Nettle *(Urtica Diotica)*

   Perennial herb distributed throughout the temperate regions of the world. Stems grow up to 120cms, carrying heart-shaped leaves 3-8cm long, toothed and covered with fine hairs which produce "sting" when touched. Found in woods and forest and any sheltered grassy place, often in large colonies. Young shoots gathered in March/April, before flowering, can be eaten fresh, provided they are dipped in boiling water to remove formic acid from "stings". Very good source of Vitamin C. Other leaves should be chopped and boiled to remove acid, but for no longer than 6 minutes, to retain as much food value as possible. Can also be used as ingredient for stew. Leaves, when dried and rubbed, make very acceptable tea.

Water Cress *(Nasturtium Officinale)*

   Perennial occurring throughout Northern Temperate Regions, and flourishing in some Southern areas. Found commonly in running water (e.g. brooks). Flowers, May/October, 5mm diameter in small groups. Leaves, which remain green in Autumn, grow on stalks from angular hollow stems which are up to 65cms long. Up to 10 leaflets grow in pairs on stalk, with larger heart-shaped leaf at end. Leaves and stalks can be eaten raw. Take care to remove snails and insect leaves. Boil plant if any suspicion of water pollution.

Watercress.

Red Clover.

Clover, Red and White *(Trifolium Pratense* and *Trifolium Repens)*

   Similar perennials, widely distributed in North Temperate Regions, especially grassy places. Red clover slightly more erect than white, stems from 12-60cms. Trefoil leaves 1-5cms long. Flowers May/September. Young leaves can be eaten raw; all leaves can be cooked, or used in stews. The dried flowers make a fine tea.

Comfrey *(Symphytum Officinale)*

An erect hairy perennial herb, 25-120cms tall, found in damp localities and edges of woods and copses in all Temperate Regions. Leaves are rough, and shaped like spear-blades. The flowers May/June are funnel shaped, 2cms long, nodding, pale yellowish-white or purple. Young shoots can be eaten raw, or with young leaves cooked or added to stews.

Comfrey.

Sorrel.

Sorrel *(Rumex Acetosa)*

Perennial with smooth erect branching stems, 20-70cms. Flowers, red (May/July), grouped on stem branches. Leaves, 3-12cms, grow from base on long stalks. Occurs throughout Northern Temperate Regions in grassy areas, wood clearings. Young shoots and leaves, rich in vitamins, can be eaten raw; all leaves usable in soups. Consume plant in moderation.

Bramble, Blackberry *(Rubus Fruticosus))*

Perennial deciduous shrub, widely distributed throughout Northern Temperate Regions, in woodlands, hedges, heath and scrub. Easily identified by long stems, armed with thorns of various kinds, which wander and intertwine, often making large clumps. Flowers pink or white, June/August. Fruits first green, then red, finally shining black. Berries can be eaten raw, or collected and used for drinks and in salads. Leaves can be dried – but very slowly – and crushed, when they will make very good tea. They can also be used for tea if very fresh. **N.B.** Do NOT attempt to make use of wilted leaves from the blackberry, raspberry, peach or plum or cherry. All can be poisonous in this condition.

Bramble, Blackberry.

Dog Rose.

Dog Rose *(Rosa Canina)*

Deciduous shrub up to 4 metres tall, found throughout Northern Temperate Regions in woods, hedges, scrubland and rough hillsides. Stems erect or arching with stout curved thorns. Leaflets are toothed, oval, up to 4cms. Flowers June/July, 5 petalled, pink or white, 5cms dia. Rose hips are egg-shaped, 2cms long, smooth, shining and scarlet. Gather from August/December. Good source of Vitamin C. Hip must be cut open and seeds and fine hairs removed. Can then be eaten raw or cooked in pie or soup.

Daisy *(Bellis Perennis)*

Perennial herb widely distributed in grassy places. Leaves in basal rosette, paddle-shaped, 2-9cms long. Flowers white, 2cms diameter, solitary on erect stem 40-100cms tall. Young flower buds and young leaves can be eaten raw in salads or added to soups. Available all year round.

Daisy.

Cat's Tail.

Cat's Tail *(Typha Latifolia)*

Aquatic herb, found throughout the world, except in the extreme North and South. Occurs on banks of rivers, ponds and lakes. Erect round stems, 1-4 metres; leaves (up to 2 metres) erect, 2-6cms wide, sheathing at base. Flower in spike 15-30cms, very dark brown. Often dominant plant in slow-moving water. Young leaf shoots edible (boil 3-8 minutes). Yellow pollen can be used like flower. Rootstocks, rich in starch and sugar, edible boiled or raw. Remove outer covering, grate or chop inner white parts.

Goat's Beard *(Tragopogon Pratensis)*

    Annual to perennial herb, found in all but Northern extremities of Northern Temperate Regions. Stem 20-70cms tall, grows from half-sheathing base which itself tapers to long point and is clearly white-veined. Upper leaves clasp stem. Flowers June/July solitary, yellow, on long stalks thickened at top. Seed-head hairy (like "dandelion clock"). The stems with young buds can be treated like asparagus: young leaves, tips of shoots and dried tap root can be used as salad ingredients. The whole plant is usable when cooked in stew or soup.

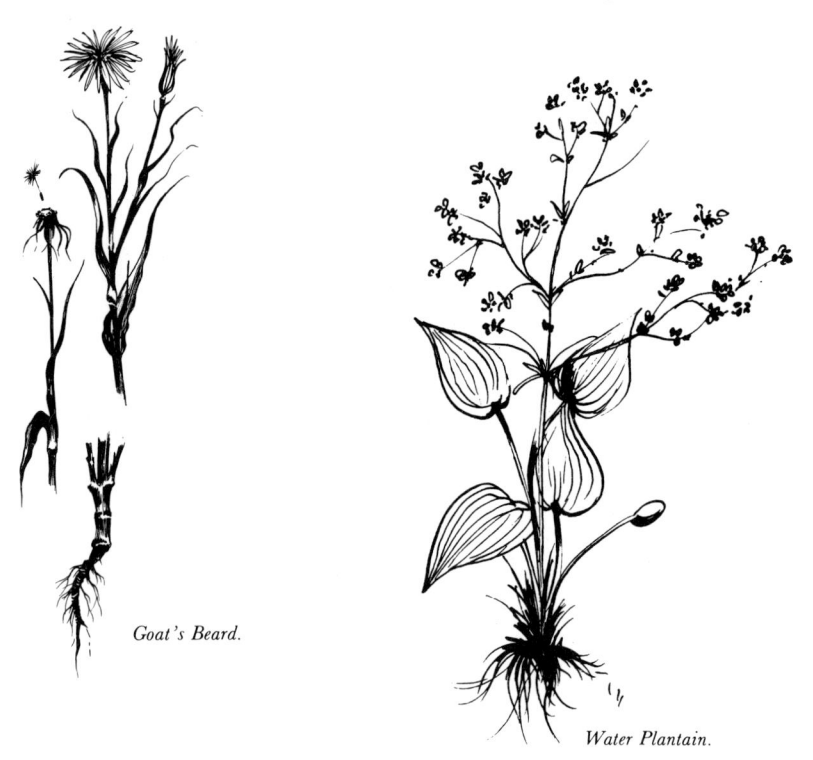

Goat's Beard.

Water Plantain.

Water Plantain *(Allisma Plantago Aquatica)*

    Erect aquatic or semi-aquatic perennial, up to 1 metre, occurring throughout Northern Temperate Regions. Leaves few, almost heart-shaped, 15-20cms, on long stalks. Flowers numerous, 1cm., white or pink. Flowerstems from 30-120cms forming loose pyramid. The thick rootstocks below ground lose their bitter taste when dried; are cooked like potatoes.

Hawthorn (May) *(Crataegus Monogyna)*

Deciduous shrub or tree up to 6 metres, thorny, much-branched. Occurs Northern Temperate Regions, in woods, hedges and scrub. Flowers April/May, white, small, bunched. Fruits July/October, red, 1cm diameter. Young shoots can be eaten raw, edible fruits fleshy, not bitter.

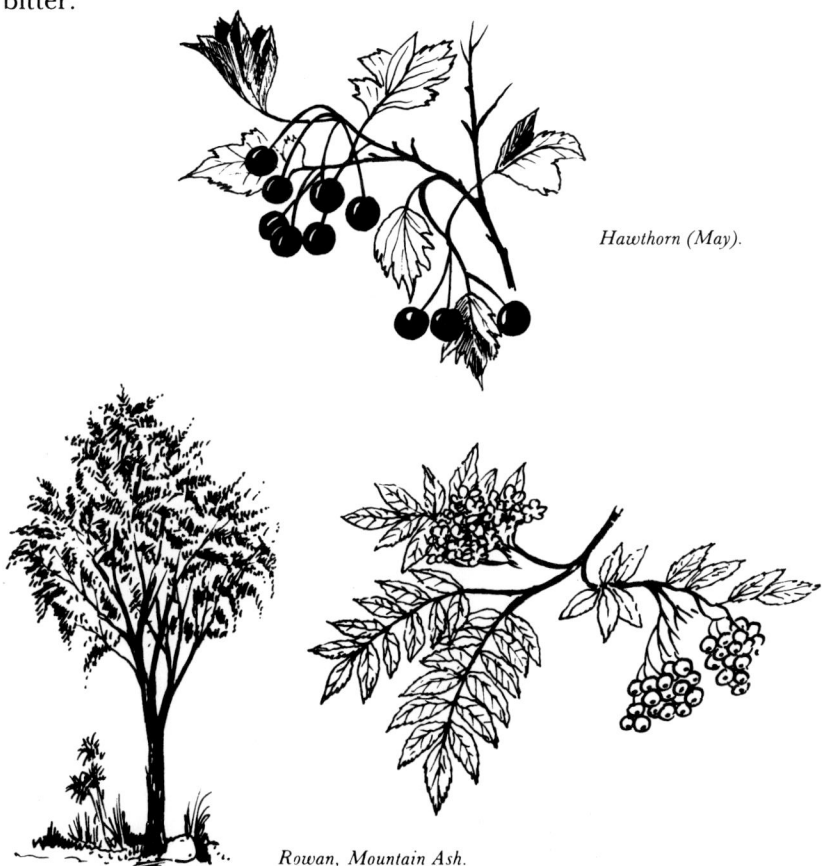

Hawthorn (May).

Rowan, Mountain Ash.

Rowan, Mountain Ash *(Sorbus Aucupaira)*

Deciduous slender tree up to 20 metres, distributed throughout Northern Temperate Regions, found in woods, mountains. Leaves up to 26cms long, made up of up to 9 pairs of leaflets, dark green. Flowers 1cm., white, in clusters, May/June. Fruits 1cm, red with yellow flesh, clustered. Fruit edible. Boil briefly, discard water to remove bitterness. Use in soups.

This list makes it possible to practice locating and identifying some edible plants. Use the varieties given here as a guide to discovering and testing others of the same species in the Temperate Regions. Other areas of the world are included in the Distribution Chart below, showing some common plants grouped according to their edible parts. A further note on each plant follows:—

	Tropics	North America	South America	Asia	Aust.	Africa	Desert	Temp. Regions
A. ROOTS and ROOTSTOCKS								
Bullrush		✔		S.E	✔	✔		✔
Ti Plant	✔			Tropical				
Flowering Rush				Temperate				Europe
Manioc	✔							
B. TUBERS								
Wild Potato		All — especially Tropics						
Soloman's Seal		✔		Northern				Europe
Water Chestnut	✔	✔		✔	✔			
Taro	✔							
C. SHOOTS and STEMS								
Mescal				✔		✔	✔	Europe
Wild Desert Gourd				SE India		Sahara Arabian		
Bamboo	✔							Warm
D. LEAVES and LEAFSTALKS								
Baobab						✔		
Spreading Wood Fern		Alaska		Siberia				
Wild Rhubarb				✔				SE Europe
Prickly Pear		✔	✔	✔		✔		Mediterranean

Distribution Table.

C. STEMS and SHOOTS

Mescal

Typically a desert plant, which grows, additionally, in moist tropical areas. Has clustered erect leaves, tough, thick and sharply pointed. Stalk rises, centrally, carrying yellow flowers in loose spike. Shoot is edible before the flowers are fully developed. Best roasted.

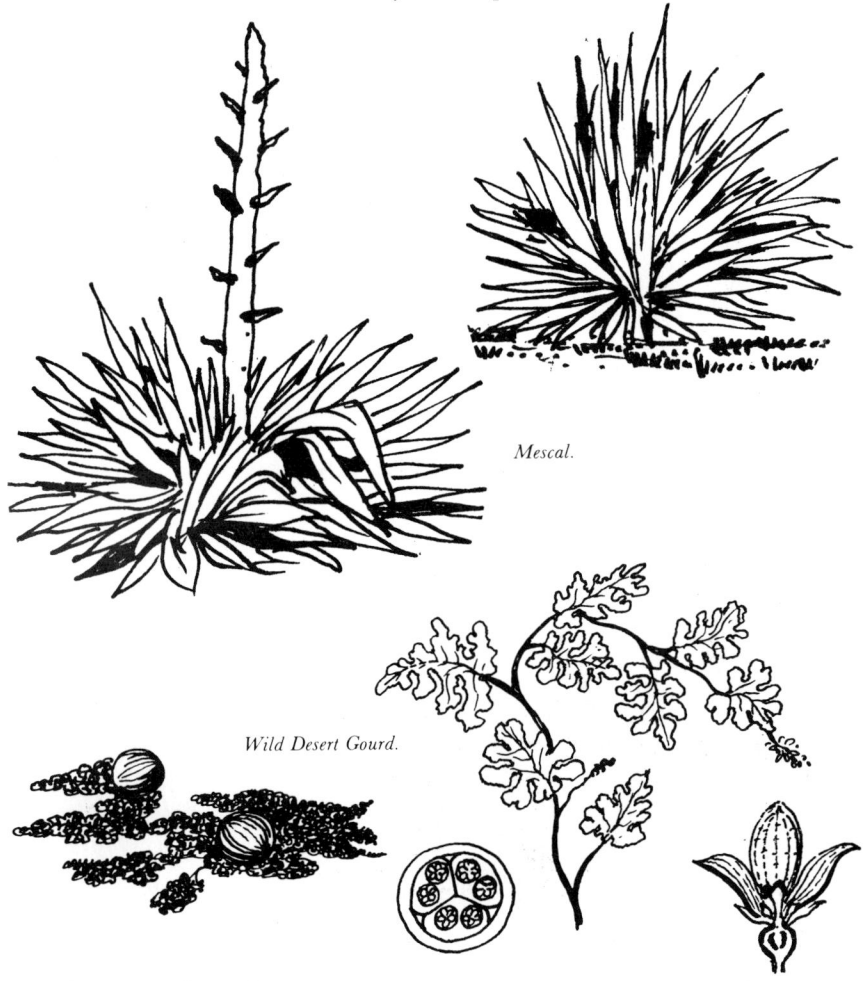

Mescal.

Wild Desert Gourd.

Wild Desert Gourd

Creeping plant up to 4 metres long. Produces edible flowers and orange-sized gourd, containing seeds edible if boiled or roasted. The stem shoots can be chewed to extract water.

Bamboo

Found in moist areas of forest and river and stream banks. Mature stems 5-25 metres, jointed. Young shoots edible. Boil with one or two changes of water to remove bitter taste. The seeds of the bamboo flower are edible if boiled like rice.

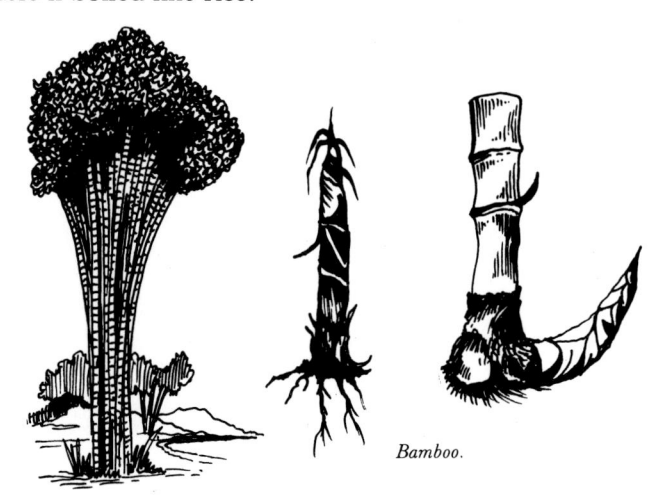

Bamboo.

D. LEAVES and LEAFSTALKS

Baobab Tree

Baobab Tree.

Found in open tropical bush. Massive girth compared with normal height identifies (i.e. trunk diameter equals half height). Leaves edible in soups. May also provide water (See Chap.9). Fruit, which follow large white flowers, also edible.

Spreading Wood Fern

Abundant in indicated regions and found in woodland and mountains. Rootstocks, below ground, carry old leafstalks resembling fingers. When roasted, and with shiny brown covering removed, the inner parts are edible. The young coiled fronds are also edible when cooked.

Spreading Wood Fern.

Wild Rhubarb.

Wild Rhubarb

Found on mountain slopes in open aspects on edges of woods and stream banks. Long stout stalks have large leaves growing from bases. The stem is edible after boiling to alleviate its strong, bitter taste.

Prickly Pear

Occurs in many desert areas. The plant has a thick stem (2-3cms) which holds water. Carried on the stem are clusters of pads covered with sharp prickles. Yellow or red flowers grow at the top of the upper pads, producing egg-shaped fruit, up to 10cms long. These are edible if opened and the outer layer removed, when the pulp and seeds inside can be eaten. The inner portions of the pads can also be eaten either raw or boiled, and are best cut into strips for cooking. This plant does not produce any milky juice – AVOID any similar plant that does.

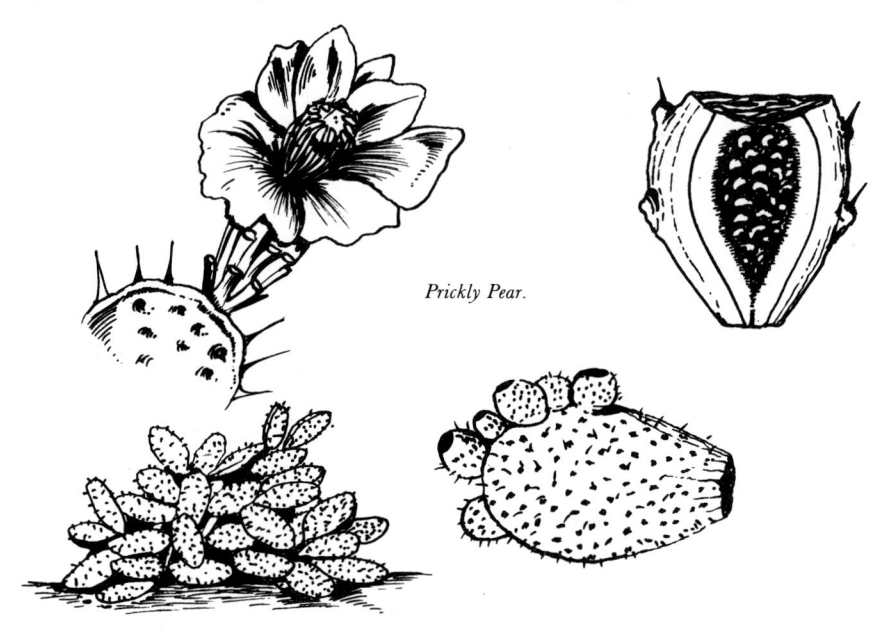

Prickly Pear.

Using this guide as your starting point, read further about these and other plants which are to be found in any area through which you may travel. Seize any opportunity to acquire first-hand information on this topic. Do this BEFORE beginning any activity which could lead to any emergency situation. When practising the technique of using wild plants as food, remember always that there are many plants which are poisonous or harmful, or which have unpalatable or unpleasant structures. Your first safeguard against the dangers presented by these plants is –

EAT ONLY PLANTS THAT YOU HAVE IDENTIFIED WITH COMPLETE CERTAINTY – and make sure that no other species is mixed in with it.

If you are not certain of a plant's identity, or need to find if any particular plant is edible, follow these steps through the Edibility Test.

1. Never collect plants from polluted waters or areas. Always clean them thoroughly before attempting to eat or cook, and remove damaged or inferior parts.

2. Do not assume that every part of a plant is edible because you have found that any one part is.

3. Do not waste time in testing any plant unless it is abundant. It is a waste of time and effort to test any plant if it is not easily and plentifully obtainable.

4. Test for the presence in the plant of any contact poison. Crush the leaf and rub some sap on to the skin of the inner wrist. Wait for 15 minutes. If no itching, blistering or burning occurs go on to step 5.

5. Hold a small portion in the mouth for 5 minutes. If no unpleasant reactions occur, chew the plant, again looking for unpleasant signs (extreme bitterness, burning or soapy taste). If none, swallow the juice, but spit out the pulp. Allow another 8 hours.

6. If no ill effects develop, (sickness, dizziness, sleepiness, stomach aches or cramps), eat a slightly larger amount – a teaspoonful, for example – and watch for similar effects for a further 8 hours.

7. If no negative effects are revealed, eat about a handful of the plant. A final 24 hours without trouble indicates that the plant is safe and can be eaten in larger quantities.

8. Eat only healthy plants, avoiding all with rotting parts, mould, diseases or insect infestation.

9. Avoid any plants with milky sap, (except Dandelion, Goat's Beard and Coconut), or a bitter or burning taste or having caustic sap. Always boil leaves which have prickly hairs (e.g. Stinging Nettle).

10. Test only one plant at a time, on one person at a time, so that the cause of any ill effects can be pin-pointed.

11. Even palatable wild plants may prove detrimental to health if eaten in large quantities or over a long period. Wherever possible, make a salad or vegetable stew, combining leaves, berries, nuts, inner bark and rootstocks. You will achieve a more balanced diet, as well as a tastier meal. This is one occasion when variety really is the spice of life!

12. This test does NOT apply to fungi – see below.

The Edibility Test may seem to be time-consuming and over-cautious, but one of the basic strands of any Survival Technique is to choose the safest option. Consider the alternatives to the careful testing of unknown plants. They range from mild inconvenience, through temporary disablement to fatal poisoning. Start testing available plants before food stocks are exhausted. Even better, practise edibility testing as a survival technique as part of your general preparation for outdoor activities.

TREES

Trees can provide food in two other ways – from their nut-crops and their bark. There are certain exceptions. The survivor should remember that a number of trees produce substances harmful or poisonous to man. Some of the more common are listed below. It would be dangerous to eat any part of any of them.

1. Black Locust   2. Buckeye   3. California Bay
4. Cedar   5. Hickory   6. Horse Chestnut
                  7. Moosewood   8. Yew

There are other less common varieties which should be avoided. Take any opportunity to read further about the trees to be found in any area of interest to you.

However, the inner bark of many trees – the thin, white layer next to the wood – is both edible and nutritious. Its food value is particularly high in early Spring, when the sap is rising.

To obtain it, cut or scrape away the outer bark, and peel the inner bark from the trunk. Alternatively, take it from any large exposed roots, where it is often even thicker and has more flavour. Avoid the outer bark, since it contains large quantities of tannin.

The inner bark may be eaten raw, but lengthy boiling – which will produce a jelly-like mass – makes it more digestible. Long roasting will also aid digestion. Alternatively, it can be dried and ground into flour.

A selection of the best trees to use as sources of this food include:—

1. Alder
2. Aspen
3. Basswood
4. Birch (esp. Black Birch)
5. Hemlock (American Larch)
6. Maple
7. Pine (Rich in Vitamin C)
8. Poplar
9. Willow
10. Slippery Elm (Best source)
11. Spruce
12. Tamarack (American or Black Larch)

All these species, with the exception of the Spruce and the Tamarack, have edible buds and young shoots. They can be eaten raw or cooked.

Trees also produce nuts, which are among the most valuable of all plant foods, providing fats, vitamins and protein. Plants producing edible nuts occur in all continents and every type of climate except the Polar Regions. Nuts found in the Tropics include coconuts, brazil nuts (or shoenuts), and cashews. Temperate Regions produce hazelnuts, beechnuts, sweet chestnuts, walnuts, acorns, almonds and pine nuts among others. Wild pistachio nuts grow in some desert and semi-desert areas in parts of East Asia.

Most of these nuts may be eaten raw, or chopped or ground for addition to soups. Some nuts – acorns for example – are bitter. Their taste can be improved if they are boiled for two hours and then soaked for 3 or 4 days in cold water. They can be ground into paste, which can either be dried to make flour, or used, with water, as the basis of stew or soup, or on its own as a gruel.

Nuts are excellent food. If they are available, gather and store as large a quantity as you can. If they are shelled, they provide a rich and easily-portable food store. They see squirrels through the Winter – and they can keep you going, too.

SEEDS

Many plants produce edible seeds. All grass seeds are edible, – and some, including the cereals, are rich in plant protein. (N.B. Do not use any grain heads carrying black spurs instead of ordinary seeds.) Healthy seeds can be ground, mixed with water, and cooked as porridge, or parched ready for consumption or storage. The Bamboo, with its flowers producing edible seeds, has already been mentioned.

Rice is another edible seed producer. Found in wet places in both tropical and warm temperate regions, it usually appears as a cultivated crop. Wild rice does occur in Africa and Asia, as well as suitable areas of the United States, growing 1 metre tall, with long, sheathing leaves up to 5cms wide. The seed-head is made up of hairy light-brown husks. The seeds can be roasted and ground into flour. This makes a very valuable portable food-store, and can be baked into cakes. The seeds can also be boiled.

FRUITS

Edible fruits should not be overlooked as a food source since, during their seasons, they can be plentiful. Do not be tempted to over-eat if a good supply is found. Like most wild plant foods, they will make you sick if too many are eaten at one time. Take the opportunity to collect and dry as many as possible against future needs. They are produced in all but the most extreme of the climatic zones.

Bilberries, (Whortleberries, Blueberries).

As far North as the Tundra, (Asian, American and European), Bilberries (whortleberries or blueberries) are to be found. In slightly milder conditions they grow with heather. Further North, or higher on mountain sides, they replace it completely, usually growing only 15-45cms high. Further South they may grow to 2 metres. The berries are dark blue or black.

Another inhabitant of these regions is the Cloudberry. It grows to 10-20cms, has simple leaves and carries an orange-red fruit at the plant top. It can occur in large colonies. The Cranberry and the Cowberry, (both with red berries), can be found in similar areas, but are less abundant. Their fruit is rather acid.

Cloudberry.

In the warmer areas of the Temperate Regions Mulberries occur, dense shrubs or trees up to 15 metres, with stout branches and dark brown scaly bark. The fruit, up to 4cms long, is blackberry-like but dark purple in colour.

Mulberries.

The Crabapple is also common, in these regions, and found in woods, exposed heaths, field and hedges. The fruit can be sliced and dried as part of the food store.

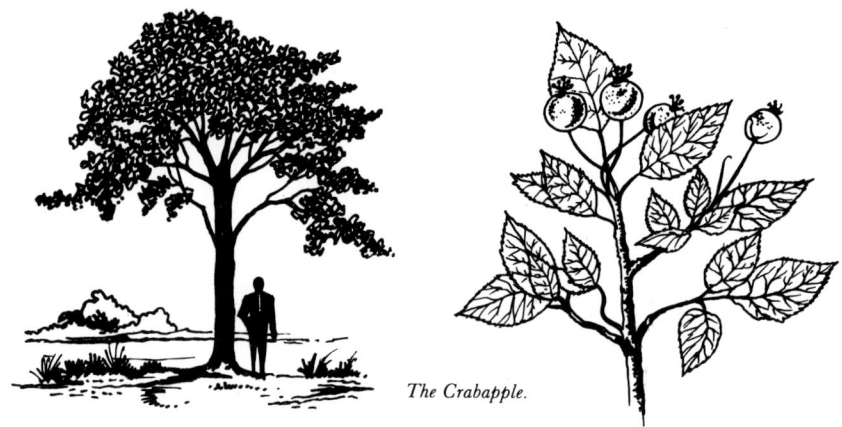

The Crabapple.

Wild grape-vine grows in warm temperate and sub-tropical areas, and is widespread. Its fruit is rich in sugars. A relation of the mulberry – the wild fig – is found in the tropics and the sub-tropics. The fruit of its many varieties grow directly out of the branch-wood. Figs which are edible will be soft, and coloured black, green or red. Another mulberry relative is the Breadfruit – a common tree in the tropics. Up to 13 metres tall, it has tough smooth leaves 30-90cms long. The fruit can be eaten raw or cooked in the embers of the fire.

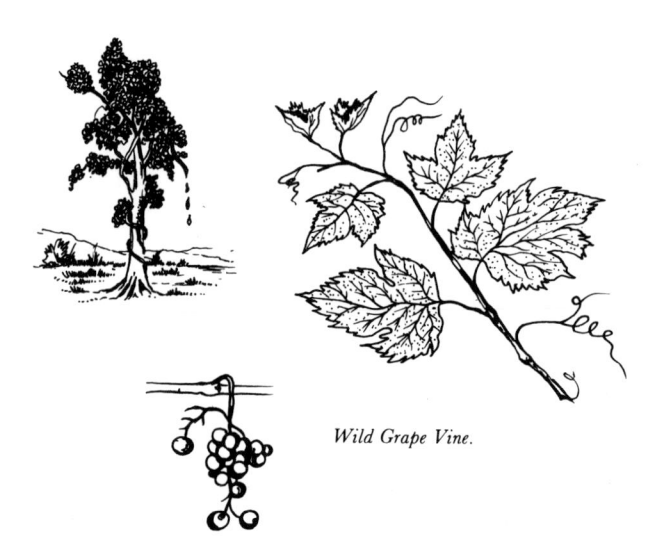

Wild Grape Vine.

SEAWEEDS

Any survivor on a sea shore is almost certainly within reach of a wild plant food source – seaweeds. They are to be found between the high and low tide lines. The most plentiful growth available occurs in shallow water just below the low tide line. This is because seaweeds grow by absorbing their nutrients directly through their fronds from sea water. Their growth depends on the amount of time they are submerged. They have no roots – merely a holdfast by which they are anchored to their chosen bases. The species are not described in the order in which they might be found searching from the high tide line downwards into the shallows beyond the low tide line.

When gathering seaweed to eat, look for fresh plants – either still attached to rocks, etc., or freely floating in the water. Many seaweeds spoil quickly if left exposed to the air. Always wash the crop in clean water, with as many changes as necessary to remove any sand or minute crustaceans from the plants. Species which provide good food include green, brown and red varieties, and all are good sources of Vitamin C and iodine. Seaweed dries best when hung in a dry, well-ventilated area for 2 or 3 days.

1. Enteromorpha Intestinalis

No common English name, but second half of Latin name helps to identify. Plant is green, tubular, 1-3cms diameter, and constricted at intervals to resemble an intestine. From 5-60cms long. Grouped on rocks or in rock-pools near upper tide line. Widely distributed. Eat raw, or dry and use in soups.

2. **Bladder Wrack** *(Fucus Vesiculosus)*

Found on North Temperate coasts which are rocky or stony. Occupies distinct zone at mid-tide level. Olive-brown to dark greenish-yellow, thick, leathery, 15-90cms long. Stalks have distinct midrib, fronds carry paired air bladders. Fresh or dried fronds can be used, boiled in soups or stews.

Bladder Wrack.

Sea Lettuce.

3. **Sea Lettuce** *(Ulva Lactuta)*

Found in Atlantic and Pacific Oceans. Lettuce-like appearance, light to dark green. Habitat rocks and pools, usually between tide-lines. Can be eaten raw, or used as a vegetable.

4. Dulse *(Rhodomenia Palmata)*

Occurs all around Atlantic, on Pacific coasts of America and Australia, as well as Mediterranean. Dark-red or red-brown plant with single deeply-divided frond 8-40cms long, no stem. Found on rocks and stones – sometimes attached to larger seaweeds; middle and lower shores and in shallow water. Easily digestible, best eaten raw, or can be added to stews or used as vegetable. If thoroughly rinsed in sea-water it can be dried for storage. Collect plenty, as it shrinks considerably when drying. Dried dulse can be fried or boiled.

Dulse.

Laver.

5. Laver *(Porphyra Umbilicus)*

Common to Atlantic, Pacific and Mediterranean, Laver grows on rocks and large stones between middle and low tide zones, as well as on sand covered rock surfaces. Thin, leaflike, folded appearance, red, purple and brown. Can be eaten raw, boiled long and gently and/or fried.

6. Irish Moss, Carragheen *(Chondrus Crispus)*

Found on temperate coasts on both sides of Atlantic, on rocks on lower shore and in shallow water below tide line. Red-purple to purple-brown (may be green in bright light). Tough, leathery, many branched, 3-16cms long. Boil before eating, or stew with fish, meat or other vegetables.

Irish Moss, Carragheen.

Dabberlocks.

7. Dabberlocks *(Alaria Esculenta)*

Found in the North Atlantic, this olive-green to dark-brown plant grows on the lowest shore and in shallow water. A short stem secures a long, blade-shaped frond, with a flattened midrib, 10-90cms long, 5-15cms wide. Stem carries finger-like spore producers. The midrib and the stem can be eaten raw or in soups. Frond, with midrib removed, should be soaked in fresh water for 24 hours, then boiled.

8. Oarweed *(Laminaria Digitata)*

Temperate Atlantic and Baltic coasts, low tide line to water 4-5 metres deep. Often in large colonies, this plant is olive to dark brown, 1-25 metres long, with frond divided into leathery strap-like strips, and set on stalk 10-50cms long. Grows on rocks and stones. Can be used in soups after preliminary boiling.

Oarweed.

Sugar Kelp.

9. Sugar Kelp *(Laminaria Saccharina)*

Occurs Atlantic and Pacific Oceans below tide line on rocks and stones. Shaped like crinkled sword-blade up to 3 metres long. Frond is chestnut to olive brown, on stem up to 40cms. Smaller plants best for eating; young stems can be eaten raw, whole plant edible if boiled

The two plants which follow are not seaweeds, but they are of interest to the survivor. They grow near the sea shore in Temperate Regions, at least. Both are edible.

Sea Kale *(Crambe Maritima)*

On North Temperate coasts, found on cliffs, rocks, shingle and dunes. Perennial, up to 60cms. Lower leaves up to 25cms, upper leaves small. Both blue-green, smooth, with wavy margins. Small white clustered flowers, February/May. Shoots and young leaves edible if immersed briefly in boiling water, then chopped and boiled in changed water for 20 minutes.

Sea Kale.

Sea Arrow Grass.

Sea Arrow Grass *(Triglochin Maritima)*

Found near North Temperate coasts, salt marshes and grassy areas near shore. Narrow erect leaves grow from base, 5-30cms. Small green flowers in loose spike on stem, 15-45cms. tall. Can be eaten raw, but best added to soups or boiled as vegetable.

FUNGI

Opinion about the use of fungi as a survival food source is divided. On the one hand it can be said that many fungi provide food high in nutritional value, that only 2 to 3% of all species are poisonous, and that fungi often occur in places where other edible plant foods are scarce.

On the other hand, the problems of including fungi in the survival diet arise from these facts:—

(i) Of the small percentage of poisonous species, some are deadly if even a small portion is eaten.

(ii) Any symptoms of poisoning may not occur until 10-40 hours after eating, by which time only hospitalisation offers any hope of recovery, should the poison be deadly. Even a relatively mild attack can lead to serious repercussions in a survival situation.

(iii) This delay in the appearance of symptoms, combined with the extreme virulence of some species, means that there is NO Edibility Test suitable for use with fungi.

(iv) Individuals react differently, even to non-poisonous species. One survivor eating a specimen with impunity does NOT ensure that others can rely on the same successful result.

The only way to make use of fungi with safety is to learn to recognise a few species so that they can be identified beyond doubt. The only way to identify any fungus is by visual examination and comparison with examples illustrated and described in a good guide. Even then, some authorities advise that beginners in the study should have their initial identifications confirmed by another person with experience of edible fungi. This is good advice, for reference books themselves disagree, from time to time, as to whether a specimen is edible or poisonous.

Sticking to the survivor's routine of assessing the situation and deciding upon the safety option, the rational choice, as far as fungi are concerned, is to avoid them all unless:—

(i) You, or someone in the group, has sufficient knowledge and first-hand experience to be able to select edible varieties with certainty;

    or

(ii) There is NO other food source available.

To help in achieving (i), above, the following list contains some of the species known to be edible, reasonably common, and widespread. To make use of any of them, study their characteristics with care, and take every opportunity to identify them positively in the field – with experienced help. Unless you are able to do this, fungi are best left alone.

Agaricus (Psalliota) arvensis	Horse Mushroom
Agaricus (Psalliota) campestris	Field Mushroom
Boletus badius	Cep
Boletus edulis	
Boletus testaceao-scabrum	Sponge Cap
(Leccinium versipelle)	
Camarophyllus pratensis	Buff Meadow Cup
Craterellus cornucopioides	Horn of Plenty
Cantharellus cibarius	Chantarelle
Fistulina hepatica	Beef Steak Fungus
Macro-lepiota procera	Parasol Mushroom
Macro-lepiota rhacodes	Shaggy Parasol
Lycoperdon perlatum	Common Puff Ball
Lycoperdon (Calvatia) gigantea	Giant Puff Ball
Morchella esculenta	Common Morel
Pleurotus ostreatus	Oyster Fungus
Lepiota personata	Common Blewit

To assist in meeting the situation in (ii) above, these guidelines are suggested:—

(i) Do not collect old fungi, or any which are insect infested or partly eaten by insects or maggots.

(ii) Avoid very young specimens, especially if still in "button" stage. This is because many of the identifying characteristics do not develop until the fungus is approaching maturity.

(iii) Boil any fungus before eating, and discard the water. There are some species whose poison is destroyed by boiling. NOTE. There are others (e.g. the Amanitas) which remain poisonous AFTER boiling.

(iv) Always examine any fungi for the presence of a cup or volva at the stem-base BEFORE picking the specimen. There is a considerable risk that the volva could be destroyed, damaged or left in the ground when fungi are picked.

(v) Ignore or discard ANY fungus having a cup or volva at its base. Do the same if there is a ring of scales on the base of the stem, or if the top surface of the cap is speckled with small white patches or fragments.

(vi) Avoid any specimens which are red on the underside of the cap, or are producing reddish spores.

(vii) Eat no fungus with white gills, nor any gilled mushroom with milky juice.

(viii) Reject any other "method" of determining whether fungi are edible or poisonous. FULL RECOGNITION is the ONLY safe way.

The majority of cases of fungus poisoning have been caused by eating species of the Amanita family, many of which are deadly – even in small quantities. They include Death Cap, Fly Agaric, Destroying Angel and Panther Cap.

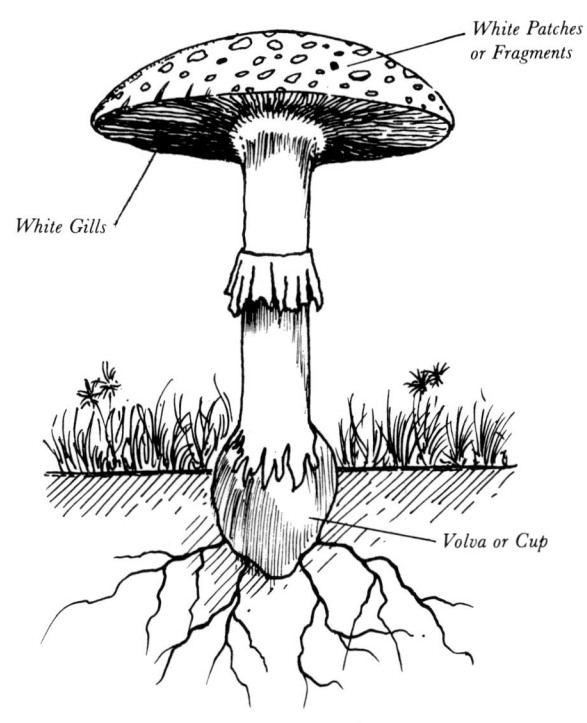

Amanita Characteristics.

The illustrations above show some of the common features of this family, and any mushroom showing ANY of these should be discarded. Look particularly for a cup or volva, white gills, or fragments of the cap. Their typical smell is like potato or radish. They grow singly in woods on the ground, and never in fields or other open grassy spaces. Study this family, using a good guide – together with any of the edible varieties you may wish to identify.

SUMMARY

The Survival Routine regarding food from wild plants follows this pattern:
>Take stock of all food in hand.
>Allocate and plan its use.
>Conserve it as far as possible.
>Aim for one cooked meal each day.
>Begin, immediately, to search for wild plant foods.

It will be possible, of course, to combine this search with your efforts to track, hunt or trap animals for food, (See Chapter 12).

Learn, remember and PRACTISE the Edibility Test. Do not forget the special considerations regarding fungi. Your best safeguards, when using wild plants as a food source, will always be IDENTIFY or TEST – with only the FIRST of these applying to fungi. When you have located palatable species, eat any particular one in moderation. The aim should always be variety.

Remember that this chapter is only intended as a starting point. Further detailed study of reference books is necessary – and practical field research essential – if you intend to develop a serious, useful technique in this aspect of survival. Properly practised, this technique can, and will, save your life. There are very few areas of the world where wild plant food cannot be found, if the survivor searches with diligence and knowledge.

Finally, the occasional plant offers more than food alone. The Houseleek occurs throughout the North Temperate Regions and its shoots and young leaves can be eaten raw. But its Latin name – Sempervivum Tectorum – sums up the survivor's creed. Loosely translated it means:

>"Always Live, Sheltered."

And its old English name offers even more:—
>"Welcome Home Husband, However
>   Drunk You May Be"!

Use wild plants to help you to be there for the greeting.

The Houseleek.

CHAPTER TWELVE

ANIMAL FOOD

Hunting, Traps and Snares

Your Survival Routine should, by now, have covered the following decisions or actions:—

a. First Aid or treatment to any injured or sick survivor.
b. Proper use of all available clothing.
c. Collection of all water and food stocks and their allocation for future use.
d. Identification of all survival equipment, together with any other useful items.
e. Whether to move out or to make camp where you are.
f. Finding or building shelter.
g. Getting a fire going.
h. Location of water supplies.
i. Setting up location signals and preparation of signal fires.
j. Surveying your immediate locality to determine its nature and potential for survival and/or travel.
k. Investigating – and probably collecting – some local edible plants.

Now is probably the time to consider animal food sources, which will provide a wider, more varied diet for your longer-term needs. Even if the food in stock seems plentiful, it is vital to begin living with the land as soon as possible. Non-perishable food stocks should be kept for use in any secondary emergency – e.g. foul weather preventing any collection of food from the wild. In any event, it is far more rational for the survivor to establish his wild food sources while he is still well fed and efficient.

The sources of wild animal food include mammals, birds, reptiles, fish, crustaceans and insects. Any of these can provide food which, pound for pound, has much higher food-value than most material derived from plants. They do not provide it willingly, however, and have to be hunted, trapped or caught – and to do any of these, information and technique are required. It is also vital to employ methods which are "cost effective".

This means that the amount of time and energy put into hunting, trapping, snaring or catching any animal must be weighed against the value of the food it supplies. There is little profit in even a successful hunt if the hunting takes more out of you than the resulting food puts back.

Hunting

Without a firearm, the odds are against your success as a hunter – unless you are one of the comparatively few people who possess the skills needed to get near enough to wild animals to be able to deal with them with a club, spear, or self-made bow. The best chance of success lies in ambush hunting. To do this, look for animal trails leading from feeding grounds to water. Early morning and late evening are the times of most animal movement. Smear mud on your face and hands to break up their outline. Hide well before any movement is expected.

The wait may be long, but you must keep still, since the only chance of success lies in seeing any animal before it sees you. Take note of the wind direction, and set your ambush on the downwind side of the trail. It will help if you are able to rub any aromatic herb or leaf on to your skin to dilute or conceal your own scent. It only remains to be certain that any opportunity of catching or killing the quarry is taken as positively and vigorously as possible.

SMALL GAME

Snares

The better alternative is to employ traps and snares to catch the game needed. If properly made, and effectively sited and set, they will do the waiting – 24 hours a day. Any food they provide will be highly cost-effective. Set out to catch small game at first. They are among the easiest to trap, are relatively common and simple to carry back to camp. They are also easy to prepare. To achieve success with traps and snares the survivor has to decide what animal he is trying to catch. He then has to determine if these animals are in the area and if so, what they usually do – and then set his trap to catch them while they're doing it. Perhaps rabbits will serve as an example.

They are social animals, always living in groups, usually remaining in one area. They occupy burrows, sometimes with a number of entrances. Their habitats are grasslands, open woodlands and dry, sandy localities in lowland places. Banks and slopes with light tree or shrub cover are chosen for the burrow sites.

Conspicuous runs, regularly used by the rabbits, are seen between the burrows. These runways, as well as the burrow entrances, show the animals' small dark round droppings if they are in current use. It will be more effective, if there is a choice, to set the snares in the runs a little distance away from the burrow entrances. This is because animals are naturally on the alert as they emerge from underground. They are therefore more likely to spot and avoid the snare. When setting snares, take care not to step on or disturb the run in any way, and rub the snare and your hands with animals droppings. This will help to conceal your own scent.

The Drag Snare

The simplest – and quickest to set – is the drag snare. It is a simple noose, and kills the animal by strangulation. The most efficient material is brass snare wire, but steel wire, nylon cord, hide strips or even a wire saw can make good working alternatives. Use 50cms. or so of wire. Put a 1cm. loop on the end, pass the other end through the loop, and the noose is ready. Check that the loop slips easily and, if wire is being used, that it has no kinks.

Simple Drag Snare.

The snares must be securely fastened to a stake driven into the ground, or hung from any natural deadfall above the run. Set a noose about the size of a fist so that its lower edge is about 10cms. off the ground. If the site is suitable, place dead twigs and branches on either side of the snare to help channel the rabbit into it. Do not use green twigs – the rabbit may stop to eat them. Use the twigs to hold the snare off the ground if you are using anything other than wire.

It is a good idea to set a number of snares — but site them some distance from each other. There are two reasons for this. First, if an animal is caught the disturbance created will bring all nearby animals to the alert. Second, it is more likely that other snares will produce results if they are set in a different groups' territory. Check all the snares the following day. It is unfair to allow any animal caught but not killed to suffer unnecessarily. In addition, if you leave it for too long, some other four-legged hunter may make off with your catch. Collect any animals caught and re-set the snares.

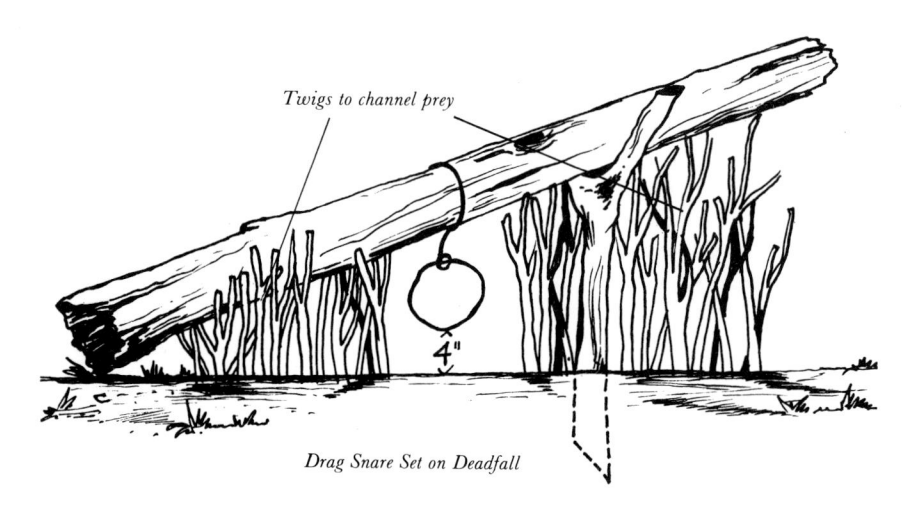

Twigs to channel prey

Drag Snare Set on Deadfall

It follows that a round of, say, ten snares set some distance apart will involve a trip which may take some time and cover some distance. It is important to make full use of this time and effort.

Carry some kind of container — a purse net is ideal — and search for edible plants as you go. If you have chosen your snare sites properly there will be animals in those places. The animals will have chosen the best feeding areas — those rich in vegetation. The fact that animals each particular plants does not mean that they are suitable for you — but, if some plants grow well in an area, so will others — which means that you should be able to find edible plants, too.

Besides looking out for edible plants, watch out for evidence of other small game — squirrels, rats, mice, birds, water fowl, etc. They will reveal their presence by their nests, burrows or dens, as well as their tracks and runs, meal remains, droppings, territorial markings and maybe calls, songs or even smells. Remember that birds' eggs are good safe food — don't neglect them as a food source.

The Balanced Pole Snare

If signs of other game are seen, the survivor must consider plans to catch it, too, although something other than a simple snare may be required. Further suggestions will be given later. Game detected could include fish and other aquatic animals. The chapter, "Aquatic Foods", will offer advice and information on catching them. In the meantime, there are some useful modifications available to the simple snare. It can be developed into a balanced pole snare. This has the advantage that it lifts the snared game clear of the ground – so making sure that your catch is not some other creature's meal. The details of this snare are shown below.

The first step is to tie a suitable pole to a convenient tree so that its lighter end can be pivoted downwards to be directly above the animal run.

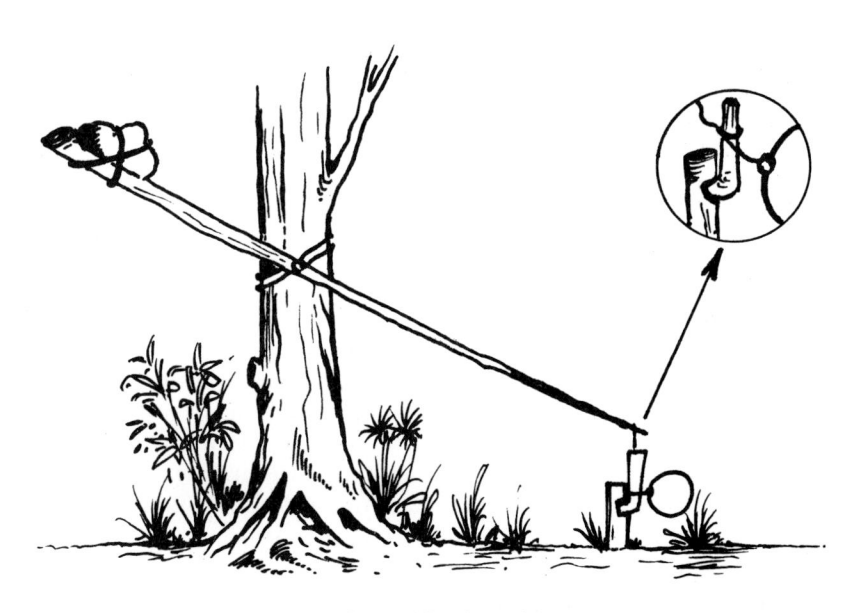

The Balanced Pole Snare (Set)

Tie the loose end of the snare firmly on to this end of the pole after knotting it, at a convenient point, around the movable half of the snare trigger. Next fasten a rock weight to the other end, so that when released, the pole holds the snare at least one metre clear of the ground.

Drive the other half of the trigger into the ground alongside the run. Engage the trigger halves, and the snare is ready. Check that the loop runs freely and that the noose is set at the correct height above the ground.

The Balanced Pole Snare (Triggered)

The Half-Reef Trigger

If snares are being made from cord or line, a simpler variety of trigger is available for use with the balanced pole. Fasten a metre or so of cord to the light end of the pole so that about 10cms. hang down at one end, and the remainder at the other. Tie a simple knot on the end of the short line. Use an overhand or bowline knot to put a 1cm. loop on the longer end. Bring the light end of the pole down, and tie both ends of the snare line using half a reef knot around the anchor stake. Support the half knot against the stake while allowing the pole to rise gently. The half knot will slip, but eventually the knot on short-end will bear against it and hold the pole in position.

Use the looped end to form the noose and set the snare. When an animal jerks the noose end, the half-reef will twist, release the knot, and allow the pole to rise. The illustration shows the trigger just before final tension is taken up. Practice will enable you to set this snare easily and quickly.

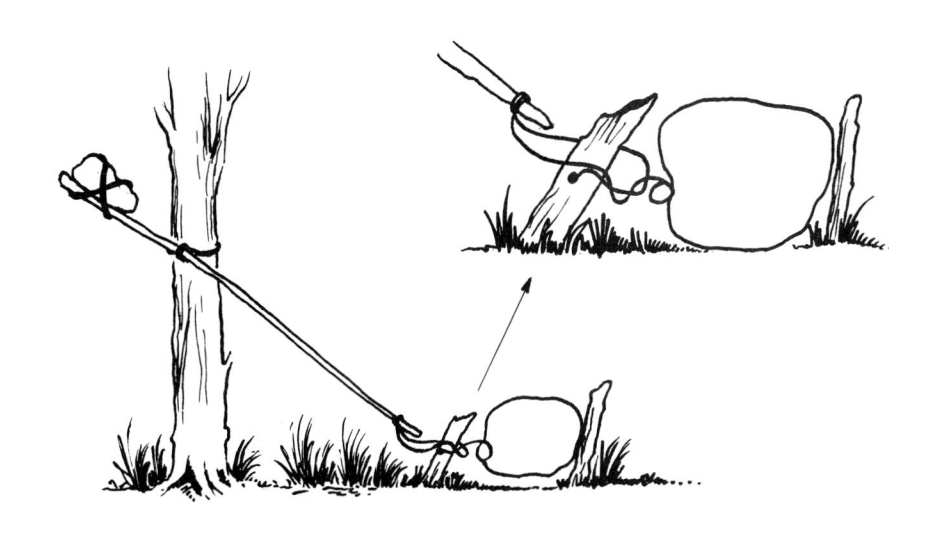

The Half-Reef Trigger

Three peg trigger

The Spring Snare

An alternative to the balanced pole is the spring snare. The function of the balanced pole is performed by a small sapling or bent branch held under tension. The half-reef trigger is probably unsuitable for use with spring snares.

The Spring Snare.

Trigger Variation

When the trigger is tripped the animal is lifted clear of the ground and strangles itself. If cord or nylon is being used, the snare noose will have to be supported in some way to keep it open.

Trigger Variations

Other types of trigger become possible if longer lines are available. One of the simplest is shown below, in use with a spring snare.

If line or wire is available, this trigger can carry a snare at each end.

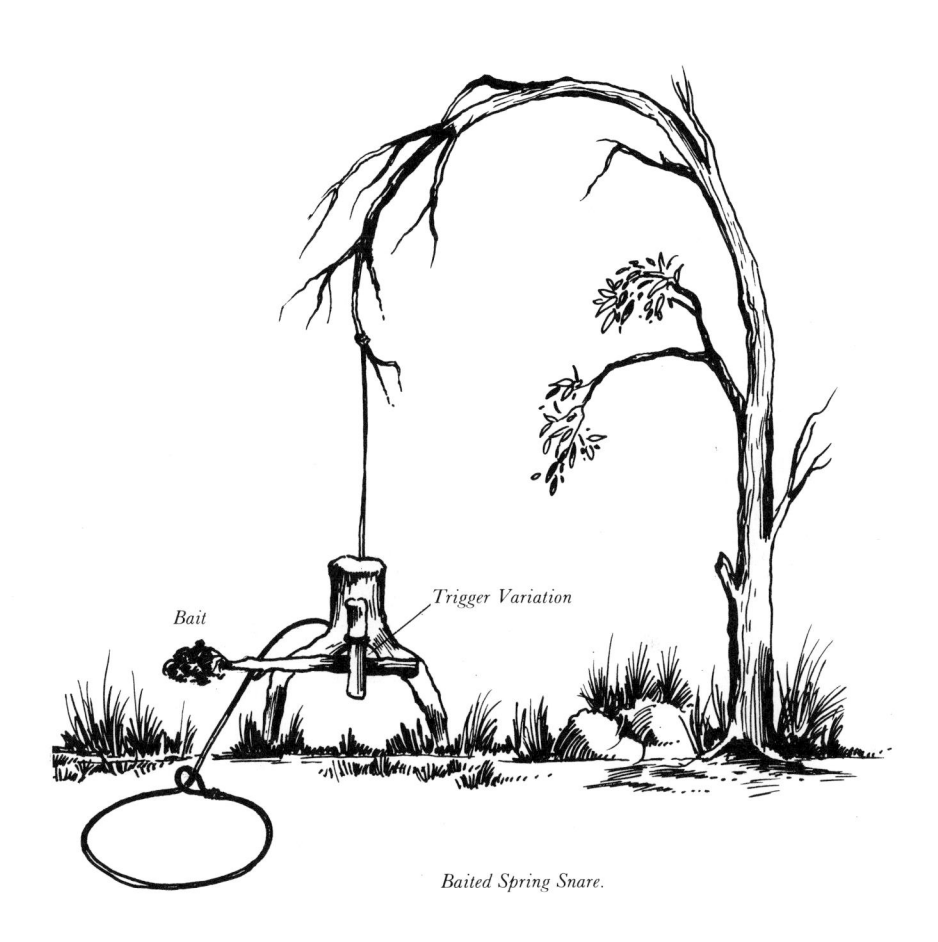

Bait

Trigger Variation

Baited Spring Snare.

The Figure Four Trigger

The Figure Four trigger is a little more difficult to make, and may be not as easy to set, but it can be very sensitive, especially with deadfall traps.

Bait

Rock Deadfall

Disturbance of the trigger causes the rock to fall, trapping the animal. One advantage of this trap is that the pieces of the trigger can be carried and used repeatedly if travelling.

Squirrel Snares

If any signs of squirrel have been seen, snares can be set for them – if snare wire is available. The signs will include pine cones stripped of their scales (except, perhaps for a tuft at the top) and the scales themselves, scattered at the base of a tree. In deciduous woods, look for nut shells which have been split in two. The tree trunk will probably show claw marks. Old mushrooms, wedged into forks near the trunk, also indicate squirrel occupation.

The first step is to provide the animals with an easier route up into the tree. Do this by propping a suitable pole, 4-5m. long, at an angle against the trunk, wedging it into a fork if possible. Prepare 3 or 4 snares, using about 60cms. snare wire for each, and setting nooses about 7cms. across.

Tie the snares on to the pole, using the extra length to form a curve so that each noose hangs vertically about 10cms. above the pole. Leave a metre clear at each end of the pole. This is one set-up in which snaring one animal will not necessarily lessen the chance of catching others –

Squirrel Snares

who may well be attracted to the disturbance, come to investigate it, and snare themselves.

Bird Snares

Small drag snares can be adapted to catch birds. Shown below is a method of hanging snares on and around a well used perch. Such a perch can be identified by droppings on the branch or ground below.

Birds can also be caught using a snare on a baited perch.

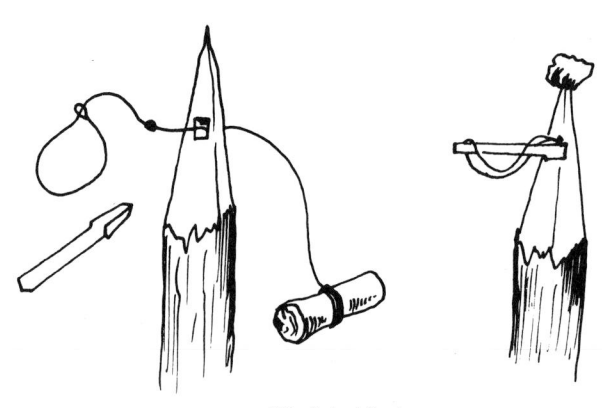

The Baited Perch

The square ended perch must be a loose fit into the upright, being held lightly in place by the knot in the snare line. When a bird dislodges the perch the weight falls, being no longer held by the knot, and draws the noose around the bird's legs. Do not use too heavy a weight – 0.5kg. is sufficient.

It is always worthwhile, if near water, to bait a fish hook and leave it anchored on the shore or bank. There is a good possibility that a bird will peck at it. Water fowl may be caught by a floating trap on the lines illustrated. If no vessel is available a weighted piece of wood can be used.

Fowl Trap

If you have a purse net – or make a gill nett as shown in "Aquatic Foods," – there is another method of catching small game (e.g. rabbits). Having located a burrow, stake the net over one of the entrances showing signs of recent use. Block all but one of the adjacent holes, and then blow smoke or pour water into it.

There is a good chance that the rabbit or other occupant will make a panic exit into the net. If no net is available, use a snare set outside the open hole.

A gill or purse net can also be adapted to catch birds.

Gill/Purse Net *Water or Smoke*

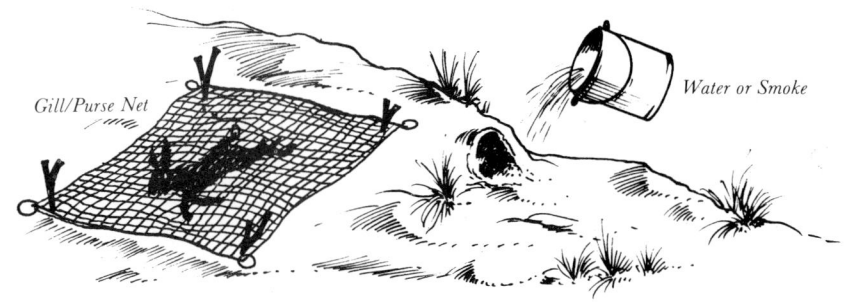

LARGE GAME

Deadfall Traps

The deadfall principle can be employed in larger traps according to the size of game being sought. The limiting factors are the time and energy a large trap will demand in construction, the weight a survivor can handle safely and the length and strength of lines and cords available.

Large traps can be dangerous to the survivor as well as to the intended prey. Great care needs to be exercised. In any event, positive sighting of a reasonable number of the big game would be sensible before investing in the building of such a trap.

A simple example of a baited deadfall is shown here.

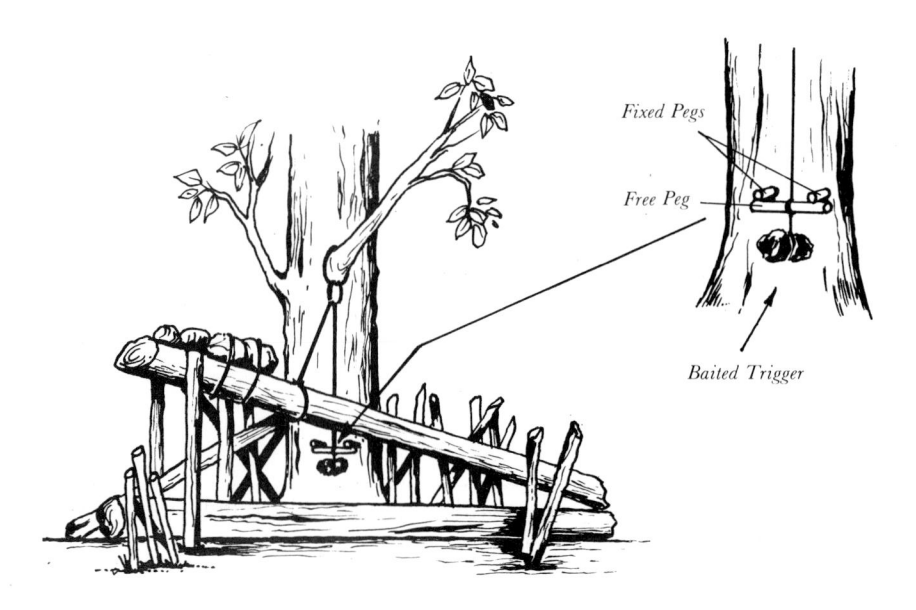

Fixed Pegs

Free Peg

Baited Trigger

The trigger release line is used here with a trip-line operation, baited if required. Another variation would be to use a snare attached to the tension line via the trigger, so that the deadfall becomes a bigger-game version of the balanced pole snare.

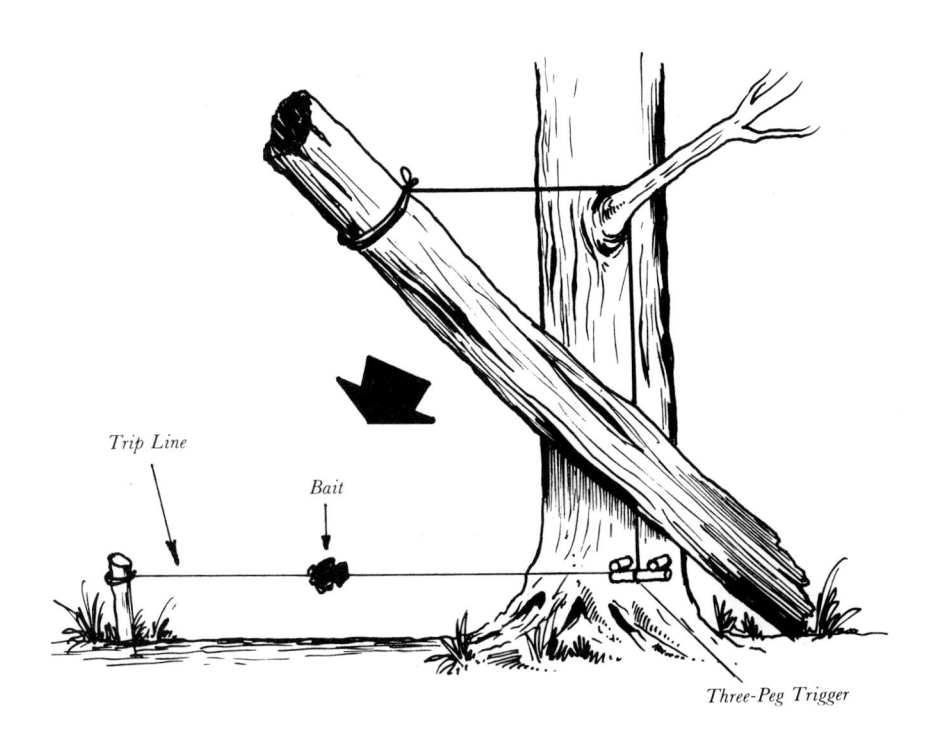

Trip Line

Bait

Three-Peg Trigger

The adaptable and inventive survivor might even combine the two operations – using one trap with two trigger lines, covering baited trip line and snare operation.

The Baited Hole Noose

In addition to the snares and traps already described, there are traps aimed at capturing the quarry whether or not it is killed. The least complicated of these is the baited hole noose. The illustration is self-explanatory.

The Baited Hole Noose.

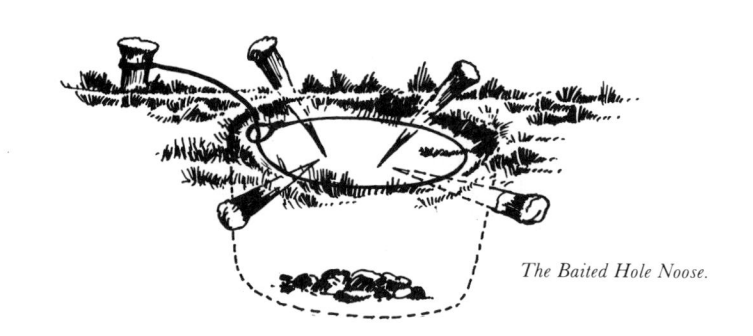

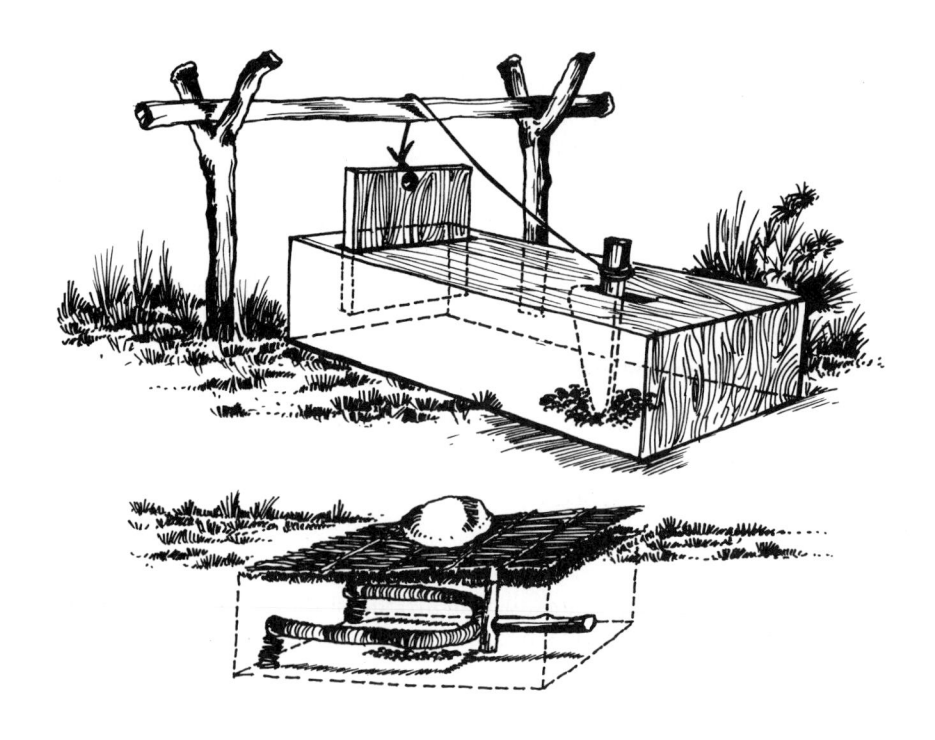

Baited Traps.

The spear pit is a development of the previous trap, but it demands a great deal of time and energy in construction. Allied to these must be positive knowledge of the animal's habits and considerable skill in siting the concealment of the trap. In addition, the better prepared this form of trap is, the more dangerous it becomes to the trapper himself – and even more so to fellow survivors.

As a last resort, the survivor must remember that anything that walks, crawls, creeps, flies, jumps, wriggles or swims can be eaten. There is usually an initial repugnance – not to say disgust – at even the thought of eating some of the more outlandish creatures. There is an old saying, however, that "Hunger is the best sauce" – and any survivor might have to consider insects, worms, grubs, hairless caterpillars and other unlikely creatures as possible foods.

If that time arrives the best approach is to dry them by roasting or baking, or add them to vegetable stew. Not only will their identities disappear, but they will be safer to eat, since cooking will destroy any danger present from parasites. It may help, when catching and preparing food of this type, to reflect that many of them are rich in protein – and are regarded as delicacies by people ranging from the cuisine-conscious French to the aborigines with the simplest of life-styles.

SUMMARY

(a) Animals provide food of much higher value to the survivor than the great majority of that food derived directly from plants. However, more effort, more knowledge and more patience are required to make their food available.

(b) Particular, specialised knowledge is required to be able to hunt successfully with primitive weapons. A firearm will give the survivor a much improved chance.

(c) Early morning and late evening are the best hunting times, since animals will be moving between feeding and bedding grounds and their water source.

(d) All animals survive by being constantly alert. Their senses are more acute than ours. Their physical capabilities are generally greater. The only chance a human hunter has is – as with so many other aspects of survival – to use his intelligence to overcome his physical deficiencies. Observation, camouflage, a low profile, silence, smooth careful movement downwind while the animals are feeding and patience – all are needed if the hunt is to be productive.

(e) Any wounded animal is highly liable to be extremely dangerous, and the greatest caution must be exercised when returning to traps or snares.

(f) Do not discard any part of a carcase without careful consideration. Nearly everything is of some use. Skins can be used as clothing, bones as arrow heads, needles or fish-hooks, intestines provide gut, sinews make thongs, and so on.

(g) It is always a good idea to set snares in and around any spot which has been used to clean or butcher an animal. The entrails will act as very effective bait.

(h) If startled into motion, rabbits and hares may be checked by a sharp whistle. They can sometimes be attracted towards you by a high-pitched kissing sound made between the curled forefinger and thumb.

(i) If a good torch with a focussed beam is available, it can be used during darkness to "mesmerise" a rabbit so that a quiet approach can be made to within arm's length. Keep the beam steadily on the animal throughout the approach. Survey the feeding grounds by day before the attempt.

(j) Watch birds carefully. Their movement will often reveal nest-sites containing young or eggs, which should never be overlooked as a food source.

CHAPTER THIRTEEN

AQUATIC ANIMAL FOODS

Life is generally supposed to have originated in the sea. Whether this is true or not, animal life is certainly more abundant in water than on land and is, usually, more easily caught. Any survivor's chances are very greatly increased if near a lake, stream or river. Make camp near any of these and a water supply – either fresh or purified – is assured. The prospects of a food supply are also greatly enhanced. Its attraction for land animals will bring them into your trapping grounds. But it can also be a rich food source in its own right. Never overlook or under-estimate the food possibilities offered by any sizeable body of water, for there will be fish, reptiles and crustaceans to be found.

Fish are the most attractive and obvious of the aquatic foods – as well as being the most difficult to catch. They can be caught using hooks, nets, traps, snares and spears – or even by hand alone. All the methods require observation, some knowledge, thought – and above all, patience. You need to know – or find out – when, where and how to fish. If you do, fish can be caught using relatively crude equipment. Even so, it would be folly to expect to produce a fish dinner at your first attempt. It may call for repeated efforts and a variety of approaches, but it **can** be done, with patience and your skills and techniques. In some circumstances fish can also be obtained by poisoning or stunning.

Angling

Very few general rules are valid as far as fishing is concerned. Different species of fish vary as widely in their diet and habits as do land animals. In addition, the time of day, the kind of water area and the weather all have an effect on fish and their feeding activity. One acceptable generality, however, is that dawn and dusk are the two most likely periods when bait fishing will be successful, although some species feed at other times of day or night. Other favourable times for fishing would be:-

(i) When fish (especially minnows) are seen to be rising or jumping.

(ii) When a river or stream is in full spate after rain. Fish very often feed at this time, even though the water is muddy, to take advantage of any extra food carried down by the high water. A small backwater, served by a minor tributary, is then a good location.

(iii) When waterfowl are in a group on the surface, or are actually diving.

(iv) When a storm is impending.

(v) Just before and just after full moon.

(vi) From the seashore, during the hours on either side of high tide.

Fish will react to hot weather by looking for cooler water. This is water which is generally deeper or shadier, or both. In hot weather, cast for fish in the deeper river pools and under shaded banks. An ideal combination could be found along the outer bank of a river bend. If the river level is low, by far the best chance lies in such places as these. If using natural bait, try to move it downstream at the water's pace, to pass near underwater rocks, logs, or undercut banks. These are the places where fish look for cover. Similarly, deep fishing is the best bet in lakes when it is hot.

In cooler weather, and at dawn or dusk, fish the shallower areas of stream or river, or around the edges of lakes or ponds. With less warmth and lowered light levels the fish will search for warmer water — and in any case they tend to feed more readily in the shallower places. Always let your bait move with the water in stream or river. Fish always lie in the water facing into the current so that (a), they can spot anything drifting downstream and (b), they ensure an easier flow of water over the gills. Allowing natural bait to move in this way gives the angler the best chance of its being seen, accepted and taken.

Another good fishing spot is at the foot of a small waterfall – especially if it is tumbling into a pool. Fish frequent these places because the water is well aerated. If natural bait is in use, cast it into the falling water and let it drift down and across the pool, or for a short distance downstream. Then haul the line in as smoothly and quietly as possible and repeat the cast. Having the line on the end of a slender, pliant pole makes this action much simpler, as the line can be lifted out of the water rather than pulled back through it. The pole also enables casting and recovery to be achieved with the minimum of movement by the angler.

Some species, such as carp, catfish and eels, feed on the muddy beds of ponds and slow-moving rivers. Bait should be cast on the bottom and moved very slowly.

Fishing Tackle

1. Hooks

When buying or making fishhooks it is important to remember that small hooks are the best choice. Big hooks will only be taken by big fish, but a small hook can catch both big and small fish. If no manufactured fishhooks are available, working alternatives can be made from almost any available metal. Safety pins, paper clips, split pins and stiff wire are among the obvious sources. Hooks can also be carved from hardwood. A hook can be shaped from the angle of a small branch. Even a large thorn on its stem can be used for the purpose. Adaptation and improvisation are the name of the game. Some possible approaches are illustrated below.

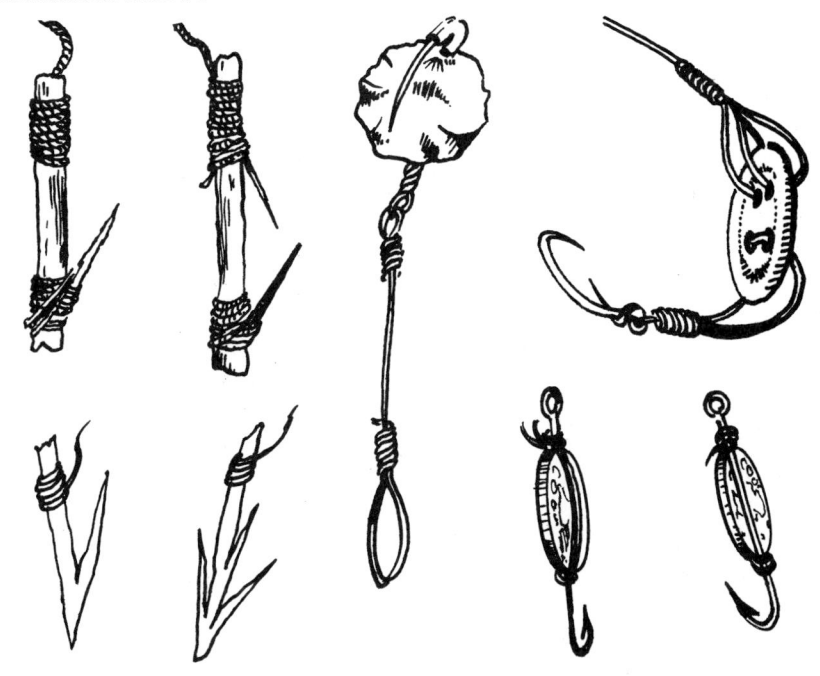

One of the simplest is the skewer or gorge hook.

If any thin, flexible wire is available, it is a good idea to use about 20 cm as a trace. This has the hook fastened to one end and the line to the other. Its purpose is to make it impossible for the hooked fish to bite through the line. The thin inner core of a nylon cord is an alternative choice for a trace. An ordinary small button can be used to join the trace to the line, or the hook directly to the line if no trace is available.

If the aim is to float the bait on the surface, then the lighter and simpler the hook arrangement the better. To fish deep, add a small weight a short distance up from the hook. A float tied on to the line will hold the bait at any depth required. This is particularly useful for keeping the bait off the bottom, or for carrying it past submerged rocks, etc., where fish may be lying.

Two things must be kept in mind when making or using fish hooks.

(i) Small is beautiful – and effective.

(ii) The points MUST be kept as sharp and fine as possible. If needed, very nearly any stone or pebble will serve as a honing surface.

Fish Spears

2. Line

If no manufactured fishing line is available, there are other possibilities. Most thick ropes or cords can be unravelled into their smaller strands for use as lines. Any hand-knitted garment can, with care, be unpicked to provide sizeable lengths of lines, which can be used singly or doubled up as necessary. Cloth fibres, fibres from the inner bark of trees or the stems of climbing vines can be spun (i.e. twisted) into a usable line.

A thin, flexible pole or rod will enable the line to be manipulated more easily and accurately, and with less personal movement.

Baits and Lures

(i) Baits

Two general rules regarding bait are:—

(a) Look for natural food that is already there, and offer it to the fish on your hook.

(b) Small offerings are more likely to be taken than larger ones.

Study the water in which you are going to fish, along with its surrounding banks or shore. Look for signs of insects, shrimps, grubs, worms, minnows, shellfish, etc. Make these your first choice for bait, for they will be the food normal to the fish. If one bait produces no result, try the others in turn. If no natural bait can be found, make use of alternatives such as scraps of meat or artificial substitutes.

When a fish is caught by any method, examine its stomach contents closely to find out what it has been eating. Then try to find and use that type of food as bait for other fish of the species. In any case, make use of the fish eyes, intestines and any other portions which are inedible for you, as bait in later fishing.

Periwinkle

Limpet

Live bait can sometimes be used to attract fish. A grasshopper or beetle thrown on to the surface will start kicking, and may then be taken by a fish. If this happens, another insect, carefully impaled on the hook so as not to kill it, will provide a good chance of securing a catch. Minnows can be used in the same way under water. The hook should be placed through the body under the backbone to the rear of the minnow. Use a float to keep the bait off the bottom.

The float will dip under the surface when a bigger fish goes for the bait. Do not take this as the moment to strike – i.e. to pull the fish in. The big fish must be given time to turn the bait and take it fully, so that the hook has a chance to engage. If the strike is too early, the chances are that the "catch" will be half a minnow.

When fishing from the seashore the most effective – and most easily obtainable – bait is the meat of shell fish – limpets, mussels, clams, dog whelks and periwinkles.

Mussel

Clam

These shellfish are themselves edible provided they are cleaned and thoroughly cooked.

(ii) Lures.

These are all forms of artificial bait and aim to deceive the fish by simulating the appearance of insects or smaller fish. The angler has to make his contribution to this deception by imitating, as closely as possible, the movements of living bait.

Other possibilities include lures made from a tuft of hair (your own, if necessary), a piece of fin from any fish with a scrap of flesh attached, brightly coloured scraps of cloth or pieces of feathers made up to suggest an insect. Any of these should be made up around the hook so as to conceal it. Use and move the lure in the manner of the creature it suggests.

Fishing Hints

Most fish are alert, and react very rapidly to anything not in the ordinary pattern of events by departing from the scene to take cover. Their bodies have a lateral line containing many very highly sensitive vibration detectors. It is essential, therefore, to approach the water's edge slowly and gently to avoid any ground vibration. Keep a low profile, use a minimum of movement and be as quiet as possible. Do not allow your shadow to fall on to the water.

Present your bait upstream of where you believe fish to be and allow it to move downstream with the current until it has passed you. Recover it gently and repeat the process. Change your fishing pitch if no bites are forthcoming – again moving slowly and carefully. If the fish are not biting, try fishing the same area again at the other end of the day or even – if the water is clear and shallow – after dark.

Many anglers throw groundbait into the water they are fishing. This is free bait, and its only aim is to attract fish by persuading them that they have found a good feeding ground. Do the same if you have any bait to spare. In the lake, pond or pool situation you can try another very effective version of groundbaiting. Tie any unwanted offal or carrion to an overhanging branch. This will soon attract blowflies, which will lay eggs in the rotting meat. The maggots so produced will steadily fall into the water and certainly attract fish. One of them on your hook should produce results.

The survivor may make meticulous preparation. He may have efficient tackle and suitable bait. He may use it at a favourable location and at the right time. But he must appreciate that angling can NEVER be guaranteed to produce a catch on a given occasion. Do not be discouraged if this happens. There is always another time and place for the survivor. In addition, there are also other ways of catching fish.

The NIGHT LINE is simply a line carrying one or more hooks which is left in the water overnight. It can be secured to a rock or stake on the bank, or hung from an overhead branch. The major point to note is that the hooks should be baited with strong bait – a small fish, or piece of meat – which can be securely placed or tied on to the hook. Soft bait, such as a worm, would probably be lifted off the hook by eels, with no resulting catch. The lines should be checked each day, any catch removed, and bait replaced where necessary. The gorge hook is very suitable for use with night lines.

Nets.

If sufficient line is available, such as might be found in parachute rigging lines, the survivor has the capacity to make and use what is probably the easiest and most effective method of catching fish – the gill net. These nets can be set across a small stream, but in a larger river would be most effective when set above or below an eddy. In any case, the net should be set in quiet water. It should be laid out at right angles to a lake shore, the favoured location being off any small headland. If it is to be used in a small stream, aim to make the net as long as the stream is wide, and as wide as the water is deep. For other locations, make a net as large as your resources allow and you are able to manage.

Having decided on the length of the net to be made, tie a line between conveniently spaced saplings or stakes to mark the top of the net, and another below to mark the net width. If nylon lines are available strip out their inner cores. Double a piece of this inner core and tie it to the upper line. Use an overhand loop, letting both ends hang down loose. These hanging strands should be about 30% longer than the net width required.

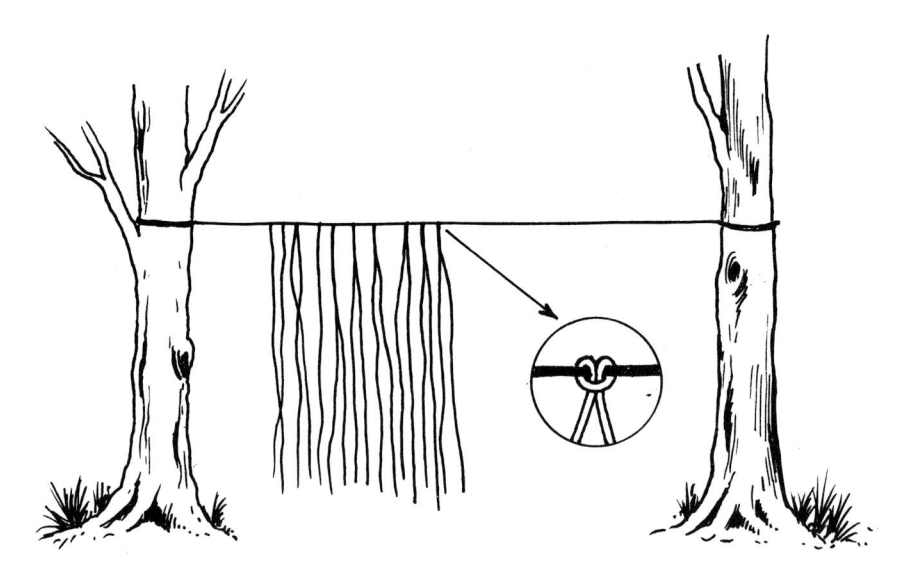

Repeat this across the length of the upper line. Position the knots so that the space between each is slightly less than the width of the target fish. If in doubt, 3 to 4 cms would be a working compromise for fresh water use, and 4 to 5 cms for use in the sea. The next step is to tie a horizontal guide string below the upper line, placed to indicate the mesh depth. Pick up the second and third hanging strings. Tie them with an overhand knot level with the guide string. Repeat this with each succeeding pair. There will be a single line left hanging free.

Move the guide string down one step and tie the next row of knots. Start this time with strings one and two so that you finish with the final pair. Complete each row before lowering the guide string and starting the next. Remember to alternate the numbers of the starting strings in each succeeding line. The illustration shows how the net should look during manufacture.

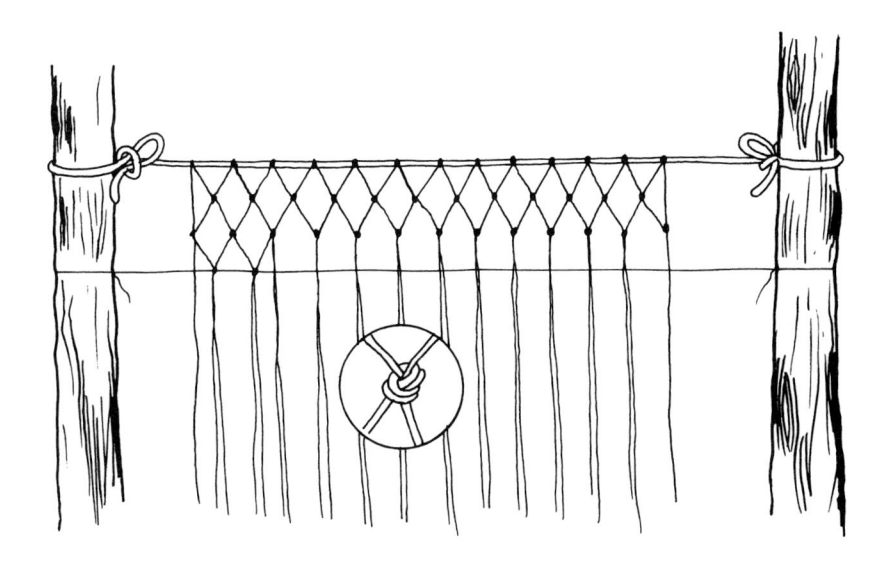

To use, the net can be supported by a line stretched across a small stream. The lower edge should be anchored to the stream bed by stones. Should it be impracticable to make a net long enough to stretch the full width of the stream, stones or brush wood could be used to narrow the channel at the point where the net is used.

Off lake or sea shore, use wooden floats along the upper edge of the net, and pebbles or metal weights along the lower. The off-shore end will require a large float and a stone on a longer line to serve as an anchor. The anchor-stone could be ferried out to position using a log or small raft. If this is done, suspend the anchor-stone on a shortened line beneath the raft or log. This will give the operation some stability, while the water displacement will reduce the apparent weight of the anchor.

Although resources sufficient to make a gill net may not be available, a smaller net will be of use in gathering fish too small to catch by other means. Even small areas of water support these – and minnows are nearly always present in the shallows edging rivers and lakes. Schools of small fish can also be found in the shallows of a calm sea. A purse net can be adapted for this use if the mesh is fine enough.

Stiff wire can be formed into a frame, or a convenient fork on a small branch can be tied into a rough circle. A vest or underpants will form a net if tied or stitched so that the sac is closed. A pair of tights is very suitable, if rather fragile.

The net can be used to scoop up any small fish. Move it against any current so that it comes from behind the fish, and sweep it around rocks or boulders. The resulting catch, with heads and tails removed, make a valuable addition to a vegetable stew. It is important to note, in this context, that fresh water fish should never be eaten raw, since many carry or contain parasites dangerous to humans.

Traps

There are several types of fish traps a survivor can employ, usable in the sea as well as in fresh water. Some make use of tidal movement; some are better in more restricted waterways. They can be permanently sited or moveable. Some employ bait. Basket-type traps can be made on the general pattern shown below.

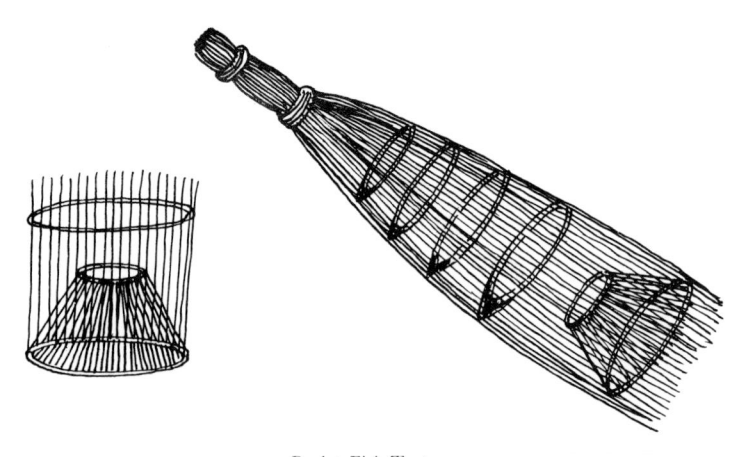

Basket Fish Traps.

The cone-shaped entrance makes it easy for the fish to enter, but difficult to get out. Any light, flexible twigs can be gathered and fashioned into this general design. The key to the trap is the "lobster-pot" entrance, but the overall shape is immaterial. Placed in a stream, river or rock pool, a few of these pots will provide a supply of fish. Their effectiveness will be increased if suitable bait can be tied inside.

It is possible to make the body of the trap from a metre or so of stout bamboo. Wrap a few turns of binding around the stem a few cms, from one end. Then split the length down from the other end as many times as is convenient. The split pieces will form a cone if forced apart. The ends can be tied to a hoop with line, wire or vegetable fibre. A funnelled top can then be added. This can be made in the same way from a shorter bamboo piece.

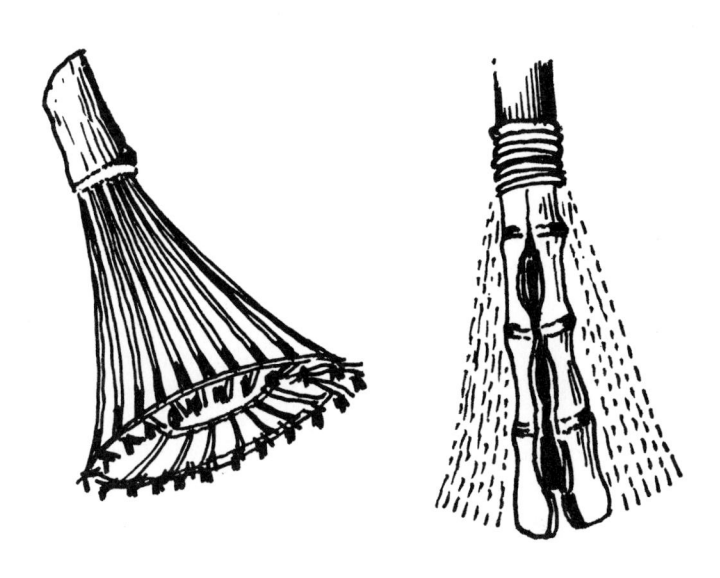

Bamboo Fish Trap.

The same principle — though of different scale and construction — can be employed on the seashore to make use of tidal movement. Schools of fish habitually come inshore with the tide. They move along the inter-tidal zone, and can be deflected by obstacles. The survivor can construct such an obstacle in the form of a stake fence or stone wall to guide the fish into his trap. It should be built so that its closed end is towards the open sea, about two-thirds of the way down between high and low water marks. Built lower than this, it may be not uncovered at low neap tide.

Make the sides of the trap from wooden stakes driven into the sand and tied together if necessary. Something on the lines of split fencing supported by additional stakes would be effective. The shape of the trap is not critical, as long as it incorporates a version of the funnel entrance. Some possibilities are illustrated.

Seashore Fish Traps.

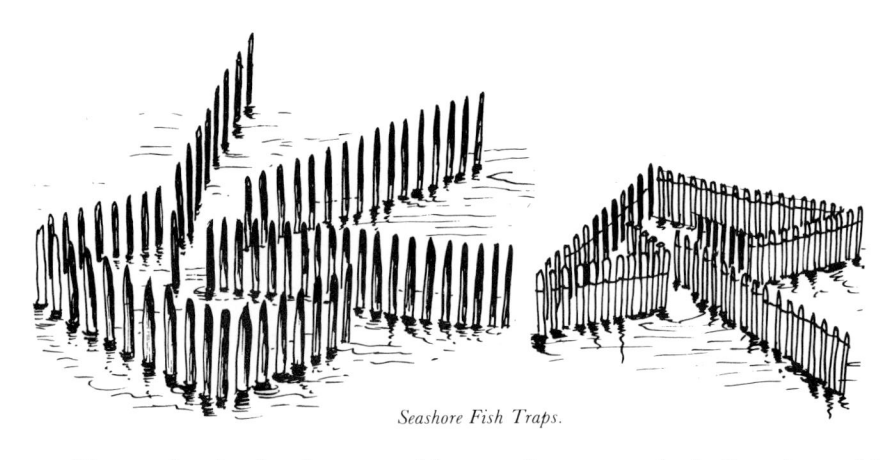

 Choose the site for the trap with care, for a great deal of work would be saved if any natural rock ridge could be incorporated during its construction. On a sandy shore, make use of the depressions which lie inshore of sandbars. In this particular situation it may be possible to build the simplest trap of all. This takes the form of a low crescent-shaped wall, horns pointing up the beach. This should retain enough water, when the tide falls, to strand the fish. If rock pools are present, consider how to use one as the body of the trap, with low stone guide walls added. These traps demand some time and effort, but they will provide fish. Whether they are worth building will depend on how long you plan to remain in that location and what other food is available.

 Do not overlook the possibility, if on a rocky shore with deep water, of a basket-type lobster and crab trap. These traps need to be baited and let down to the bottom on a line.

 The seashore funnel traps already described can be successfully used in rivers and streams, and are easier to construct, since light stakes and brushwood can be used. The guide fences should lead fish into a pen or side pool from which they can be taken. It may be possible, after observation, to herd them into the trap by wading into or disturbing the water.

 If any suitable box is to hand, it can be used as an eel trap in fresh water. Make a small hole or two in each side near the top, and bait the box with a piece of ripe meat. The weighted box can then be left in the water, and needs only to be checked every two or three days. Take the box out of the water and partially empty it before opening and checking the contents. Eels are so slippery that it is almost impossible to grasp them and lift them clear of the water.

Fish Snares.

Snaring fish is not simple, but it can be done with time, care and observation. Study of a stream or river will reveal where fish tend to lie. They can be caught if the snare is brought upstream from behind, passed over the tail and dorsal fin towards the gills. A quick snatch will then bring the fish on to the bank. A wire snare tied to a pole is the simplest way to operate.

Fish Snaring.

A development of the method is to use a hollow pole, such as bamboo, with a longer length of wire, which is passed through the tube and securely attached to one end. The other end is provided with a simple wooden toggle. Now a variable loop is available and can be used to catch fish of all sizes.

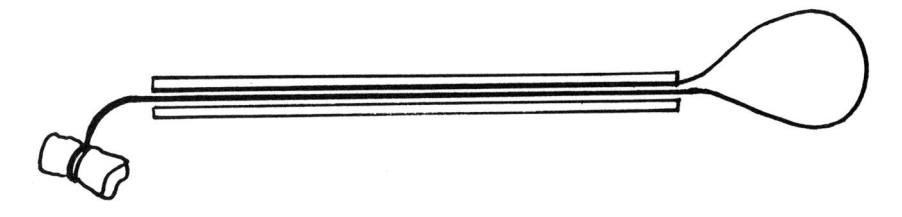

Variable Fish Snare.

Spearing

In daylight this is not the easiest way of catching fish, but it can be done. It is essential that the spear is rigid and that the point is kept sharp. A blunt tip will merely glance off the scales of any sizeable fish. If a three pronged spear can be made, it will very much improve efficiency. Do not throw the spear. A stab or thrust is better controlled and more effective. Try to find a position over a fish run and strike directly downwards. This method has the twin advantage of minimising the effects of refraction and of pinning any speared fish to the stream bed.

If two people are available they can work together over a stretch of stream which contains rocks. Starting at the downstream end, one slowly lifts rocks in turn while the other attempts to spear the fish as they are revealed.

At night, the spear can be much more effective. Any sort of light will attract fish, and they will be much easier to spear. If no portable light source is available, moonlight can be used by placing a shiny piece of metal or a mirror on the stream bed. The reflected moonlight will also attract the fish. They can be seen as they pass over the reflective surface, and become relatively easy targets.

Tickling Trout

Trout are only found in clear running water. As they are very nervous fish, they tend to lie hidden. They choose places such as undercut banks, rat holes in stream and river banks, under rocks – or anywhere providing good cover. Even though it is impossible to get anywhere near a trout in open water, they can be caught by hand while lying in cover.

There is less need for caution when approaching what looks a likely spot. Lie on the bank, put both hands into the water, and wait until they are at or near water temperature. Then, keeping them together, start at the downstream end of the cover and feel gently and carefully under the cover, working upstream. The tail of the fish should be felt first. Stroke it gently a few times and then, still stroking the body, work slowly towards the gills. As the gills are reached, grasp the fish firmly and quickly and toss it up on to the bank.

The two major factors in tickling trout successfully are:—

(i) Choosing the right cover under which fish will be found. Study of the water will assist in this choice. Watch where fish head for when startled – or, rather more difficult, where they emerge from into open water.

(ii) Avoiding nervousness. While tickling trout tends to be a fairly tense undertaking, nervousness must be controlled while feeling for the fish with your fingers. They must be relaxed, or it will be difficult to avoid an involuntary start when first the fish is touched. This will alarm the fish and scare it away.

Poisoning or Stunning

In some of the warmer parts of the world native people make use of different plants containing substances poisonous to fish but harmless to humans. Such plants include the derris (S.E. Asia). The powdered roots of this plant, thrown into a stream above a pool, will render its occupants unconscious. They will surface and can be collected. The crushed seeds of the barringtonia, a tree growing near the seashores in Malaya, have a similar effect. Lime will kill fish when put into streams. It can be obtained by burning fragmented limestone, chalk, coral, bones or shells. If more fish are obtained by any of these methods than can be eaten at one time, be sure to clean and dry them for future use. (See Chap. Types of Fire, Stoves and Cooking).

Crustaceans

Crabs, crayfish, lobsters, shrimps and prawns are found in both salt and fresh water all over the world. All are edible, but they will not keep. They must be cooked as soon as possible after catching. Never eat any crustacean before it is thoroughly cooked. Many are caught more easily at night – especially freshwater shrimp – if a light is held near the surface. The gills and intestines of lobsters, crabs and crayfish should be discarded, but all meat inside the shell or claws can be eaten.

As noted earlier, clams, mussels, periwinkles and limpets are all edible when cooked. Scallops, starfish and sea urchins can be added to this list.

Scallops

Sea Urchins

Starfish

In areas of fresh water as well as the land surrounding them, do not forget the small amphibians, newts and frogs. Frogs will reveal their whereabouts at night by croaking. Patience is needed at the outset, for if they are plentiful, they can always be heard somewhere other than the place you are. They will have fallen silent as you approach. Keep still for a while, however, and they will soon start up again near you.

In general, fish provide very good food, but there are some poisonous species. These occur in tropical waters, especially in lagoons, and around reefs and atolls. Avoid fish showing any of the following characteristics:

odd shapes; box-like appearance; spines or thorns; lack of scales; slimy covering; sunken eyes; horns; glossy gills; an unpleasant smell; horny or protruding lips; irregular rows of teeth;

Do not eat any eggs, gills, intestines or livers of any fish from tropical waters. They contain poisons which are not destroyed or weakened by even the most thorough and prolonged cooking.

As with all Survival Skills and Techniques, those needed to catch fish require practice and familiarity. Many of them can be interesting and rewarding in themselves. They are well worth any time and effort devoted to them for their usefulness and interest in ordinary life – quite apart from their inestimable value in any survival situation.

At all events, the survivor will agree with the saying, "Give a man a fish, and you have fed him for a day. Teach him how to fish, and you will have fed him for life".

To this we would add "One who learns to fish can be a Survivor".

CHAPTER FOURTEEN

TRAVELLING FOR SURVIVAL

Assessment of your Survival Situation may have identified the need to travel – to move to a safer, more favourable location. Perhaps the need is to undertake a longer journey to find help and safety. If this is the case, the same careful deliberation must be applied to this part of your Plan for Survival as you would give to any other.

Review all knowledge of your present location. Re-take any bearings and re-work any calculations used to pinpoint your position, so that it is done as exactly as possible. Do the same with regard to your intended destination. These two positions are the foundation upon which the travel plan will be based. The more accurate they are, the more likely is your travel to be successful. Make sure that everyone in the group is fully informed and that the plans are fully discussed. Check that you are sufficiently equipped to provide food and shelter each time you camp. Observe the following Survival Routine before setting out.

A. Make sure that everything that can be of use is included in your pack – subject only to the limitation of a reasonable load. If there are a number of survivors, share what is to be taken equitably among the party. Take care not to concentrate all resources of any one type into a single individual's pack. Split supplies of first aid materials, matches, water purification tablets etc., if this can be done without damage or harm to the supplies. In this way, the loss of any single pack will not rob the group of the means of fire-lighting, water purification or any other vital resource. In any case, ensure that crucial items (compass, knife, flint and steel etc.,) are securely stowed. It is wise to attach them to your person with a line.

B. If possible, survey the area through which the line of march will take you. Use any high ground available, or climb a tree for this purpose. When climbing a tree, keep as close to the trunk as possible. This will be of help in maintaining balance and will provide the strongest hand and foot holds. Never put your weight on to any hold before testing its strength. Do not release any sound hold until secure anchorage is obtained elsewhere – preferably at two points. Your intention is to climb and descend the tree safely – not to emulate Tarzan or any of his friends . . .

C. Many factors can affect the choice of route. Among these factors will be the type of area, the climate and weather, and the equipment and supplies available. Whether you are alone or with other survivors will be an important consideration. Your route possibilities may include following a river, a stream or the coastline, or travelling along hill ridges or valley floors. If moving through forest or jungle, paths or trails are likely to be the best option. You must always, as a survivor, be looking for the safest route. Only in very rare instances will the safest route also be the shortest or easiest.

Extra effort or longer distance covered are a reasonable price to pay for safety. The survivor will usually be the one who is ready to pay it when making his choice.

D. Work out a travel routine before you start. Modify it as you gain experience and further knowledge of the country. Base the routine on an easy, steady pace. Do not rush. Plan for a break of 5 to 10 minutes at the end of each hour. This will provide more than just a physical rest. It will allow consideration or discussion of your route. Any repairs and adjustments to clothing and equipment can be done. There will be a chance of refreshment, and an opportunity to check for and remove leeches, thorns or other nuisances. It is also recognised that a repeated combination of 50 minutes' effort followed by 10 minutes' break is actually more productive than successive hours' of continuous work.

Start early each day. Aim to pitch camp with time enough to be organised, fed, and ready to settle down for the night before the sun sets. Keep well within your physical capabilities. There is little point in exhausting yourself by the end of each day. If you do this, you will begin each succeeding day with a little less to offer. It is far more effective to be able to start each day with something in reserve. This approach will, as the days pass, gradually build up your stamina.

E. All survivors must be aware of the importance of personal hygiene. While travelling, some of the most important precautions are concerned with the feet. It is literally true that you won't get anywhere without them! Prevention of damage is always better than cure, so be sure to remove all footwear at the end of every day's march. Wash your feet, as well as your socks, stockings, puttees or foot-rags and boots or shoes. Dry the footwear overnight by the fire, so that it is fresh, dry and ready to wear next morning. Greasing boots or shoes will keep them supple and waterproof. It will also give them protection against cracking or rotting. Do not lace boot or shoes too tightly – but avoid any movement of the foot within the footwear which produces chafing. If any tender spots begin to develop, take what measures you can

BEFORE a blister is formed.

A second pair of socks, a plaster over the area, some extra or alternative binding on the boot or shoe, or candle-grease rubbed on the sock where the chafing occurs – all or any of these will help. The aim is to AVOID blisters – and the lowering of personal efficiency that they can cause. Soaking the feet in very hot salt water can be a great relief and will help to harden the skin. Start the soaking process with the feet in warm water, and raise its temperature by the careful addition of extra hot water. (See "First Aid.") Part of your preparation for outdoor activities could include soaking the feet in surgical spirit, which will harden the skin.

F. Boots, into which the ends of long trousers can be tucked, would be a very good choice for survival travel – but such ideal footwear may not be available. You must consider carefully what can be done to adapt what is available to the conditions around you.

In the desert, for instance, it is essential to keep sand, stones or insects out of your boots or shoes. It can be very frustrating and demoralising to be forced to stop repeatedly to empty them. Try to improvise puttees. These are strips of cloth wrapped over the boot or shoe and then wound upward around the lower leg. They will exclude most of the sand. Each puttee should be at least one metre but preferably two or three metres long by 10cms. wide. They can be cut or torn from any available cloth. Take care not to wind them too tightly. Circulation must not be restricted.

The opportunities for foot washing are likely to be few and far between during desert travel, but the survivor should remove shoes and socks during rest periods. However, do this briefly to begin with, replacing footwear before the feet begin to swell. Do not be tempted to walk barefoot – it will usually cause deterioration of the feet. Improvise sandals or overboots, roughly made from canvas or other stout material. Good soles can be cut from old tyres. Be sure to keep the upper surfaces of your feet covered. Any significant degree of sunburn on these areas can immobilise you.

Many of the same techniques are important in arctic conditions also – although the problems are almost completely reversed. Puttees will help in keeping legs and feet warm and dry. Two pairs of socks will do the same. They will also lessen the risk of blisters. Added insulation between the socks will conserve more body-warmth. Improvised overboots have an obvious role in cold conditions. The washing routines are, however, still important – and every effort must be made to keep your feet dry while walking.

The major additional threat to survival while travelling in jungle or tropical lowlands comes from leeches, insects etc. These can cause discomfort and damage unless dealt with effectively. In wet areas or in lowland forests after rain, leeches can be plentiful.

Watch out for them, and check your legs and feet frequently. Use the heliograph mirror to check your back if you are alone. Knock off any which have not yet taken hold. Do not attempt to pull them off it they have already bitten. (See "First Aid," – Leech Removal). In tropical or jungle conditions, **always check your footwear before putting it on.** Something unpleasant – a scorpion, perhaps – may resent your foot's intrusion into his newly-occupied home.

G. Before leaving your original location make certain that you have left behind clear signals which:—

(a) will be clearly visible to anyone searching for you from the air or on the ground,

and

(b) indicate your direction of travel.

On the ground, leave a written statement of your situation, your intentions and requirements. Include the time and date of departure. Repeat this on whatever scale you can comfortably manage at each of the camps en route.

CHOICE OF ROUTE

Jungle Travel

It is hardly ever possible to travel a direct line through jungle. You will have to make use of streams or rivers, game trails, dry water courses or ridge-crests. There may be native paths. Make use of them, since cutting a way through the vegetation is exhausting and slow. 1km. per hour would be a very favourable speed and 5km. in a day would be very good progress.

These suggested ways through the jungle share one common feature. They follow the general lie of the land, running along, or parallel to, the valleys. They will often run in directions which do not match your intention. Follow any which lie within 25 degrees or so of your required track. Use pre-determined landmarks to maintain your general heading if that is possible. If none are visible, use the compass, or a watch set to local time in conjunction with the sun.

During the middle period of the day, the tropical sun is too high in the sky to be of much help with navigation. A watch can only be used to obtain accurate direction during the morning and late afternoon. Use the easterly rising and westerly setting of the sun to determine whether it is to the North or to the South at noon. The answer will confirm whether your location is in the Northern or Southern Hemisphere.

These paths and trails become the animals' highways at night – so do not use them outside the hours of daylight. If a choice exists, a trail or path along a ridge is usually a better route than those low in the valley. The lower trails will generally pass through thicker vegetation, and may involve river/stream crossings. They may lead through marshy ground or swamps. Lowland trees with split roots give warning of this kind of terrain. Always avoid it if possible, for it is invariably difficult going, and can become impossible. However, you may not always be able to detour around every such place.

If forced to cross an unstable area, try to bridge it with foliage, branches or logs – even large bundles of reeds and grass are worth a try. If this is impossible, or if you have stumbled into a bog, quicksand or similar hazard, remember that it will support you if most of your weight is immersed. Your body may be 90% water, but it does contain air-filled spaces. It is lighter than the material surrounding it. The heaviest part of the body, size for size, is the head. The much-feared sensation of being "sucked down" is caused by the unsupported body and head weight pushing the legs further down into the mud or sand. Keep cool. Simply lie forward with legs and arms spread. Keep your body level and "swim" your way through. If carrying a back-pack, take it off and tow it along with you.

Another probable advantage of a ridge trail is the much better chance of observation which will allow you to keep your orientation. Of course, the direction in which the ridge lies may be too far off your required heading. Even so, it might be useful in making progress towards, and keeping sight of, any possible alternative valley or ridge, or river crossing. A compromise between the valley floor and the ridge could be a trail that follows a contour. Since this maintains a constant height, it minimises the climbing to be done. On the other hand, it will generally be a longer route. The choice can only be made by a thoughtful survey of the terrain.

If the chosen track runs along the sides of a thickly forested hillside, watch out for gullies or other places where boulders and debris may have collected. If overgrown with vegetation, they can present a false appearance of solidity, and with it a real danger of falls and leg injuries.

It is always worth thinking seriously about using a stream or river as a route – especially if you have no compass. Followed downstream it will lead to human habitation, if there is any in the area – although it may very often take a roundabout course.

In addition, there is the possibility of using a raft (or aircraft dinghy) for travelling – and the river is a ready-made source of food and water. Use bamboo or other light wood when building a raft. Remember that palm logs and many hard-woods will not float. One method of construction, using very little binding, is shown below.

If plenty of binding is available, construction will be easier. Use punting poles at each end of the raft if you are not alone. Secure supplies and equipment to the raft (or your own person, in small amounts) to avoid loss in the event of an upset. Do not secure so many bits and pieces to yourself that their weight will be insupportable if you do fall into the water. Proceed with care, keeping a keen eye out for white water or falls ahead. If any are seen, tie up and reconnoitre on foot. Choose the option of by-passing rapids etc., on foot if there is any risk of losing supplies or equipment.

Keep a lookout for possible camp sites which are a little away from and above the water. There will be fewer mosquitoes, midges and other insect nuisances to ruin your night's sleep. Light a fire as soon as convenient. Ash from the fire, spread around your bed, will hold back the insect pests which crawl along the ground. Be sure to moor your raft securely – dragging it up out of the water if possible. River levels can rise sharply, even if there is no local rain. Rainfall in the upper waters may arrive at your location without warning.

If following the waterway on foot, expect to encounter thick vegetation and other causes of unavoidable detours. Be ready to ford the river to gain better going on the other bank. When you have to cross, choose the widest, slowest point. Avoid bends, as the speed of the current will increase when wading from the inside of the bend to the outside. So will the depth of the water. Wade through rather than jump from stone to stone. Even a simple slip can result in an immobilising sprain or other injury – and perhaps loss of equipment.

If possible, anyone crossing should be secured to the bank by rope or line. Use a solid stick as an extra point of contact with, or as a probe for, the river bed. Take off your trousers before entering the water, as they are better kept dry, especially if the water is cold. You will need them to conserve body heat when you have made it to the other bank. Wet clothing can lose up to 90% of its insulating properties. Keep your boots or shoes on, however, when wading. If the shoes are slip-on, tie them with cord to lessen the risk of losing them in the water.

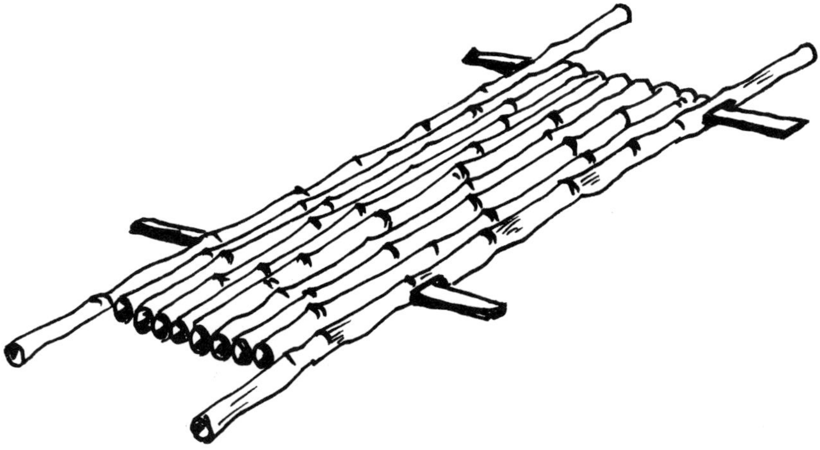

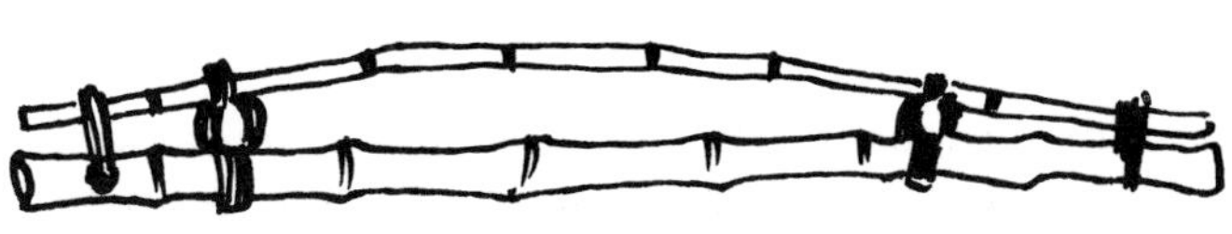

Make use of any flotation assistance available if the river depth is suspect. If nothing else is available, trousers tied at the ankles and waist and then filled with air will give support for a while. After tying the ankles, fill them with a sharp downward flick, holding the waist open.

NEVER attempt to ford a river above falls of any kind. You should never try to follow a waterway downhill at night, for it will always find and take the shortest, steepest course. Such a course often incorporates waterfalls and rock-clefts of varying heights.

Movement through jungle is best achieved by taking your time, moving deliberately and steadily, and going around obstacles rather than trying to force a way through. Never rush blindly forward. Look ahead, through the foliage, trying to spot hornets' nests or other difficulties. Watch out for snakes lying in your path. Occasionally bend down and look along the floor of the jungle. Don't tread or sit on rotting tree stumps or trunks. They are often home to a myriad ticks or other insects.

If you want to attract attention, do not shout, for this is exhausting. Hit the trunk of any tall tree with a stout, solid stick. This noise will be heard over much greater distances than even a loud shout. However, do check that you are not standing under a dead branch when you do it.

Coastline Travel

Following a coastline has both advantages and disadvantages. It offers a good chance of encountering any native help, or of rescue from any passing boats or ships. It offers a variety of probable sources of food and water (See ''Water Procurement'' and ''Aquatic Food''). On the other hand, the going can vary from easy walking on firm sand to difficult scrambles on rocky shores. You may encounter near-impossible swampy terrain, as in a river delta. It will almost certainly be a roundabout route – but is probably worth following until a better alternative presents itself. As usual, do not forget to leave ground signals and information behind when you leave.

Desert Travel

Too much heat and light, and too little water are usually the major problems of travelling in the desert. Additionally, accurate position fixing can be extremely difficult, if not virtually impossible. This difficulty is due to the featureless nature of much of the terrain and the uncertainty and inadequacy of detail on many desert maps. It is essential, however, that the best possible estimate of your start position is made. It is essential because you cannot decide on the direction of travel until the start and finish points are known. The more accurately they can be located, the more realistic will be the bearing on which you move.

The choice of destinations can only include any area known to be inhabited, any water source, a coastline or any known travel route (caravan, road, rail – even an airway offers some chance of rescue). In the absence of any easier or more certain choice, a coastline offers good possibilities. Sea-water can offset or lessen sweating. There is a chance of food. There is a chance of finding fresh water. If you can set up a survival still, fresh water will be available. There may also be marine traffic from which help might be obtained.

You should be reasonably sure of the accuracy of your position-fixing. You should be reasonably sure that you will be heading towards a known objective. If these conditions cannot be fulfilled, good survival routine will now entail re-consideration of your decision to move. You must be convinced that travel is your best, if not your only, course. If any doubt exists, remember that it will be easier for searchers to find your vehicle or any wreckage than you, when you are on the move. (In the Australian Outback, for instance, there is a positive instruction to remain with a broken-down or wrecked vehicle).

But the Survivor makes an informed, reasoned decision – and the circumstances or information may still result in a decision to travel.

Once the direction of travel has been decided, move only in the early morning and late evening. Remember the vital importance of conserving body-fluids. Rest, in the shade if possible, during the hot middle hours of the day. Use what clothing is available to gain maximum protection against sunlight – direct and reflected. (See "Shelter Construction"). Improvise a mask with the smallest convenient slits to protect your eyes against the light.

In desert conditions, effort is costly in body-fluids, so avoid all unnecessary exertion. One way to do this is to look for the easiest walking. The valleys between dunes usually offer a firm surface, and struggling over soft sand can often be side-stepped. In the same way, any desert trail or track leading in your general direction is worth considering, as it will have fewer stones or rocks on its surface. However, do not assume that watercourses – dry or otherwise – lead eventually to the coast. Unless their direction matches your required heading, ignore them – after checking them for water. Many desert wadis lead only to inland depressions or wet-season lakes. Of course, if you encounter any water source – even a place in which a desert still can be operated – the wisest option will almost certainly be to remain there.

If you have no compass, use the stick and stone method to determine the cardinal points during the rest period. Scratched on the ground, they will give directions from which you can determine the line of march when it is cooler. Try to pick up a landmark at some distance, and use it when walking.

Estimates of distance are likely to be far short of actuality, due to the lack of reference points and features. This diminishes perspective and judgement. Check direction using the rising and setting sun. Use the stars to give guidance after sunset, again marking your heading on the ground when the night's travel is completed.

Use ground direction marking also if bad weather prevents travel. Sandstorms are the most probable cause, for they will cut visibility to nil, besides being extremely unpleasant to face. Take shelter if possible. If none is at hand, lie with your back to the wind and take the opportunity to sleep. Covering your face with a cloth will provide easier breathing. You can afford to relax, for the sandstorm cannot harm you. There is no danger of being buried by blown or drifting sand.

Arctic Travel

The Arctic and sub-Arctic present very difficult conditions for Survival Travel. Perhaps surprisingly, one of the causes is the very great range of temperatures – especially inland. Within the Arctic, extremes of – 56 degrees C. to more than 18 degrees C. have been recorded. In the sub-Arctic even greater temperature variations exist. The regions include an equally wide variety of terrain – plains, mountains, hills, icefields, snowfields, glaciers and, in Summer, marshes, bogs, lakes and waterways. Some areas are wooded. Some are apparently without vegetation or animal life in Winter, but covered with thick plant growth and abounding with insects in Summer.

The Arctic summers are short. The blood sucking insects are particularly voracious as they have a lot to achieve in a very short time. It is necessary to take all the anti-insect precautions that have been indicated in the "First Aid" Chapter.

As in desert travel, it is necessary to establish your position as accurately as possible, and to determine a realistic destination before setting out. The destinations likely to be available will include any area known to be inhabited, a coastline, or a significant river. A river should be followed downstream as it is likely to lead to any village or settlement. The exception to this suggestion would be any river flowing in a northerly direction.

Allow the contours to play a full part in determining your route. In

Winter the valley floors may provide easier going if a river or lake is frozen – but make camp some way up the valley side if possible. It will be warmer there than on the valley floor. Ridge-line travel may be a good option, but take full account of the chill-factor if it is windy. Do not attempt to move in blizzard conditions. Take shelter and sit it out.

Obtain a stout stick to use on the march. It is invaluable for probing snow ahead, testing ice-strength, stream-crossing and drumming to attract attention if the opportunity occurs. Improvise a slit mask to guard against snow-blindness. Even if you have a compass, check your heading regularly using the stick and stone method with the sun. There are two reasons for this precaution. The first is that compass deviation can be uncertain in some Arctic areas owing to the possible proximity of the magnetic pole. The second is the fact that unbroken snow coverage can be disorientating.

If you are in an area of deep, loose snow, normal walking becomes virtually impossible. Some form of snow-shoes are essential. There is no problem if commercial snow-shoes are available – except to remember that they are put on so that the free ends of the footstraps are on the outer side of each foot. This avoids stepping on a strap if it becomes undone.

When walking with snow-shoes, aim to pass the inside edge of each shoe over the other, using as comfortable and normal a stride as possible. If you adopt an abnormal gait, your leg muscles will soon protest very painfully. If no snow-shoes are available, it is worth trying to improvise. Anything that can be conveniently attached to your footwear, can spread your body weight over about 0.5 sq.m., and is of usable shape should be considered.

The following are some of the possibilities:—

(i) A small, dense evergreen bough fastened to each foot, with its shoot tips to the rear.

(ii) Thin flexible tree branches formed into a suitable shape, with binding and webbing made from parachute shroud lines.

(iii) If aircraft wreckage or a broken-down vehicle is available, metal or wood panels, seat parts, inspection covers etc., can all make usable snowshoes.

Bear in mind that the body requires more food when travelling than when in camp – i.e. a minimum of 2-3000 cals/day when on the move compared with 1000 cals/day when static. Remember that you will need to provide yourself with shelter each night – and that in these regions the nights can be long. Do not forget that you will need facilities to dry your clothing if you are to keep warm. All these aspects of survival call for equipment and supplies. If they are not available in portable form, be absolutely certain that moving is the best – if not the only – answer to your survival problem. If you do decide to travel, remember to leave behind your location signals, as well as the information the searchers will need.

GENERAL ADVICE

(i) When you have decided that a move is necessary and practicable, it is better to implement the decision sooner rather than later. You will be stronger, your resources will be intact and your resilience and mental ability will be at their best.

(ii) Travel well within your own – or the group's – capabilities. If there are some people more active than others, they should be organised as trail-finders and blazers. The less able will then be saved the effort involved in false trails, backtracking, etc. You must have a regular rendezvous schedule so that there is no risk of the group becoming separated. The only circumstances in which division of a group is acceptable are those in which fit, experienced members go to obtain help for others who are unable to travel.

(iii) Even if you are taking it easily, and keeping within your limitations, you will still be giving your body a testing time. For this reason, take all the normal precautions to keep fit – and try to check that all other members of the group do the same. Attend to any scratches, cuts, bites, etc., immediately. Deal with incipient blisters at once. If necessary, rest for a day or two to recharge your physical batteries.

(iv) Do not attempt to conceal any of your transit camps. On the contrary, mark them as clearly as time and effort required permit. They could lead your rescuers to you.

Robert Louis Stevenson once wrote, "To travel hopefully is a better thing than to arrive". The Survivor would write that differently, and would use his skills and techniques to prove that his version is right – **"To arrive is a better thing than to travel hopefully"**.

INDEX

A

Adaptation	24,122
Ambush Hunting	188
Angling	205/7
Animal foods:	
baited perch,	198
cooking,	94,95,100,103/4
eggs,	104,190,204
hunting,	188
netting,	199/200
preparation,	97/9
preservation,	105/6
small game,	188
snares,	188/195,197/9
sources,	187
summary,	203/4
traps,	197,200/202
value,	187,203
Ants	49
Aquatic foods:	
amphibians,	220
angling,	205/7
baits,	209/210
crustaceans,	219
eel trap,	216
fish poisoning/stunning,	219
fish snares,	217
fish spearing,	217/8
fishhooks,	206/8
fishing line,	207
fishing hints,	211
lures,	210
nets,	211/4
nightlines,	211
poisonous fish,	51
shellfish,	210,219
traps,	214/6
trout, tickling,	218
Arctic:	
travel,	231/4
shelter,	83/6
water sources,	131/2
Assessment, of Situation	22

B

Baking	102
Bag, survival	12/3
Bait	209/210
Baited Perch	197
Barracuda	50
Battery, multicell	64
Bees	48
Birds:	
cooking,	98
preparation,	97/8
trapping,	197/8
Bleeding	36/7
Blisters	223/4
Body-heat Loss	12
Boiling	100/1
Boredom and Isolation	4
Bow Drill	66/9
Breathing, assisted	30/2
Burning Glass	62
Burns	43

C

Candle	61
Carbon Monoxide:	
poisoning danger,	97
Cassiopeia	115/6
Centipedes	49
Clothing	19,20/1
Chest Compression	32/3
Choking	33/5
Containers, water,	11,101
Coastlines:	
food sources,	177/182,210/1,219
routes,	229
water sources,	129/130
Cold	2
Compass:	
button,	12,110
improvised,	121/3

C

Cooking:
    fires, 92,94
    general hints, 103
    stoves, 93
    pits, 95,96,98
Cooking, Methods of:
    amphibians & reptiles, 103
    crustaceans, 103
    baking, 102
    boiling, 100/1
    bread, 104
    eggs, 104/5
    fish, 103,214
    fruit, 104
    herbs, 104
    molluscs, 103
    nuts, grains & seeds, 104
    roasting, 100
    roots and tubers, 104
    small game, 100/3
    steaming, 102

D

Deserts:
    food sources, 167/9,186
    shelter, 87/8
    travel, 229/231
    water sources, 132/3
Dew Trap 134/5
Dehydration 132/3
Direction Finding:
    improvised compass, 121/3
    map, 110/1
    moon, 119
    shadow, stick & stone, 112
    sun and watch, 113/4
    star movement, 118/9
    stars, 115/8
    vegetation, 120
    prevailing winds, 120/1

E

Edibility Test, plants 171/2
Enemies of Survival 2

F

Fatigue 3,4
Fear 2
Fire(s):
    base, 80
    bow-drill, 66/9
    cooking, 92,94
    dangerous fuel, 66
    damping down, 58
    essentials for, 55
    from friction, 66
    fuel grading, 55
    heat, 56
    heat sources, 59/62
    importance of, 24
    kindling, 56
    lighting, 57
    other uses, 92
    pits, 94,102
    reflector, 80
    starter, magnesium, 62
    thong, 69/70
    tinder, 55
    tinder sources, 58/9
    warming, 70,80,90,97
Fire Types:
    cooking, 92/3
    drying/smoking, 96,105/6
    hangi, 95
    pyramid, 90
    signal, 91/2
    star, 91
    steaming pit, 102
First Aid:
    assisted breathing, 30/2
    bites and stings, 47
    bleeding, 36/7
    burns, 43
    casualty assessment, 30
    chest compression, 32/3
    choking, 33/5
    coma (recovery) position, 36
    concussion, 42/3
    fractures, 42
    frostbite & hypothermia,
    causes/prevention, 43/4
    treatment of, 45/6
    hyperthermia, 71
    immersion (trench) foot, 46/7

F

First Aid (Cont.)
   immunisation, 47
   insect bites,
     precautions against, 48
   internal bleeding, 39
   personal hygiene, 47
   poisonous fish, 51
   pressure application, 36/7
   pressure points, 38
   shock, 40
   shock, treatment of, 41
   situation assessment, 29
   snakes, 51
   snake bite treatment, 52/3
   water animals,
     dangerous, 49-51

First Aid Kit 17

Fish:
   poisonous, 51
   preparation & cooking, 98
   preserving, 106

Fishing:
   angling, 205/7
   netting, 211/4
   snaring, 217
   spearing, 217
   trapping, 214/6

Flint & Striker 62
Flies 48
Flukes & Hookworms 50

Food:
   animal, 187/201
   aquatic, 205/220
   cooking, methods of, 94,100/4
   plant, 151/186
   preparation, 97-100
   preservation, 96/7, 105/7
   storage, 105

Food Supplies:
   assessment of, 151, 187
   conservation, 151

Fractures 42

Fungi:
   dangers of, 183
   identification needed, 185

H

Health:
   cleanliness, 47
   inoculations, 47
Heating with stones 80, 102
Hygiene, personal 47/8
Hookworms & Flukes 50
Hornets 48
Hunger 2
Hunting, ambush 188

I

Immunisation 47
Insect bites:
   precautions against, 48

J

Jellyfish 48
Jungles:
   beds, 89
   travel, 225/6, 229

K

Kit, Survival 7
Kit, First Aid 17
Knife, Survival 15

L

Lantern, Simple 10, 147
Leeches 49, 225
Lice 49
Lighters 61
Location:
   identifying 108, 110/111
   signalling, 145/150

M

Magnesium Fire Starter 62
Magnet 122
Magnetic Variation 110/1
Maps:
   orienting, 109/110
   using, 110/111
Mental Preparation 5

M

Moon:
   full, 119
   quarter, 119
Morse Code 147

N

Navigation:
   choice of route, 111
   compass, 110
   compass, improvised, 121/3
   destination choice, 111
   direction finding, 112/121
   map use, 110/111
   moon as guide, 119
   orientation, 109/110
   position fixing, 108,110/111
   sun, 112/4
   stars, 115/8
   starting position, 108,111
   vegetation, 120
   watch, 113/4
Nets:
   gill, 211/3
   improvised, 214
   purse, 17, 190, 214

O

Orienting, maps 109/110
Osmoration 127/142
Oxydisation 65

P

Pain 2
Personality Requirements 5
Pinhole vision 53
Planning for Survival 25/6
Plant foods:
   cooking, 95, 104
   distribution table, 162
   edibility test, 171/2
   fruits, 161, 174/6
   fungi, 183/5
   general, 153/161, 170, 182, 186
   leaves & leafstalks, 168/9
   roots & rootstocks, 163/4
   seeds, 173/4

P

Plant Foods: (Cont)
   seaweeds, 177/182
   stems & shoots, 167/8
   summary, 186
   survival routine for, 151
   trees, 172/3
   tubers, 165/6
   value, 151
Poisonous Fish 51
Pole Star 115/6
Position Fixing 108, 110/111
Preparing Wild Foods:
   animals, 97/100
Preserving Wild Food 104/6, 177
Prevailing Winds 120/1
Psychological Factors 2
Psychological reactions 1

Q

Quarter Moon 119
Quicksands 226

R

Raft-making 227/8
Reading Glasses, loss of 53
Real Time 113
Roasting 100
Route choices:
   coast/seashore, 229
   jungle, 225/9
   ridge, 226
   river, 226/9
   river crossing, 227/9
   study of terrain, 221
   valley, 225/6

S

Sandflies 48
Scorpions 49, 225
Sea ice 144
Sea water, warning 130, 142
Seaweeds 172/182
Sharks 50

S

Shelters:	71/2
desert,	87/8
fallen-log,	76
fir tree,	84
grassland,	78/9
igloo,	86
jungle,	88/9
layered tree bivouac,	77
lean-to,	73/4
para-tent,	81/2
sanga,	73
siting,	71/2
snow cave,	85
snow trench,	83
Shock:	
causes, symptoms,	40
treatment,	41
Signalling:	
camp signs,	150
equipment,	145/6
fires,	149
ground to air,	149
heliograph,	147/8
location,	225,234
Morse Code,	147
passive,	149
at sea,	150
sound,	148
Snakes	51/2
Snake Bite Treatment	52/3
Snare Triggers:	
figure 4,	196
half-reef,	192/3
three-peg,	193,200
simple,	191
Snares:	
balanced pole,	191/2
bird,	198
drag,	189/190
fish,	217
fowl,	199
setting,	188/190
spring,	194/5
squirrel,	197
Snowshoes	233
Spectacle Loss	53
Spiders	49
Southern Cross	117

S

Stars	115/8
Star Movement	118/9
Steaming Pit	102
Sting Ray	51
Stoves:	
improvised,	93
yukon,	96
Streams and rivers:	
crossing,	227/8
following,	226/7
Survival:	
enemies of,	2
equipment for,	7,27/8
first aid,	29/54
movement decision,	26,221
parameters,	28
planning for,	25/6
priorities,	24/5
routine,	22,24
situation assessment,	22
Survival Kit:	7
candle,	10
compass,	12
condoms,	11
fishing tackle,	16
flint and steel,	9
knife,	15
matches,	8
needle,	11
optional items,	17
packing,	11,12
purification tablets,	14
snares,	16
survival bag,	12
wire saw,	14
Survival (Desert) Still	135/7

T

Thirst	2
Ticks	49
Time, real	113
Traps:	
baited,	200/2
baited perch,	198
deadfall,	200
fish,	214/6
fowl,	199

T

Travel:
- arctic, 231/4
- bog/swamp crossing, 226
- camp sites, 227
- choice of route, 225
- coastline, 223,229
- desert, 229/231
- foot care, 223/4
- footwear, 224
- general advice, 234
- jungle, 225/6,229
- river, 226/7
- river crossing, 227/9
- signals, 225,229,234
- survival routine for, 221/5
- travel routine, 223
- travel hygiene, 234

Tree Climbing 221

Triggers:
- figure 4, 196
- half-reef, 192/3
- simple, 191
- three-peg, 193,200

V

Vegetation Still 138
Ventilation, need for 97

W

Wasps 48
Water:
- boiling, 126
- charcoal, use with, 127
- collection, 137/8,143
- conservation, 124/5
- containers, 11,101
- dangerous animals in, 50/1,125
- dangers from impurity, 125
- dehydration effects, 132/3
- filtering, 125/6
- need for, 124
- purification, 126/7
- storage, 143
- survival time without, 142
- table, 127

W

Water Discipline 133
Water Location/Collection:
- in cold weather areas, 131/2
- in desert areas, 132/3
- in earthy areas, 128/9
- in rocky areas, 127/8

Water Location/Collection:
- at sea, 142/4
- on seashore, 129/130

Water Sources:
- animal body fluids, 144
- choice, 125
- dew trap, 134/5
- ice and snow, 141
- plants, 137/141
- survival still, 135/7
- vegetation still, 138
- water table, 127
- at sea, 142

Wild Food, preparation 96/7
Wild Food Sources:
- animal, 187/202
- aquatic, 205/218
- plant, 151/186

Wind Chill 44
Wire Wool 63

Y

Yukon Stove 96